A GUIDE TO GYMNASTICS

FRANK F. MUSKER Ed.M., C.A.G.S.
Gymnastics Coach
Massachusetts Institute of Technology

DONALD R. CASADY Ph.D.
Course Chairman,
Physical Education Skills Program for Men
University of Iowa

LESLIE W. IRWIN Ph.D.
Professor of Health and Physical Education
Boston University

55172

The Macmillan Company, New York
Collier-Macmillan Limited, London

Library of Congress catalog card number: 68–10105

THE MACMILLAN COMPANY, NEW YORK
COLLIER-MACMILLAN CANADA, LTD., TORONTO, ONTARIO

PRINTED IN THE UNITED STATES OF AMERICA

PREFACE

Gymnastics, one of the most popular sports for decades in many European nations, is now one of the fastest-growing sports in the United States. Aside from its inherent appeal because of the fun, challenge, and satisfaction it offers, the present popularity of gymnastics to both the participant and to the spectator may be attributed to a number of factors. The televising of gymnastics competition in national championships, Pan-American Games, and Olympic Games has entertained audiences numbering in the millions, many of whom were viewing the sport of gymnastics for the first time. During the past few years national gymnastics teams from various nations have toured the United States and have given many exhibitions (as well as competing against gymnastics teams representing the United States) in locations scattered around the country. The tours made by the men and women of the 1960 Russian Olympic Championship Teams and the 1964 Japanese Olympic Championship Teams provided immense enjoyment for many Americans. The number of competitive gymnastics teams for men at the high school and college level has increased greatly during the past few years. The United States Gymnastics Federation, which promotes gymnastics competition for men, and which was originated a few years ago as a governing body for gymnastics somewhat in competition with the Amateur Athletic Union of the United States, has aggressively promoted the sport of gymnastics. Both the U.S.G.F. and the A.A.U. have contributed to the growth of the popularity of gymnastics in a number of ways. Gymnastics clinics at the local, state, regional, and national levels have aided this growth by not only helping gymnasts to improve their gymnastics skills but also by helping gymnastics instructors and coaches improve their coaching techniques. In 1965, for example, National Gymnastics Clinics were held during the latter part of December—the Eastern Clinic met in Fort Lauderdale, Florida, and the Western Clinic met in Tucson, Arizona. Efforts to attract an increased number of girls and women into gymnastics practice and competition have also been highly successful. Another factor that has enhanced the growth of gymnastics has been the important role of gymnastics in combating the low level of physical fitness displayed in recent years by a large number of American youth.

The appearance during the past few years of a considerable number of

iii

well-written and clearly illustrated books of gymnastics has also been an important factor. These books have been exceedingly helpful in aiding the competitive gymnast and gymnastics coach to acquire skill in and knowledge of many difficult skills and stunts. Consequently, the question may logically be asked, "If several worthwhile and informative gymnastics books are currently available, then what is the need for yet another one?" This question can best be answered by citing the ways in which this book is unique—the needs in gymnastics that it fulfills that are not satisfied in other gymnastics books.

This book of gymnastics is not designed to help the highly skilled gymnast, as many gymnastics books are designed to do. Instead, this book is designed to lay a solid groundwork in gymnastics for the beginning gymnast or the gymnast with only a fair amount of training and practice. An understanding of the explanatory information concerning the value of gymnastics, how to prepare for participation in gymnastics, and an acquisition of the basic through intermediate gymnastics stunts will provide the potential gymnast an excellent base on which to develop himself into a highly skilled gymnast. The material in this book should aid the aspiring gymnast to understand thoroughly how to prepare himself for gymnastics participation. This feature is often missing or is only briefly discussed in the majority of the other books that deal with gymnastics. Because this book is written for the beginner and assumes that the reader has little or no knowledge of gymnastics, each stunt presented is thoroughly discussed and its correct performance is also illustrated. Therefore, the stunts listed in each chapter are not at all a complete compilation of all gymnastics stunts through an intermediate skill level for that event. Rather, these selected stunts are representative and should enable the beginning gymnast to prepare himself for gymnastics participation in each event. Experience indicates that presenting the entire spectrum of gymnastics stunts to the gymnast of no, little, or limited experience is likely to be more confusing and bewildering than helpful to him.

Because of these reasons, this book should be ideally suited to use by students in gymnastics classes and instructors in gymnastics, particularly those who are not highly skilled in teaching or performing or who are unsure of the reasons that some gymnastics stunts should be performed in a particular way.

In order to facilitate the reader's comprehension of the material in this book, it is presented in two parts. Part I is concerned with the preliminary information and essential knowledge that is a prerequisite to successful practice and workouts in gymnastics. This material, then, should answer many of the why questions that arise in gymnastics. Part II is concerned with the methods and techniques of successfully performing basic, elementary, and intermediate gymnastics stunts. This material, then, should answer many of the how questions that the gymnastics performer and instructor frequently ask.

F. F. M.—D. R. C.—L. W. I.

CONTENTS

Beginning Tumbling Stunts   82

Elementary Tumbling Stunts   86

Intermediate Tumbling Stunts   92

Tumbling Routines   100

KNEE-SHOULDER BALANCE
LOW SHOULDER-TO-SHOULDER BALANCE

Intermediate Single Stunts   142

FOREARM STAND (TIGER STAND)
HEAD-IN-HANDS BALANCE
FIFTEEN-SECOND HANDSTAND
HANDSTAND PRESS FROM HEADSTAND
SQUAT HANDSTAND PRESS TO HANDSTAND
CHEST ROLL TO HEADSTAND
BACK EXTENSION ROLL TO HEADSTAND
FORWARD ROLL TO STRADDLE STAND
HEADSPRING TO STRADDLE SEAT
SIDE SCALE
HALF LEVER ON FLOOR ("L" POSITION)
FRONT SPLIT
SIDE SPLIT

Chart for Rating Balancing and Flexibility Skills   147

8 Floor Exercise   148

SAMPLE FLOOR EXERCISE ROUTINE

9 Side Horse Stunts   150

Beginning Side Horse Stunts   151

DEVELOPMENTAL EXERCISE
SQUAT VAULT
FLANK VAULT (SIDE VAULT)
REAR VAULT
FRONT VAULT (FACE VAULT)
FEINT—LEFT OR RIGHT
FIVE SETS OF FEINTS
WOLF VAULT
STRADDLE MOUNT
STRADDLE VAULT
KNEE VAULT (COURAGE VAULT)
CUT LEFT OR RIGHT
FOUR SETS OF CUTS

Elementary Side Horse Stunts   157

SQUAT VAULT TO REAR SUPPORT
FLANK VAULT TO REAR SUPPORT
CHEST STAND
SEAT HOPS
HIGH FRONT VAULT (HIGH FACE VAULT)
CORKSCREW VAULT
THIEF VAULT

Part I THE WHYS OF GYMNASTICS

The material presented in Part I of this book appears in the first four chapters, which deal with (1) the values derived from gymnastics participation, (2) a history of gymnastics, and (3) how to prepare for gymnastics participation, including a discussion of the mechanics of gymnastics. An understanding of this information should enable the person interested in gymnastics to prepare competently for successful participation in gymnastics and to remain motivated to continue to participate in gymnastics for many years, whether this participation is for the purpose of ranking high in national competition, of mastering a limited number of gymnastics stunts in order to enjoy a sense of achievement or as a means of maintaining an above average level of physical fitness.

After a period of gymnastics training and practice, the gymnastics performer should find that he has gained many of the benefits listed in Chapter 1. Although the benefits derived by a group as a whole do not always accrue to all the persons comprising the group, any given gymnastics performer should expect to derive most of these values if he follows the suggestion given for gymnastics training in Chapters 3 and 4. The beneficial physiological effects that result from regular, strenuous participation in gymnastics training and exercises should, in particular, occur to some degree in all who practice gymnastics.

A knowledge of the history of gymnastics, which is discussed in Chapter 2, should enable the gymnastics performer to appreciate its present status and how it has evolved into its present form.

The suggestions given in Chapter 3 for preparing for gymnastics participation should allow the gymnastics performer to efficiently and effectively ready himself physically and mentally to master rapidly the many diverse skills of which gymnastics is comprised. The knowledge that he is following correct training procedures should increase his self-confidence and permit his progress to proceed at an optimum rate.

Many gymnasts and even gymnastics instructors and coaches sometimes disagree about the correct method of performing various gymnastics stunts. An understanding of the mechanics of gymnastics

1

will usually enable the correct method or technique to be determined when such disagreements arise.

In summary, a knowledge of the material in Part I of this book should enable the aspiring gymnast to prepare himself physically and mentally for successful training in gymnastics.

1 THE BENEFITS DERIVED FROM GYMNASTICS PARTICIPATION

Why should a person spend his time trying to learn how to do a handspring or a handstand when he can find recreation in basketball, golf, and other sports? In answering this question and other questions a considerable array of information concerning the beneficial effects of participation in gymnastics needs to be examined. The first question to be considered is "What qualities of gymnastics cause it to be one of the fastest growing activities and sports in the United States?" The second question is "Why do millions of people of a large age range in Europe, Russia, and Japan regularly engage in gymnastics as a sport and as a healthful, satisfying activity?"

The answers to these questions lie in the fact that the regular practice of gymnastics provides an opportunity to develop many physical and mental factors that might otherwise not be fully developed. The many desirable and beneficial outcomes that may be expected to occur because of systematic participation in gymnastics are considerable and well worth the effort. However, if such benefits were not forthcoming, gymnastics would still possess a strong attraction to many simply because of the fun and challenge that it offers. An example of its universal appeal can be seen in the instinctive drive of small children to tumble, roll, swing, climb, and perform other movements that are duplicated in gymnastics. Because of the many facets of which gymnastics is composed, almost anyone can find one or more events that interest him and in which he has aptitude.

DIRECT LASTING BENEFITS OF GYMNASTICS PARTICIPATION

Many of the worthwhile benefits that accrue to the person who practices or participates in gymnastics are a direct consequence of this participation and can often be readily observed in the experienced gymnastics performer. In all instances the concern is with the long-lasting benefits that occur over a period of time; not with the immediate temporary effects of exercise such as an increase in the heart rate or rate of breathing.

Although some findings of the benefits of gymnastics participation have resulted from scientifically conducted research studies, the bulk of the evidence in this area is the result of empirical studies and observations. One needs only to attend a gymnastics meet and observe the superior physique and muscular development possessed by the participants to be convinced of the effectiveness of gymnastics for these purposes. However, most authorities agree that the gymnastics participant who performs regularly can acquire the benefits listed in this chapter. In part the reason that a large number of research studies are not cited is because few questions have been raised concerning the desirability of participating in and the benefits to be gained from gymnastics participation. Consequently the major portion of the research performed in physical education has not dealt with this aspect. In two separate studies conducted at the University of Iowa, an analysis of the data revealed that (1) the college students enrolled in gymnastics classes had a higher level of physical fitness than did the students enrolled in any of several other classes; and (2) students participating in a trampolining class had a definite increase in the flexibility of the ankle joint.

Contributions to Physiological Development

One of the basic tenets of any training program designed to increase physical fitness and muscular development is that the overload principle must be properly utilized. This is done when the performer periodically increases the resistance against which he works, as for example, is exemplified by a systematic increase in the poundage of the barbell used in weight training exercises. In gymnastics the performer works against his body weight (a heavy resistance) and frequently supports or moves it while in a variety of positions. Consequently because the major muscles of his entire body are forced to work against such a large load the gymnast develops a superior physique when compared to most sports participants who manipulate only light equipment such as a golf club, tennis racket, or basketball. The superior body development and physical fitness that the gymnastics performer develops are two of the major reasons for adoption of gymnastics in the physical education programs of schools at all levels.

Components of physical fitness.   The considerable evidence that participation in gymnastics enhances physical fitness and the development of the body will be discussed in detail. In order to do this intelligently the names and definitions of the common components of physical fitness will first be given and then the ways in which each component benefits are discussed. The improvement of these components is concentrated and often requires a shorter developmental time when gymnastics is the choice of activities than if almost any other single activity is instead participated in.

Agility (*nimble, brisk*)—The ability to change quickly the direction and/or elevation of body movements.

Balance—The ability to maintain a desired body position, when in a static position or during movement, regardless of the size of the base of support.

Coordination—Muscular teamwork in accomplishing a movement or series of movements.

Endurance—The ability of the body to continue in motion without rest. This is usually considered as having two aspects: (1) circulorespiratory endurance that demands wind or the ability to move the entire body for long distances while supplying sufficient oxygen and nutrients to the body cells (and removing waste products), and (2) local muscular endurance; that is, the ability of a muscle or group of muscles to continue to perform repetitious movements (such as sit-ups).

Flexibility—The range of motion exhibited at the joints of the body.

Neuromuscular skill (*coordination and timing*)—The ability to perform simple and complicated movements involving the body and other implements without making excess motions and with a high degree of efficiency.

Speed—The ability of the body or parts of the body to move rapidly from one place to another.

Strength—The ability to exert muscular force.

Gymnastics Compared to Other Body-Building Systems

In an interesting study performed a few years ago, a panel of experts compared the values of gymnastics participation with those derived from participating in other activities. In this comparison eleven physical values, three mental values, and the carry-over value were compared for various body-building systems. In evaluating the factors, the value scale for each factor compared ranged from one to three—one representing a low quality of development of a factor, two representing a medium development, and three representing a high quality of development. Of the thirteen body-building systems compared, gymnastics (heavy apparatus, tumbling, and trampolining) was found to contribute more to the all around development of a person than any other single system; the score for gymnastics being forty-three points. The results of this comparison are presented in Figure 1.1, Body Building System Evaluation Chart.

What are some of the specific lasting physiological benefits that you might reasonably expect to take place as you begin and continue to participate in gymnastics? These are many and some would often occur as a result of regularly engaging in almost any type of vigorous physical activity. In addition, some of these specific benefits are indirect and may be considered secondary benefits that are not a direct result of the reaction of the body to a strenuous exercise.

Agility. The gymnast is constantly called upon to make agile movements as a routine consequence of practicing gymnastics. Such practice naturally leads to a marked increase in the degree of agility that the gymnast possesses.

Balance. The successful performance of gymnastics requires a mastery of many stunts in which dynamic or moving balance movement and static or stationary balance positions must be practiced. This practice not only sharpens the general sense of balance and the accompanying kinesthetic

THE BODY BUILDING SYSTEM EVALUATION CHART

	Physical Factors											Mental Factors				
	Ability	Balance	Body-Alignment Posture	Carry-Over Value in Later Life	Coordination	Flexibility	Endurance	Muscular Bulk	Speed	Strength	Symmetrical Proportions	Alertness	Courage	Perseverance	Skill Transferable to Other Activities	SCORE
Gymnastics (Heavy Apparatus, Tumbling, and Trampolining)	3	3	3	3	3	3	3	2	3	3	2	3	3	3	3	43
Swedish Gymnastics	3	3	3	3	3	3	3	2	2	2	3	3	3	3	2	41
Track and Field	3	1	1	2	2	2	3	1	3	2	2	2	2	3	3	32
Winter Sports	1	3	1	3	2	2	3	1	3	2	1	2	3	3	2	32
Combatives	2	3	1	2	3	1	2	2	2	2	1	3	3	3	1	31
Swimming	1	2	3	3	3	2	3	1	3	2	3	1	1	2	1	31
Relays	2	2	1	2	2	2	2	1	3	2	1	3	2	2	3	30
Team Games	3	1	1	3	2	2	2	1	2	1	2	3	2	2	3	30
Weight Lifting	1	2	2	3	2	1	1	2	2	3	3	2	2	3	1	30
Group Games	3	2	1	2	3	2	2	1	2	2	1	3	1	1	3	29
Body Building ar Weight Training	1	2	3	3	1	1	1	3	1	3	3	1	1	3	2	29
Calisthenics	1	2	2	3	3	2	2	1	2	1	3	2	1	2	1	28
Dancing	2	3	2	3	3	3	2	1	2	1	1	2	1	1	1	27

(Figure 1. 1)

sense that enable one to know his body position at all times but also enables the gymnast to master many specific balancing positions and movements.

Coordination. The many single isolated movements that must be integrated and executed in order to perform one skill demands coordinated movements. Because gymnastics, tumbling and trampolining consist of many skills, a high degree of coordination is developed by the gymnast as he progresses to advanced gymnastics movements. Because of this almost incessant practice of a wide variety of skills most advanced gymnasts can easily accommodate the tasks met during their daily duties and in learning the skills of other sports.

Circulorespiratory endurance. The effect of tumbling, vaulting and apparatus activities on the circulovascular system have been demonstrated through scientific experimentation to be highly beneficial. The heart becomes stronger and more efficient. A heart that is larger and stronger from repeated power movements, such as dipping and chinning or from tumbling or trampolining activity pumps an increased amount of blood with each contraction, and therefore does not need to beat as often as the untrained heart. This means that a heart that is exercised through sequential gymnastics does more work with fewer beats. The slower the heart beat, providing it is healthy, the greater will be the resting period between beats. During gymnastic movements the spleen contracts, forcing the blood stored there during sedentary periods into circulation, thus increasing the number of circulating red corpuscles and amount of hemoglobin and consequently the oxygen-carrying power of the blood. A trained gymnast possesses deeper respiratory movement than does a person who is not in good physical condition. This is accompanied by an increase in the flexibility of the chest wall and a strengthening of the respiratory muscles, all of which enable the respiratory efforts to occur with increased efficiency. All of the above effects benefit the gymnast because they enable him to perform, for an increased length of time and with improved efficiency, movements and exercises that require heavy respiration and place a large load on his circulatory system.

Local-muscular endurance. Local muscular endurance is primarily determined by the amount of muscle strength one has. Until a very high level is attained, the more one performs on the apparatus, the more strength one gains, thus causing a great deal of reserve to be built up. Muscular endurance results from and is directly related to this build-up or reserve since in any movement only the number of muscle fibers needed to do the specific task are brought into action. The muscle fibers held in reserve go into action when those that are exercising become fatigued, resulting in the muscle fibers acting in relays. All the muscles of the body come into play while performing routines on the apparatus, tumbling, vaulting, balancing, and trampolining. Therefore a trained gymnast has sufficient muscular strength and power to more than satisfy his everyday needs and he will use part of his muscles in relays to perform a movement while the other part of his muscles rests. This allows some parts of his contracting muscles to lay idle and recover their chemistry while recuperating as other muscle fibers carry the load. This, in turn, allows the muscles to function with increased efficiency. In the tremendously competitive life that most of us live today, an adequate reserve of energy is extremely essential.

Flexibility. Probably one of the most important benefits to be gained from regular participation in gymnastics is an increase in the range of motion throughout all the joints of the body—gymnastics requires flexible movement at all times. One of the first symptoms of aging is often a loss of flexibility. As one grows older a well-developed musculature can be important in maintaining correct body alignment. The poor posture often seen in the aged is often caused by weak muscles that are too long or too short.

Neuromuscular skills. The many skilled movements that must be perfected as one becomes proficient in gymnastics increases significantly one's repertoire of neuromuscular skills that require the utmost coordination of the efforts of nervous and muscular systems. Thus the practice of gymnastics should result in the performer experiencing a higher degree of neuromuscular control, splitsecond timing, and coordination of movements and efforts.

Speed of movement. The practice of gymnastics should result in the ability to perform a large number of movements with increased speed because a large variety of movements are necessary for successful gymnastics performance.

Strength. The size, strength, and endurance of a muscle increases as the muscle develops through use. Gymnastics in most instances is a resistive activity that enables strength to be developed much more rapidly than occurs with most forms of exercise. The muscles of the thorax, abdominal area, and shoulder girdle, which are underdeveloped in most citizens in our modern space-age society and which are not sufficiently exercised in most sports, are especially strengthened by performing gymnastics. Vaulting, tumbling, and trampolining are particularly valuable in developing the strength of the leg muscles.

Fatigue. The sum total of the improvement in overall physical fitness that ordinarily results from regular participation in gymnastics is a tremendous increase in the ability to successfully resist fatigue, and when it does occur the ability to recover rapidly from its effects is considerably improved. Whereas many of the middle aged in the United States suffer almost constantly from chronic fatigue and its sapping effect in preventing joyous living, any improvement in physical fitness is added insurance against eventually falling victim to this condition. Consequently the physically fit person each day works and lives with increased efficiency.

Digestion. The many different types of gymnastics movements such as reaching, flexing, extending, rolling, twisting, vaulting, and swinging help to speed up the intestinal action in such a way that the digested foods are moved along by peristaltic action with increased speed. As an indirect benefit, relaxation from the beneficial effects of exercise also contribute to an improvement in digestion.

Vital Organs. Gymnastics activity is beneficial to all the vital organs. Through the demand placed on all the vital organs by an increase in circulation and increased muscular action there is an increased development of the organs such as the liver and pancreas.

Contributions to Personality and Character Development

There is almost universal agreement that participation in sports and athletics presents numerous opportunities for the development of many desirable personality and character traits. Many outstanding athletes often speak and write of the advantages that they have derived from sports participation and of being better people because of these experiences.

The importance of enhancing the additional development of desired personality and character traits can hardly be overestimated. In our modern culture the opportunities for the development of some of these traits, however, are severely restricted and sports participation is one of the few avenues readily available to large masses of people. The self-discipline imposed by the necessity of training efficiently in order to attain the pinnacle in physical fitness, sports skills, team play and strategy helps to develop many worthwhile traits and it demands the wise and effective budgeting of time. Very few other ventures are available at the present time in which one is expected to make an all-out effort for an extended length of time in order to excel.

Gymnastics, as a member of the sports family, also can contribute immeasurably to the development of worthwhile personality and character

traits. In fact because of the nature of gymnastics participation and competition, unique opportunities exist for the gymnast to develop desirable
psychological characteristics. Thus the person who regularly engages in
gymnastics for a lengthy period can ordinarily expect many of the benefits
listed in this section to accrue to him. Some of the reasons why gymnastics
participation is especially valuable for these purposes are (1) gymnastics is
a highly individualized sport in which each person is on his own and suc-
ceeds or fails solely on the basis of his own efforts—facing and over-
coming the challenges that are presented can be an extremely satisfying
experience, (2) because gymnastics is individualized no two routines have
to include the same stunts or be alike. The gymnast can thus fulfill his own
interests and specialize in those areas in which he has the most aptitude,
(3) because gymnastics routines need not follow any set order or pattern
the gymnast can make full use of and further develop his creative ability in
mastering stunts and constructing routines employing symmetry of
movement, close coordination between individual stunts within the routine, and he may include favorite stunts, (4) the gymnast, to a higher
degree than almost any other athlete and regardless of his aptitude,
ability or length of experience, is continually challenged to learn new
stunts, combinations of stunts, and routines, and (5) each gymnast may
progress in gymnastics at whatever speed he desires (within the limits of
his abilities).

Regular participation in gymnastics should enable the performer to
know himself better. He learns about his abilities and capabilities, how he
reacts under stress and when winning or losing, how he reacts to others
when in a variety of circumstances and how they react toward him. As his
mastery in this sport increases his self-confidence and self-respect should
improve. This is aided by the knowledge that he is expending his time and
efforts in a worthwhile way. Considerable enjoyment can occur because
he knows that he is physically fit and capable of handling his body well in
many situations. All of these advantages can in turn lead to a unification
of his personality and its many facets, resulting in an increase in his pride
and self-respect.

Mental alertness, courage, determination, and perseverance are all
needed in order to excel in gymnastics. The practice of gymnastics leads
to success in performing gymnastics skills and aids in developing such
qualities as self-confidence, will power, decisiveness, and daring without
foolhardiness. The ability to persevere in spite of frustration, and the
courage to continue in spite of the dangers that might arise are important
abilities that often determine how successful one is in life. It takes much
perseverance and determination to learn to do well a row of flip-flops and a
full-twisting back-airo on the tumbling mat or to do giant swings on the
horizontal bar. Participation in a sport that enables these accomplish-
ments to be made should give the participant a great deal of joy and satisfaction.

Many rich social experiences may be gained through participating with
a group or team while engaged in gymnastics practice and competition.

The gymnast becomes a close member of a group that depends on one another for spotting and coaching help. This in turn improves his social fitness as he develops and enhances such traits as cooperation, courtesy, tolerance, helpfulness, and an appreciation of the abilities and limitations of others.

INDIRECT BENEFITS OF GYMNASTICS PARTICIPATION

Many of the benefits that appear to be derived from regular participation in strenuous physical activity, including gymnastics, are not a direct consequence of the activity. Nevertheless these indirect benefits can be of the utmost value and an increasing amount of scientific research evidence is being produced that supports these claims. The case for gymnastics as the means by which these benefits are attained rests on such grounds as personal preference, the inherent challenge of gymnastics, its interest to both the participant and the spectator, its usefulness to the performer over a large number of years, the many opportunities for engaging in some gymnastics activities at almost any time or place, and the reasons previously listed in this chapter.

A large number of studies have produced evidence that the greater the amount of vigorousness of the physical activity in which people regularly participate, the less frequent and less severe is their incidence of cardiovascular and degenerative diseases when compared to sedentary people. Because cardiovascular disease is by far the leading cause of death from disease in the United States and because it and degenerative diseases begin to appear in young adults and affect large numbers of the middle aged, the importance of preventive measures can hardly be overemphasized. Although factors other than the amount or lack of physical activity are involved with these two diseases, there are several reasons why participation in physical activity is a helpful preventive measure. (1) The narrowing of the arterial walls in most adults, which is caused by degenerative changes and deposits of cholesterol and other substances on the inner walls, seems to be delayed or prevented by exercise. (2) Should a heart attack develop, the heart, because of its increase in pumping power due to exercise, is better able to withstand the resultant stress and strain. This is true because the collateral or secondary circulation in some of the ordinarily dormant capillaries within the heart muscle is quickly available to supply blood to the areas of the heart in which the blood vessel(s) is blocked. (3) Regular exercise appears to retard the clotting time of the blood which reduces the possibility of the blood forming a clot while circulating in the body. (4) The milking action of the muscles (when the muscles are contracted, the one-way valves in the veins allow the blood to flow only toward the heart) aid in keeping the blood circulation normal. (5). Exercise appears to help keep the blood cholesterol level within the normal limits and aids in preventing a narrowing of the walls of the arteries and in preventing any of the arteries from becoming plugged.

Regular exercise again and again appears to be the best way of maintaining the body weight within normal limits. Most overweight children become overweight after first becoming inactive and not because they first start eating more food. The average person requires a minimum of one hour of vigorous activity a day. People who do less than this consume more food than if they do one or two hours of exercise a day. On the other hand an increased amount of physical activity does not lead to a proportional increase in the appetite. The appetite seems to adjust itself quite accurately to the amount of strenuous physical activity performed, provided that this amount is at least one hour in duration.

Another valuable outcome of regular gymnastics participation is the help given in the ability to relax. Man's body and nervous system appears to have been developed to meet the stress and strain of living a rugged outdoor life under extremely primitive conditions in which physical action was clearly needed to respond to danger and threats. In our modern society the avenue of reacting openly with physical activity is not an appropriate or meaningful response to many of the situations that produce anxiety, strain, stress, or worry. The threat of the H-bomb or World War III, the concern with racial inequalities, the reaction to a poor examination grade or a trying social situation can quickly produce stress and worry but no easy way of relieving the stress or worry is available. In one survey of several hundred physicians, well over 90 per cent indicated that participation in physical activity relieves anxiety and stress. Therefore, the physical relaxation that follows physical activity such as gymnastics participation also seems to produce an accompanying mental relaxation. As one becomes older and more beset with tensions and worries, the ability to relax gains importance. This then emphasizes one of the more valuable long-range effects of participation in gymnastics.

Regular exercise is also valuable in retarding the aging process through the operation of several factors. It aids in preserving a youthful contour, in maintaining a normal body weight, in maintaining a large degree of flexibility, and in maintaining an erect posture.

Another indirect outcome of gymnastics training that may be invaluable is the ability to act quickly whenever necessary; which may enable one to save one's life in an emergency. The ability to quickly run, jump, or roll without injury if being pursued by an enemy or if in the path of an oncoming vehicle may well determine whether one lives or dies. Also, gymnastics participation helps one learn how to fall from low heights safely and without injury.

2 A BRIEF HISTORY OF GYMNASTICS

THE DUAL MEANING OF GYMNASTICS

Man has engaged in gymnastics activities for a long period of time and for a variety of reasons. Although written records and other artifacts reveal that various people have participated in some types of gymnastics for at least four thousand years, it is highly probable that such participation dates back long into man's prehistory. Observations of apes, monkeys, and lower animal forms indicate that such gymnastics activities as climbing, hanging, balancing, and tumbling are spontaneous and are freely engaged in by the young animals. Without previous training or instruction, prehistoric and early man undoubtedly participated in these activities for the sheer enjoyment of them as well as for the purposes of obtaining food and escaping pursuing enemies.

One difficulty encountered in tracing the history of gymnastics is that the meaning of the word has changed in recent times. For centuries the term gymnastics had a much broader meaning than does its modern connotation. In recent years the term gymnastics has been used to connote stunts and series of stunts performed on gymnastics equipment or apparatus such as tumbling mats, horizontal bars, parallel bars, and trampolines. In many instances the intent of such performance and practice is to prepare for competition in gymnastics events or contests. However, the modern meaning of the word gymnastics has existed for hardly one hundred years. Until after the advent of the twentieth century in the United States and in some foreign countries yet today, the word gymnastics has for untold years been applied to entire systems of physical activities, including various kinds of conditioning exercises, games, and dancing. When used in this sense gymnastics had a similar meaning to what is now called physical education although far fewer sports were included in the various gymnastics systems of the past than are found in modern-day physical education programs.

An overview of gymnastics as it existed in former times may aid the reader in understanding how gymnastics has evolved into its present form. For a number of reasons it is difficult to present a precise history of present-day gymnastics because various pieces of gymnastics equipment and types of gymnastics activities were developed in different eras and have been used in different ways in the past. In addition the events included in competitive gymnastics contests have changed during the past few decades and even during the past several years.

A presentation of the use of gymnastics activities in man's past, the origin and development of gymnastics activities and equipment, and the present role of gymnastics in the overall program of physical education should permit an increased understanding and appreciation of the values and uses of present-day gymnastics. Therefore in the next section of this chapter is described the history of gymnastics when the term was used to denote a part of a complete system of physical education activities. In some of these systems of physical education, some gymnastics equipment or activities, as they are presently construed, were utilized.

THE ORIGINS OF GYMNASTICS

With few exceptions gymnastics and physical education activities have been employed in various nations for centuries for the primary purpose of developing the physical fitness level of the citizens in order that the country could field highly fit soldiers for defense of the nation and for offensive warfare. In some instances gymnastics activities have been promulgated for the purpose of politically unifying the people of a nation, thus giving them a purpose or goal toward which to strive. In other instances gymnastics movements involving dancing have been utilized in religious programs and systems.

Ancient records found in China, Persia, and Egypt describe and/or illustrate the practice of skills that involve the fundamentals of gymnastics. In Egypt the small children participated in many kinds of play activities and older children participated in tumbling activities. In China, a series of light exercises called *Cong Fu* were practiced for their supposed medicinal and other beneficial effects. The Chinese of this era before Christ believed that bodily inactivity caused disease; they therefore devised exercises consisting of stretching and breathing movements that were believed to aid in maintaining good organic functioning. Most of the exercises were performed in the sitting or kneeling position. The Persian gymnastics program was sponsored by the state for the purpose of providing well-conditioned, physically tough soldiers for the army, which was employed as a political instrument to conquer and subdue neighboring countries.

Gymnastics in Ancient Greece

The practice of gymnastics played an important role in the lives of the male Greeks, particularly those from Athens, who believed that they should be proficient in all phases of life and that the physical was an important facet of the whole person. As a result glory and acclaim were bestowed upon the physically trained who often competed in various contests of physical feats.

The Greeks originated the term gymnastics, which literally means "naked art," and which is derived from the Greek word *gymnos* meaning nude. The word refers to a practice of the Greeks in which they participated unclad in gymnastic activities. The word gymnasium is derived from the same source and refers to the structure or building in which "the nude art" was performed. *Acrobatics*, a form of gymnastics in which feats of skill are performed by teams of gymnasts on mats, novelty apparatus, or trapeze, is also a word of Greek derivation. Another word of Greek origin is *calisthenics*, which means "beautiful strength." The youth of Greece practiced gymnastics in a building called a *palæstra*. Because of their love of physical activities the Greeks developed the ancient Olympic Games (and other Pan-Hellenic games) which remained in existence for eleven hundred years. The main activities included in the Olympic Games were running and other track and field events such as discus throwing, wrestling, boxing, and horse and chariot racing.

The Romans and Gymnastics

By the Second Century, B.C., the Romans conquered the Greeks and thus had ample opportunity to observe the Greek system of gymnastics. The Romans adopted those phases of Greek gymnastics that they believed to be of utilitarian value such as preparing the citizenry for war, and hence they introduced selected types of gymnastics activity to the citizens of Rome. However, the Romans rejected the Greek ideal of a well-rounded man who should be physically well developed as one facet of the ideal whole person. In training for combat the Romans made use of wooden horses, which they mounted and dismounted. This appears to be the origin of the side horse and long horse used in modern gymnastics competition.

The Middle Ages

Gymnastics and formal physical activities came to a standstill with the fall of the Greek and Roman civilizations. The advent and rise of Christianity with its resultant philosophy and religious attitude concerning asceticism (the belief that the way to elevate the soul was to neglect and abuse the body) caused most forms of gymnastics activity to virtually disappear for more than a thousand years. During this time, only the knights and warriors participated in conditioning and gymnastics activities. One widely used training device used by knights in full armor (which had considerable weight) was the wooden horse that they practiced mounting. This exercise served to continue the use of exercising on the wooden horse as preparation for combat purposes and kept alive the use of the wooden horse. Other gymnastics activity engaged in during this era was the forming of human towers during sieges. Acrobatics, tumbling, and balancing were forms of entertainment presented by traveling troupes at public performances. These forms of gymnastics activities were further developed and their usage continues to the present day.

Physical Education in the 18th and 19th Centuries

Gymnastics as it is known today originated in large part toward the end of the eighteenth century. The development of modern day gymnastics was somewhat incidental to the rise of systems of gymnastics that included apparatus, tumbling, and balancing activities which in turn were parts of larger, more comprehensive systems of physical education. Some of the trail blazers in this development are discussed forthwith.

Rise of Gymnastics in Germany

JOHANN BASEDOW (1723–1790) conducted the first course of gymnastics as part of his school curriculum. Included in the gymnastics activities were riding, fencing, dancing, music, gardening, military drill, hunting and fishing, boating, bathing, climbing and jumping, vaulting, running, wrestling, broad and high jumping, games, walking balance beams, climbing ladders, calisthenics, and manual labor and training.

JOHANN GUTS MUTHS (1759–1818), an educator who is called the Grandfather of Gymnastics, used the fundamentals of Greek gymnastics but added new exercises and published the first book on gymnastics. His teaching methods provided for children as well as adults and included carefully selected gymnastics skills for girls. His first gymnasium was out-of-doors and it contained seesaws, ropes, balance beams, and vaulting apparatus. In addition to the activities taught by Basedow, Guts Muths also included pole vaulting, weight carrying, foot races, long walks, rope ladder climbing and discus throwing.

GERHARD VIETH (1763–1836), a mathematician, adhered closely to the Guts Muths system of gymnastics when he published an encyclopedia of bodily exercises in which he stressed the mental, moral, and physical value of exercises. He developed terminology for the long horse, balance beam, jumping ropes, horse, buck, and table.

FREDERICK JAHN (1778–1852) is considered the Father of German Gymnastics. He hoped to promote national unity and a high degree of physical fitness by organizing the gymnasts into Turner Societies. He was dynamic in his efforts and possessed a vision of a master race in physical stamina, and to accomplish this purpose he developed a program of gymnastics for adults. He preferred open air activity and constructed outdoor exercise grounds (*turnplatz*). When the need arose for new forms of activity, Jahn invented the appropriate type of apparatus and introduced to his exercise grounds the horizontal bar, parallel bars, side horse with pommels, jumping standards and pits, balance beam, ladders, and the buck. Jahn is credited with creating the system of *turnen* (gymnastics) from which the *Turnverein* (gymnastic society) arose and which eventually spread to the United States.

Gymnastics in Switzerland

JOHANN PESTALOZZI (1746–1827), a noted Swiss educational reformer, was the founder of free-arm exercises or calisthenics. He believed that conditioning exercises developed the individual intellectually, morally, and aesthetically.

ADOLF SPIESS (1810–1858) of Germany, who was trained under Pesta-lozzi, utilized Guts Muths and Jahn gymnastics in the schools of Switzer-land. In addition to the gymnastics activities he added to his program marching and conditioning exercises set to music for the purpose of im-proving body posture and developing grace of bodily movement. Spiess wrote *The Science of Gymnastics* and through his promotion gymnastics became a school subject in Switzerland. He is known as the Father of School Gymnastics.

Gymnastics in Sweden

PEHR LING (1776–1839) of Sweden was considered the first of the modern educators to introduce and utilize corrective and adaptive gymnastics, hence earning the title the Father of Swedish Gymnastics. He believed in the therapeutic and corrective value of exercise and used his system, which he had derived from a study of anatomy and physiology, to improve the physically weak. He suggested that exercises for the individual should be emphasized, and he taught that gymnastics should be systematized. Ling invented the apparatus upon which he taught: the boom, the saddle, the window ladder, the low combination bench, and the Swedish box. Hjalmar Ling, Pehr Ling's son, further developed his father's system and originated the stall bars. The system of corrective gymnastics was used by one of Hjalmar Ling's students named Branting.

Gymnastics in Denmark

FRANZ NACHTEGALL (1777–1847), the Father of Danish Gymnastics, directed in Copenhagen the first recorded training school of gymnastics in which were prepared teachers of gymnastics. This school was called the Military Gymnastic Institute.

GYMNASTICS IN AMERICA

Gymnastics was introduced into the United States by a number of men and organizations. For some time the German system of gymnastics dominated the physical education programs in the colleges and high schools, particularly in those areas in which a large number of German immigrants had located. Later the Swedish system was introduced and it soon gained popularity. These two systems had many proponents but Americanized systems of physical education, which combined some of the features of both, also gained a place in the programs of physical education in the schools of America during the latter part of the nineteenth century. During the early part of the twentieth century the utilization of foreign systems of physical education was gradually eliminated and the type of physical education program currently in American schools and colleges gradually came into being. Some of the people and organizations who were instrumental in the physical education movement in the United States and the roles that they played are described in the next section.

Pioneer Physical Educators and Organizations

CHARLES BECK (1798–1866), CHARLES FOLLEN (1796–1840), and FRANCIS LIEBER (1800–1872) emigrated to the United States from Germany as political refugees and were instrumental in establishing programs of gymnastics at the Round Hill School in Northampton, Massachusetts; Boston and Amherst College, and Harvard University. Because these were among the first programs of physical education in the United States, the German system of gymnastics was introduced to the United States in its original form and it was given a head start as a system of physical education for schools in the United States. The German system of gymnastics that was introduced into the United States included a considerable number of exercises that were performed on modern day gymnastics apparatus. However, the original gymnastics programs were noncompetitive in nature.

Turnvereins. With the arrival of thousands of German immigrants, the largest group of non-English speaking immigrants in America, turner clubs were organized in many cities in the United States where the immigrants had settled in large numbers. In 1850 these clubs formed the North American Turnerbund and promoted German gymnastics in many cities in the United States. In 1866 the clubs established the Normal College of Gymnastics which was housed at different times in several cities and for decades supplied many teachers for gymnastics clubs and public schools throughout the United States. It is now located in Indianapolis, Indiana, and has been an affiliate of Indiana University for more than twenty years. In 1881 the Milwaukee Turners Gymnastics Team competed in the National Turnfest in Frankfurt, Germany, becoming the first American gymnastics team to compete at an international level. At this time track and field athletic events were also included in all-around gymnastics competition.

Sokols and Swiss Societies. The Sokol movement was founded in Czechoslovakia in 1862 for the purposes of promoting physical fitness, power, and other ambitious aims by means of exercise on German gymnastics apparatus and through gymnastics competition. Large numbers of Czech immigrants settled in the United States in the mid-nineteenth century and soon formed Sokol units and engaged in gymnastics. In 1879, when the first national Sokol festival was held, 120 Sokol units were in existence. Other Slavic immigrants than the Czechs organized additional Sokol groups between 1890 and 1908. During the latter part of the nineteenth century Swiss gymnastics societies made their appearance in the United States. Their programs were similar to that of the German Turners and helped to develop competitive gymnastics in this country.

The Young Men's Christian Association. The YMCA has made a great contribution to the spread of gymnastics throughout the United States by installing in its gymnasiums complete sets of gymnastics equipment. In 1887, the association's International Training School at Springfield Massachusetts (now Springfield College), established a Physical Training Department that gave and presently gives students a thorough background in gymnastic skills and methods of teaching. Its gymnastics teacher, Leslie Judd, recently retired, is renowned throughout the world for his gymnastics courses, his exhibition teams, and his enthusiasm in encouraging national programs of gymnastics.

Boston Young Men's Christian Union. The BYMCU was established in 1850 and since its inception has encouraged participants of all age groups to use gymnastics as a means of gaining a high degree of physical condition. One of the outstanding teachers of gymnastics, Arthur Fox, a German directed the gymnastics activities here for forty-five years. His students teach in many schools throughout the United States.

Dudley A. Sargent. One of the first American contributors to gymnastics as a program of physical education, Dudley A. Sargent (1840–1924), taught gymnastics at Bowdoin College. He directed the Heminway Gymnasium at Harvard and he developed many pieces of gymnasium apparatus, including pulley weights and leg and finger machines.

Hartvig Nissen. A native of Norway, Hartvig Nissen came to America in 1883. He settled in Washington, D.C., and immediately began to acquaint the physicians with the value of corrective and medical gymnastics and massage, based on the Swedish system of gymnastics, and he also operated the famous Swedish Health Institute located in that city. The Swedish system includes calisthenics exercises and light apparatus exercises.

Baron Nils Posse. A native of Sweden and a graduate of the Royal Central Institute of Gymnastics of Stockholm, Baron Nils Posse in 1889 organized and taught gymnastics at the Boston Normal School of Gymnastics, which received its financial support from Mrs. Mary Hemmingway, a wealthy Bostonian, with the stipulation that the Ling System of Swedish Gymnastics be taught to the prospective physical education teachers. He later founded and managed the Posse Normal School, which promoted the teaching of Swedish Medical Gymnastics.

A.A.U. In 1897 the Amateur Athletic Union of the United States assumed national control of gymnastics competition in the United States. Competition in gymnastics has stimulated many clubs and schools to promote courses in gymnastics. Year after year, the monopoly that foreign born or first-generation Americans have had on the national titles in the various gymnastics events has weakened and been lost as fourth, fifth, and sixth generation Americans have taken up the sport.

Modern Gymnastics

It is apparent that some forms of the sport of gymnastics have occupied man for many centuries. Man has participated in and been entertained by tumbling and balancing activities since at least the dawn of history. Man has exercised on a form of the long horse for over two thousand years. But man has practiced on and competed in most types of gymnastics apparatus for only slightly more than one hundred years. The modern sport of gymnastics originated in large part from the heavy apparatus employed in the bodily exercise form of German gymnastics. Floor exercise or free calisthenics have a large part of their ancestry in the Swedish and Danish form of gymnastics. It is probably only a trait of human nature that when several people exercise on a piece of apparatus, they soon begin competing among themselves in feats of strength, skill, balance, flexibility, and agility.

This process of making a sport of gymnastics was undoubtedly stimulated by the individual and mass shows or demonstrations that were held by various gymnastics clubs, Turnvereins, Sokols, and school clubs in their own areas or districts and before long at a national level. The German Turnvereins were holding demonstrations over one hundred years ago; this idea originated in Germany and they brought it with them when their members emigrated to the United States.

Gymnastics competition as a sport developed in the United States shortly after the end of the Civil War. For many years this sport was mainly confined to the gymnastics clubs, which were mainly composed of members who had not been in the United States too many years. During this era the high schools and colleges did not sponsor sports of any type because they were then regarded as not a part of education and as a waste of time for the students. Eventually the schools were forced to assume control of sports and athletics in which their students participated in order to assume safe and sane competition under just rules and to avoid the exploitation of the students by outside interests who desired to make a large profit. But even with these changes gymnastics as a sport was slow in being accepted into the sports programs of high schools and colleges and for many years it was lightly promoted—mainly by private gymnastics clubs and public organizations such as the YMCA. Because gymnastics stunts were included in the physical education programs of those schools that had gymnasiums and some gymnastics equipment (the number of such gymnasiums increased rapidly in the colleges in the late 1800's, in the high schools in the early 1900's, and in the grade schools after World War I) the opportunity for gymnastics competition, but not the appeal, was present for many years. The lack of appeal of gymnastics as a sport was based on several factors: (1) gymnastics was an activity developed by foreigners for a foreign culture that was not compatible to the environment in the United States or the background of Americans, (2) gymnastics was taught in a stiff, formal, and precise manner in somewhat of a military fashion that destroyed much of the enjoyment that might otherwise have been derived from it, (3) many teachers were poorly trained in the techniques of teaching gymnastics, (4) the influence of John Dewey, the noted American educator, and his pragmatic philosophy caused in the 1920's and '30's a shifting of physical education program content to mainly sports and games, and (5) the depression of the 1930's forced many schools to curtail their programs of sports competition, especially in the minor sports. During this era very few high schools and colleges had competitive gymnastics teams. A few college teams did present gymnastics exhibitions to the public and competed in A.A.U. and other gymnastics championships outside of the college level, but relatively few college gymnastics teams competed with those of other colleges. As a consequence, the sport of gymnastics has undergone its major growth in the United States since World War II.

Immediately following World War II, a revitalization of the national sports program was ordered by the national headquarters of the A.A.U. Many new district chairmen were appointed and meets ranging from the novice meet to the national championship were held. The late Roy Moore, then chairman of the National A.A.U. Gymnastics Committee, and one-time national horse champion (1912–13), directed this revival with much enthusiasm. In spite of the lack of experienced officials and poor gymnastics facilities in many areas, meets were conducted all over the nation with the assistance of oldtime gymnasts. Due in part to the efforts of this committee, college gymnasts, who increased their gymnastics proficiency by competing in regularly scheduled district A.A.U. and college meets, are now serving as gymnastics coaches in junior and senior high schools, colleges, boys' clubs, and recreation centers. These coaches have had increasing opportunities to upgrade their qualifications and coaching skills by attending numerous gymnastics clinics, workshops, and special college courses in gymnastics.

Within this decade, 1960–66, the number of high school gymnasts has increased tenfold. Many of the high schools in the New England District are now supporting both boys' and girls' gymnastics teams. At the end of the season, the districts conduct team and individual competition. The states of California and Illinois have many outstanding high school gymnastics teams; some of these performers have placed high in national A.A.U. and the US Gymnastics Federation competition. Most states now have some high school gymnastics teams; New York, Pennsylvania, and Minnesota have a long tradition of having gymnastics competition at all age levels, including the high schools—this stems from a gymnastics tradition fostered by gymnastics clubs formed by immigrants.

The gymnastics centers that first encouraged and developed the gymnastics ability of young people are still functioning. Some of these are located in Philadelphia, Minneapolis, Los Angeles, Boston, and Springfield, Massachusetts. New gymnastics centers have sprung up everywhere.

The National Gymnastics Clinic at Sarasota, Florida, which originated in the winter of 1951 and which is now called the Eastern Gymnastics Clinic, has become an annual main attraction for gymnastics enthusiasts all over the country. Recently another winter gymnastics clinic, the Western Gymnastics Clinic, which meets in Tucson, Arizona, has attracted many gymnastics performers and coaches. The energetic National Association of Gymnastic Coaches, which originated in 1950, aids in scheduling and officiating at gymnastics meets, ranging from the high school to the international level.

Within the past few years the American Gymnastics Association has promoted district and national competition for gymnasts of high school age and beyond. The most famous competition in gymnastics is that provided every four years in the modern Olympic Games, which were revived in Athens, Greece in 1896. At that time gymnastics competition on the side horse, tumbling, parallel bars, flying rings, long horse vault, horizontal bar and rope climb was held. The Olympic Games in 1964 included gymnastics competition in seven events: individual all-around, free standing exercise, side horse, parallel bars, still rings, long horse vault, and horizontal bar. At the national level, gymnastics competitions include the A.A.U. championships for men and women, the National Collegiate Championships, and the A.G.A. Championships, all held yearly. The A.A.U. Gymnastics Championships were begun in 1885 and included flying rings, horizontal bar, Indian clubs, parallel bars, and tumbling. In 1948 for the first time the trampoline event was included, an exclusively American contribution to gymnastics. The events that were generally included in the gymnastics competitions in the United States as of 1964 were free exercise, originated in 1921; the side horse, 1897; the long horse, 1897; the still rings, 1959; the parallel bars, 1885; the horizontal bar, 1885; tumbling, 1886; and rebound tumbling (trampolining), 1948.

Throughout the years the most famous United States gymnast has probably been Alfred Jochim. A member of the Turnverein of Hudson County, New Jersey, which has long been noted for the gymnastics excellence of its members; Jochim won the all-around A.A.U. championship in 1925, '26, '27, '28, '29, '30, and '33. George Wheeler won this championship in 1937, '38, '39, '40 and '41. Frank Kriz, a member of the New York Sokol, won the long horse event at the 1924 Olympic Games in Paris, the only American to win a gold medal in one of the traditional gymnastics events in Olympic competition. Other American gymnasts won gold medals in strictly American gymnastics events (the rope climb, tumbling, and Indian club swinging) at the 1932 Olympic Games; these events were abolished from the games shortly after this date. The Swiss Turnverein won the A.A.U. gymnastics team championship in 1926, 1928–39, and 1942, '44, '46, '47. Famous women gymnasts include Clara Schroth of Philadelphia who won the all-around A.A.U. championship in 1945, '46, '49, '50, '51 and '52. Some of the famous women's teams are from the Philadelphia Turners and the National Turners of Newark, New Jersey.

With few exceptions the United States has fared poorly in international gymnastics competition. This poor showing has been attributed to several reasons, including (1) choosing the American Olympic Gymnastics Team members a short time before the Olympic competition thus allowing the team members relatively little practice, (2) a lack of participation by American members in international competition with attendant unfamiliarity with a different method of judging, (3) a preference by many American gymnasts to specialize on one or two pieces of gymnastics apparatus so that they are not well prepared in all the gymnastics events demanded in international competition, (4) a tendency by the American gymnasts to attempt to include too many difficult stunts in their routines and thus not perform all of them well instead of including easier combinations of stunts done to perfection, and (5) the fact that relatively few Americans specialize in gymnastics whereas in many countries gymnastics is a national sport that attracts more participants than almost any other sport. Until after World War II, the Germans, Swiss, and Scandinavians dominated the Olympic gymnastics championships. Beginning in 1948 the Russians rose to the ascendancy and held this position until 1964 when the Japanese team won the Olympic team championship.

Gymnastics is now enjoying a tremendous growth in popularity. Each year for the past several years one or more outstanding foreign national gymnastics teams have given exhibitions throughout the US. Large crowds turned out to see the 1960 World Champion Russian team of men and women and the 1964 World Champion Japanese team when they toured the United States. For the past few years national and international competition has been televised, thus exposing the sport to millions of Americans. At the 1964 National Convention of the American Association for Health, Physical Education and Recreation, over 1,000 members attended the gymnastics section meeting. Gymnastics for many reasons truly appears to be a sport with an outstanding future.

3 PREPARING FOR GYMNASTICS PARTICIPATION

INTRODUCTION

Multiple Approach to Training for Gymnastics

The recommendations contained in this chapter are offered from the viewpoint that the most efficient and effective method of preparing for gymnastics participation is to utilize a multiple approach when training for gymnastics. By utilizing several of the facets of the physical and mental approaches to training, the aspiring gymnast should develop his gymnastics skills and abilities at an optimum rate, which in turn should cause him to be satisfied with his progress. In order for the maximum improvement to occur the novice gymnast should make use of as many of the training methods described in this chapter as appear to fit his situation and needs.

A Point of View Concerning Training

The person who wishes to become proficient in gymnastics should early decide what his goals are and then follow a training program to help him attain these goals. The type and comprehensiveness of the training program and the amount, quality, and intensity of the daily practice should be chosen to meet the goals. Certainly these goals will differ considerably for the gymnast who engages in gymnastics for the purpose of maintaining a better than average state of physical fitness than those of the gymnast who hopes to become a national gymnastics champion. In gymnastics as in any sport (and even in life) one derives from the sport only what one puts into it. A person who makes spasmodic, half-hearted attempts to improve his skills in a sport is literally wasting his time, and he should decide whether to quit the sport or to invest wisely the time he devotes to the sport and make an effort to improve his skills and ability. In arriving at this decision a person's conscience is probably his best guide as to how intensely he should devote his time and effort toward achieving his maximum potential in gymnastics. If a person decides that he wants to become as highly skilled as possible then he should regularly train five or six times a week if possible, and he should efficiently utilize his workout time for improving his gymnastics skills and practicing well-constructed routines in the various events.

WHEN TO TRAIN

When should the gymnast train? Perhaps a simplified answer to the question of when to exercise in order to develop gymnastics skill at a maximum rate and to improve selected components of physical fitness is whenever one feels like exercising, providing the feeling is sufficiently frequent. Light exercises that are not exhausting but that act as a warm-up (such as flexibility and form exercises) should be performed immediately before practicing gymnastics because they aid in preparing the gymnast both mentally and physically for the practice of gymnastics. Strenuous and vigorous exercises (such as strength and endurance exercises) should be performed either at the completion of the gymnastics workout or later in the day according to the preference of the gymnast. These exercises are physically exhausting and the fatigue induced by their performance could retard the acquisition of gymnastics skills or increase the possibility of an accident occurring during the gymnastics workout.

CONDITIONING FOR GYMNASTICS

Conditioning exercises of various types should precede or parallel the practice of gymnastics for four reasons: (1) for the purpose of conditioning the muscles, tendons, and joint structure for the full-range-of-motion movements practiced and performed in gymnastics; (2) for the purpose of providing sufficient muscular power to enable the more difficult exercises to be performed with a margin of safety; (3) for providing a warm-up before the actual gymnastics workout; and (4) for the purpose of rapidly eliminating superfluous body weight.

Although participation in gymnastics activities and the practice of a variety of gymnastics stunts will soon develop a better-than-average degree of physical fitness, carefully selected supplemental exercises can considerably accelerate the process of becoming highly conditioned for gymnastics participation. The use of efficient, modern training methods for most sports demands that supplemental exercises be done because (1) practice of the sport itself develops only that degree of conditioning needed to perform successfully in the sport and no more; once this degree of conditioning or skill has been attained, the placing, by means of participation in the sport, of an overload on the muscular and related body systems becomes extremely difficult; and (2) some of the important components comprising all-around physical fitness are ordinarily neglected by practicing only one sport. These components need to be maintained in a proper balance in order to avoid an unequal and disproportionate development of the body and because the underdeveloped components of physical fitness occasionally are vitally needed for a successful performance. For the two reasons cited above, participants in most sports supplement their training with specially selected conditioning methods. For example, basketball players often engage in weight training exercises in order to increase their muscular strength (and power), which otherwise would be little enhanced by regular basketball drills and scrimmage. Football players and wrestlers commonly perform distance running and wind sprints in order to develop a high degree of circulorespiratory endurance. Swimmers frequently practice flexibility exercises in order to utilize a full range of motion in their swimming strokes and to avoid developing additional resistance created by a failure to lift their arms and hands completely above the water during the recovery phase of the arm stroke. Track and field runners often perform calisthenics and exercises designed to increase the strength, power, and mass of their upper body and arms in order to create a better reaction and balance to their leg action while running. The universal acceptance of supplementary training methods as cited above lends support to the practice of engaging in special conditioning methods in order to effectively prepare for gymnastics participation.

General Conditioning Exercises

In order to best prepare himself for gymnastics, the aspiring gymnast needs to consider carefully how he can best develop those components of physical fitness in which he is deficient or below average. The possession of the following components of physical fitness plays an important role in rapidly and readily acquiring skill in gymnastics and in gaining a mastery of a multitude of gymnastics stunts: flexibility, strength, muscular endurance, circulorespiratory endurance, agility, balance, neuromuscular skill, and proper body weight.

Because some people have developed some components of physical fitness more than others, because some components can be developed rapidly and with less effort than others, and because participation on some gymnastics apparatus demands a higher degree of development of certain components of physical fitness than others, it is extremely difficult to make blanket recommendations concerning how much stress should be placed on developing each component of physical fitness. Instead this problem should be studied in terms of the needs of each person, and a general conditioning program should then be based on the results of this analysis. It is important, however, to remember that performing gymnastics alone is usually not the most efficient way to develop the various components of physical fitness just as repeatedly playing a game by itself is an inefficient way to perfect the fundamental skills of which the game is comprised.

THE OVERLOAD PRINCIPLE

The basic tenet of any training program designed to increase the physical fitness of the participant is the proper utilization of the overload principle. The overload principle operates whenever a person in training repeatedly subjects himself to a larger-than-normal load (an overload). His body in turn responds to this overload by slightly increasing its ability to handle that size of load. Hence during the next training session the load against which the trainee performs is slightly increased and again the body responds by making a slight gain. This procedure is continued and the body is repeatedly overloaded until the participant has achieved a high degree of physical fitness (the higher the degree of physical fitness, the more difficulty encountered in working against the overload). As soon as this state of physical fitness has been attained, considerably less training effort is required to maintain this stage of physical fitness than was required to attain it.

The reader should understand that the above explanation of the overload principle is somewhat oversimplified. Also, the process of attaining a desired state of physical fitness does not proceed at an even, uniform rate but is most apt to be characterized by periods of days or even weeks where little gain is evident followed by short periods of rapid, uneven gain. Some regression or reversal in the increase in physical fitness may occur during this process. However, if a persistent effort is made to apply an overload in the training workout, a resultant increase in physical fitness will almost invariably result over a period of time. However, the gains made in the different components of physical fitness proceed at different rates and these often vary from person to person.

The application of the overload principle is specific to the components of physical fitness that are the goals of the training program. Therefore, to gain in strength the performer must systematically work his major muscles against a resistance that is progressively increased. This is the foundation of a weight-training or progressive resistance program in which the participant, whenever he performs a predetermined maximum number of repetitions of a weight-training exercise (such as eight or ten), increases the poundage lifted in that exercise during his next workout session. In order to continually increase in endurance, the performer must regularly overload the amount of endurance work that he performs. This may be done by systematically increasing, at regular intervals, the distance that he runs without stopping, by running a fixed distance in progressively less time, or a combination of increased distances run at faster velocities may be utilized. In order to increase flexibility the overload used when performing flexibility exercises may be obtained by systematically increasing the range of joint movement over which the flexibility exercises are performed. In the above examples the gains made by these specific types of overloading would be primarily in only one component of physical fitness. This fact emphasizes the importance of following an exercise program that has been designed to achieve specific goals. On the other hand, it is entirely possible to develop rapidly more than one component of physical fitness while performing only one series of exercises or one exercise program. An example of this is performing each weight-training exercise for fifteen or twenty repetitions in order to make significant gains in both strength and in local muscular endurance. In fact, some components of physical fitness such as agility, balance, and speed of movement may be sufficiently developed as a byproduct of performing strength, endurance and/or flexibility exercises that it becomes unnecessary to train specifically for such components.

The consequences of the foregoing information are twofold: (1) the overload principle must be effectively utilized if gains in physical fitness are to proceed at the most rapid pace, and (2) in order to develop some of the most important components of physical fitness, specific exercises and activities must be selected in order to achieve, these goals.

FLEXIBILITY EXERCISES

The possession of sufficient muscular strength is extremely important for the development of artistic gymnastic movements. However, in many cases strength without flexibility may inhibit rather than enhance the advancement of gymnastics skills. The possession of sufficient flexibility necessary to perform the required movements in gymnastics without a break in form (bending the body or limbs at the wrong joint or joints) is a prerequisite to successful gymnastics performance; therefore, the beginning or less-skilled gymnast should strive to develop a significant degree of flexibility as quickly as possible. Therefore, preliminary to or when beginning to participate in gymnastics, the beginning gymnast should engage in a complete sequence of flexibility exercises that involve the major joints of the body.

Because a large number of repetitions of flexibility exercises should be performed in order to effectively increase flexibility and joint range of motion, a minimum of fifteen of each of the flexibility exercises should be performed. When sufficiently conditioned, twenty to twenty-five repetitions of these or similar exercises should be performed. The ability to (1) touch the palms of the hands to the floor while flexed forward but with the legs straight (2) perform a back-bend (bending backwards without losing the balance until the hands are resting on the floor or mat), and (3) touch the back of the hands together at shoulder level while swinging the arms backwards indicates that a desired level of flexibility has been achieved. Flexibility exercises should be performed daily if possible or at least five times weekly. Because they require relatively little energy or effort to perform they should probably be done at the beginning of the gymnastics period. When performed at this time they also serve as an excellent warm-up in addition to preparing the body for gymnastics movements requiring supple movements and a great deal of flexibility.

Each of the following sequences of exercises should be performed through a full range-of-motion for the purpose of increasing the flexibility around the important joints of the body. The exercises may be performed in any order desired and, of course, other flexibility exercises than these may be utilized. The aspiring gymnast should particularly strive to increase his forward and backward range of motion in the spinal column and in the shoulder joints.

Flexibility Exercises for the Shoulders

First exercise. From a straddle-stand position with his arms alongside his sides and thighs, the performer (1) moves his arms forward; (2) moves his arms overhead; (3) moves his arms forward; (4) recovers.

Second exercise. From the starting position used in the first exercise, the performer (1) moves his arms forward; (2) moves his arms sideward; (3) moves his arms forward; (4) recovers.

Flexibility Exercise for the Neck

From a straddle-stand position with his hands on his hips (Figure 3.1), the performer executes the following movements: (1) rotates his head to the right; (2) rotates his head forward; (3) rotates his head to the left; (4) rotates his head forward; (5) rotates his head upward; (6) rotates his head forward; (7) rotates his head downward, and (8) rotates his head forward.

Flexibility Exercise for Lateral Trunk Movements

From a straddle-stand position with his hands on his hips (Figure 3.1), the performer (1) flexes his body directly to the right, keeping his legs straight (Figure 3.2) and (2) flexes his body to the left, keeping his legs straight.

Figure 3.1   Figure 3.2

Flexibility Exercises for the Back

First exercise. From a straddle-stand position with his hands on his hips, the performer (1) touches his left foot with both hands, keeping both legs straight (Figure 3.3); (2) returns to the starting position; (3) touches his right foot with both hands, keeping both legs straight, and (4) recovers to the starting position.

Second exercise.   From a back-lying (supine) position, the performer (1) sits up and touches his knees with his hands; (2) continues to reach forward and reaches past his toes, holding this position for a count of three (Figure 3.4); (3) leans back and touches his knees, and (4) returns to the starting position.

Third exercise.   From a standing position with his legs slightly spread and his hands on his hips or alongside his thighs, the performer (1) raises both arms overhead and backward as far as possible, looking backward at the same time (Figure 3.5), and (2) returns to the starting position and then continues to repeat the above movements.

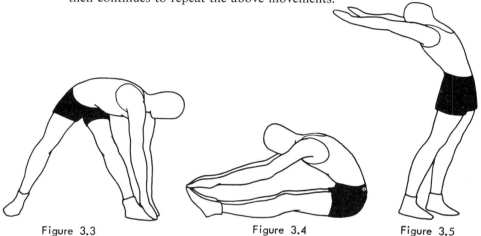

Figure 3.3   Figure 3.4   Figure 3.5

Fourth exercise.   From a front-lying (prone) position with his hands at his side, the performer (1) raises his legs, head, and chest as high as possible and maintains this arched position for a count of three, and (2) relaxes and returns to the starting position and then continues to repeat these movements.

Flexibility Exercise for the Knees and Hips

From a push-up position with both feet on the floor, with his right leg flexed and his left leg straight, the performer (1) reverses the position of his feet and (2) continues to reverse the position of his feet, keeping his hips as close to the floor as possible.

STRENGTH EXERCISES

As indicated in the previous section, flexibility exercises are recommended as a means of increasing the range of motion and to warm-up. To complete the training program for creating the gymnastics image and to develop those traits of most value when performing gymnastics, strength- and endurance-building exercises must be included in the gymnastics training program.

Several different studies have revealed that most American youths are weakest in the muscles of their shoulder area, arms, and trunk. This lack of strength in these areas is usually a great handicap to developing skill in gymnastics because the performance of many gymnastics stunts requires a great deal of power, which in turn demands the ability to apply large amounts of muscular force quickly and at the correct time. Because the rapid development of gymnastics skills depends a great deal on strength, the most logical approach for the beginning gymnast to take is to engage in a strength-building program that will produce rapid results.

Although the regular practice of gymnastics is of immense value in gaining strength in most of the muscles and in acquiring a muscular, well-developed, and symmetrical body build, the beginner or gymnast with a low degree of skill can markedly accelerate the pace at which additional strength and muscular bulk is acquired by performing supplemental strength-building exercises. Numerous research studies have supplied an abundance of evidence favoring weight-training exercises as being the most efficient type of strength exercises in terms of their efficiency in increasing muscular strength. Isometric or motionless exercises have also been found to be effective for this purpose but their performance apparently results in little other beneficial gains taking place. However, progressive resistance exercises in the form of weight training also produce secondary benefits such as improved local-muscular endurance. Improvement in speed of movement also can normally be expected to accrue. As an added argument for selecting weight training as a means of rapidly developing strength, the overload principle can be most easily applied to weight-training exercises.

Because a weight-training program requires the expenditure of large amounts of energy and is somewhat physically exhausting, strength-developing exercises should be performed at the completion of the gymnastics practice session. Because the muscles and muscle tissue need time to recuperate and rebuild themselves after a demanding training session, strength exercises should be performed only three times a week. Performing such exercises five times a week or daily in order to rapidly build up strength and muscle tissue defeats its own purpose and actually retards the acquisition of strength and increased muscle size.

After a favorable amount of strength and power has been acquired through the use of progressive weight-training exercise, the novice may wish to engage in only gymnastics, or he may choose to continue his body-building program while practicing in gymnastics.

Preparing to Engage in a Progressive Weight-Training Program

Because weak muscles can increase quite rapidly in strength when weight-training exercises are utilized, physical therapists often prescribe them (progressive resistance exercises) as the exercise medium through which asymmetrical body developments are corrected. The gymnast who is interested in performing weight training as a means of increasing his strength and body muscular development should first have a posture examination in order to determine if his body is symmetrically developed. He should then engage in a well-rounded routine of weight-training exercises with special emphasis placed on performing exercises that will correct any defect revealed in the posture examination. For example, if a person is round-shouldered, he should do two sets of an exercise (the rowing exercise) that strengthens the rhomboid muscles of the back. These, if strengthened, will pull the scapular closer together, and naturally force the shoulders into their proper position. When these corrections in body posture are achieved, the program of regular weight-training exercises only can be followed if desired.

Instructions for Beginning Weight Trainers

The general weight-training program that is presented is one that has been developed for the beginning weight trainer who has no posture defects or special weaknesses in any muscle group or body area. For those with posture defects or weaknesses in muscle groups, special weight-training exercises designed to remedy these defects should be included in the weight-training program in order to adjust it to meet the needs of such persons. For those persons who have better-than-average leg strength because of participation in sports such as track and field, football, basketball or hockey, the weight-training exercises (partial squats and heel raises) that develop the muscles of the legs may be performed for only one set or even eliminated. Because successful gymnastics performance requires extra strong muscles in the arms, shoulders, back, chest, and abdominal area, exercises that develop the muscles of these areas should be performed by everyone. The weight-training program for beginners contains exercises that put into action all the major muscle groups of the entire body. From this program, the beginning gymnast can pick those exercises that will develop only the muscle groups that he wishes to develop further. However, most persons should perform the entire group of exercises for at least the first three months of training. The number of sets that an exercise is performed may be varied if the weight trainer believes this will best serve his purpose.

The weight-training program described in this section contains the name of each weight-training exercise, the parts of the body that receive the major benefits by the exercise, the muscles chiefly used when performing the exercise, the percentage of body weight that a beginning weight trainer of average strength should first use for the exercise, and the number of repetitions to be performed. Although the percentage of weight used for an exercise is primarily determined by the composite strength of the muscles utilized in performing the exercise, the beginning poundage will, by design, be somewhat light for most beginners. Experience has shown that lifting a light poundage during the first few weight-training workouts will, in most cases, help to avoid much of the muscular soreness and stiffness that results when a beginning weight trainer lifts heavy poundages that force him to strain his muscles or exert them to their maximum effort. The number of sets of repetitions (one set means to repeat an exercise the specified number of times without stopping to rest, and two sets means to do the exercise the specified number of times without stopping; then after a short rest of one to two minutes to repeat the same exercise again) of each exercise is usually two because recent research findings indicate two sets to be superior to one set in gaining strength. For gaining strength rapidly, research indicates that six repetitions of an exercise is superior to ten or more repetitions. Therefore if the primary purpose of weight training is to gain increased strength (which is the purpose recommended by the authors) then six or seven repetitions of each exercise should usually be performed. When an increase in local muscular endurance as well as strength is the desired outcome, most authorities recommend from ten to fifteen repetitions of an exercise be performed. In order to benefit most rapidly from a weight-training program, the weight trainer should perform three times a week or every other day.

After determining the percentage of weight to be used for each exercise, the weight trainer should retain the initial poundage for about six to nine workouts before increasing the poundage used for each exercise. This practice will allow the beginning weight trainer adequate time in which to strengthen his muscles to the point where an additional load can be safely imposed, and will enable him to learn to perform the exercise while maintaining a proper body position as well as to learn to control his balance during each exercise movement. After the completion of the sixth to the ninth workout, the weight trainer should at each succeeding workout increase the poundage used in each exercise by about 5 per cent. This increase in poundage should be continued until he can not do six (or seven) repetitions of an exercise during the second set. When this stage is reached that same poundage should be retained for that exercise until the maximum number of repetitions (six or seven) is achieved during the second set. Then the poundage for that exercise should be increased during the next workout by approximately 5 per cent. The importance of increasing periodically and whenever possible the poundage lifted in an exercise cannot be overemphasized because this is the basis for applying the overload principle. As with the progress involved in almost any type of training or learning, the rate of increase in the poundage for the various exercises will not be smooth and constant but instead will be unsteady and marked by various stages, sometimes extending over several periods, in which almost no progress will be noted.

THE WEIGHT-TRAINING PROGRAM OUTLINED

Partial Knee Bend (One-Half Squat) (Figure 3.6)

Starting position. Feet spread shoulder-width apart; barbell placed behind the neck and across the shoulders with the hands positioned near the plates in an over-grip position; heels resting on a one- or two-inch high support.

Exercise movement. (1) Bend the legs at the knees until the body is in a one-half squat position, keep the back straight and head up throughout the exercise movement. (2) Extend the legs and return to the standing position.

Parts of the body benefited. Thighs and hips directly, lower legs and abdominal area indirectly.

Primary muscles used. Rectus femoris, vastus lateralis, vastus medialis, vastus intermedius, gluteus maximus, semimembranosis, semitendinosis.

Percentage of body weight to be used. 65 per cent.

Number of repetitions. Two sets of ten.

Comments. Squatting movements while supporting a barbell require the expenditure of considerable energy; hence, many weight trainers prefer to do this exercise first in order to have it out of the way. This exercise is considered by many to be the single best all around weight-training exercise.

Figure 3.6   Figure 3.7

Two-Hand Military Press (Figure 3.7)

Starting position. Feet spread about shoulder width apart, grasp the bar with a regular (palms over the bar) grip. Bend the legs, keeping the back straight, and lift the bar to shoulder height, resting it against the chest.

Exercise movements. (1) Push the barbell over head until the arms are fully extended. While performing that movement keep the legs and body straight and look forward in order to maintain proper balance. (2) Lower the barbell to the chest-rest position.

Parts of the body benefited. Upper arms, shoulders, upper back, and higher rib cage area.

Muscles used. Triceps, coracobrachialis, deltoids, trapezius, and serratus magnus.

Percentage of body weight to be used. 40 per cent.

Two-Hand Curls (Regular Curls) (Figure 3.8)

Starting position. Standing erect, the feet are spread about eight to twelve inches apart, the hands grasp the barbell about shoulder-width apart in a reverse (palms under the bar) grasp with the arms at the side and the bar resting against the front of the thighs.

Exercise movements. (1) Flex the arms, lifting the barbell in an arc until it rests against the chest. (2) Lower the barbell to the starting position.

Parts of the body benefited. Front of upper arms, upper back, and neck.

Muscles used. Biceps, brachiolis, brachioradials, pronator teres, and indirectly the trapezius.

Percentage of body weight to be used. 40 per cent.

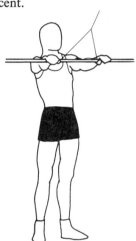

Figure 3.8   Figure 3.9

Pull-Downs Using Overhead Pulley Weights (Figure 3.9)

Starting position. Straddle-stand position with the arms extended directly overhead and grasping the pulley weight handles with a regular or palms forward grasp.

Exercise movements. (1) Lower the arms sideward and downward to the thighs. (2) Raise the arms overhead. (3) Lower the arms forward and downward to the thighs. (4) Raise the arms overhead.

Parts of the body benefited. Shoulders, upper back, chest, and arms.

Muscles used. Triceps, latissimus dorsi, levator, trapezius, deltoids, pectoral major and minor.

Percentage of body weight to be used. 20 per cent.

Pull-Overs on Bench—Alternate Exercise When Pulley Weights Are Unavailable (Figure 3.10a and 3.10b)

Starting position. Lie on the back on a bench with the head positioned at one end of the bench and, with the arms overhead above the shoulders, grasp the barbell in a regular (palms facing the feet) grasp with the hands spaced at least shoulder-width apart.

Exercise movements. (1) Slowly lower the barbell behind the head as far back as possible while keeping the arms straight. (2) Keeping the arms straight, raise the barbell upward and forward to the starting position and then continue the movement, lowering it until it rests on the thighs. (3) Keeping the arms straight, raise the barbell and then lower it past the bench and behind the head.

Parts of the body benefited. Shoulders, back, and chest.

Muscles used. Triceps, latissimus dorsi, deltoids, pectoral major and minor, and serratus anterior.

Percentage of body weight to be used. 10 per cent.

Comments. Pull-overs on a bench is an alternate exercise that may be performed in place of pull-downs or if pulley weights are not available. This exercise may also be performed with dumbbells.

Figure 3.10 a.   Figure 3.10 b.

Figure 3.11

Dead Lift (Regular Dead Lift) (Figure 3.11)

Starting position. From a standing position with the feet spread about eighteen inches apart, flex the body and legs and grasp the barbell in a regular (palms over the bar) grip, keeping the back straight and the head facing forward.

Exercise movements. (1) Keeping the arms and the back as straight as possible, lift the barbell and come to an erect standing position. (2) Slowly lower the barbell to the starting position.

Parts of body benefited. Buttocks, legs, chest, shoulders, and back.

Muscles used. Erectus spinae, supraspinatus, gluteus maximus, quadriceps, biceps, femoris, semimembranosis and semitendinosis.

Percentage of body weight to be used. 75 per cent.

Comments. The dead lift exercise is another excellent general or all-around exercise that uses many of the major muscle groups of the body. It is particularly useful in developing the muscles of the back, which are often used in performing many gymnastics stunts.

Bench Press (Supine Press) (Figure 3.12)

Starting position. Lying on the back on a ten-inch high bench the bar is grasped with a regular grasp and with the hands spread at least shoulder width apart. The barbell rests upon the chest.

Exercise movements. (1) Extend the arms, pushing the barbell upward until the arms are completely extended. (2) Slowly lower the barbell to the starting position.

Parts of the body benefited. Back of upper arms, shoulders, and chest.

Muscles used. Triceps, pectoral major and minor, serratus magnus.

Percentage of body weight to be used. 50 per cent.

Figure 3.12

Rowing Exercise (Bent-Over Rowing) (Figure 3.13)

Starting position. Straddle-stand position with the legs slightly bent and the body flexed forward at the hips. The hands are spread shoulder-width apart and the barbell is grasped with a regular (palms downward) grip.

Figure 3.13

Exercise movements. (1) Without moving the trunk flex the arms and raise the barbell to the chest. (2) Slowly lower the barbell to the starting position.

Parts of the body benefited. Upper back, shoulders, and front of upper arms.

Muscles used. Rhomboids, trapezius, latissimus dorsi, levator, biceps and deltoids.

Percentage of body weight to be used. 40 per cent.

Lateral Raises with Dumbbells (Figure 3.14)

Starting position. Feet spread about shoulder-width apart with the arms straight and the dumbbells held at the sides.

Exercise movements. (1) Raise the arms sideward to a horizontal position and then continue to raise them until they are directly above the shoulders. (2) Lower the dumbbells sideward and to the starting position. (3) Raise the dumbbells forward until they are directly in front of the shoulders; continue to raise them until they are directly above the shoulders. (4) Lower the dumbbells forward and downward to the starting position.

Parts of the body benefited. Shoulders, arms, chest, and upper back.

Muscles used. Triceps, deltoids, pectorals, trapezius, and latissimus dorsi.

Percentage of body weight to be used. 15 per cent total for both dumbbells.

Comments. Movements three and four may also be performed with a barbell.

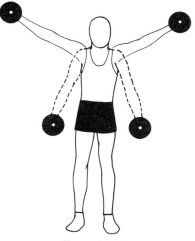

Figure 3.14   Figure 3.15

Heel Raises (Rise-on-Toes) (Figure 3.15)

Starting position. An erect standing position with the balls of the feet resting on a two-inch high block of wood and the barbell resting across the back of the neck and the shoulder with the hands spread wide and grasping the barbell in a regular (palms forward) grip.

Exercise movements. (1) Raise the heels as far off the floor as possible, holding this position momentarily. (2) Return to the starting position.

Parts of the body benefited.   Lower legs and feet.

Muscles used.   Gastrocnemius primarily.

Percentage of body weight to be used.   65 per cent.

Comments.   Because the calf muscles are subjected to frequent, almost constant exercise whenever one walks or runs, it is recommended that a minimum of twenty repetitions of this exercise be performed each set. The weight of the barbell resting on the shoulders and back of the neck can become painful; therefore, it is suggested that padding, such as a folded sweatshirt or T shirt, be placed between the barbell and the body.

Sit-Ups (Figure 3.16)

Starting position.   Supine position on the floor, with the knees so bent that the thighs and legs form an angle of 90 to 135 degrees. The feet are held firmly on the floor by another person or are placed underneath a barbell. A barbell plate or a dumbbell is held behind the neck and head.

Exercise movements.   (1) Curl the trunk forward and touch an elbow to the opposite knee. (2) Return to the starting position. (3) Sit up and touch the other elbow to the opposite knee. (4) Return to starting position.

Parts of body benefited.   Abdominal area primarily.

Muscles used.   External and internal obliques, rectus abdominus.

Percentage of body weight to be used.   10 per cent.

Comments.   This exercise may also be performed on an inclined sit-up board in which the feet are hooked under a strap and positioned one or two feet higher than the head. Because the muscles in the abdominal area appear to respond differently to exercise, twenty repetitions (instead of six) of two sets of the above exercise are recommended. The aspiring gymnast should note that strong abdominal muscles are a prerequisite to successful gymnastics performance.

Figure 3.16

ENDURANCE EXERCISES

Endurance is usually considered to have two aspects: (1) circulorespiratory endurance, commonly referred to as wind, which over a prolonged period of time involves a sustained effort of the entire body and which is exemplified by the qualities demanded for running or swimming long distances, and (2) local muscular endurance which involves strength of the working muscle or muscle groups and which demands the ability to continue to perform repetitious movements involving some parts of the body such as repeated sit-ups or pull-ups (chins). A high degree of local muscular endurance is frequently demanded when performing gymnastics stunts and routines; hence, the need to do specific exercises in order to develop this component is not great as its development is a by-product of the regular gymnastics workout. By rapidly repeating a number of times the special exercises described in this chapter and the gymnastics stunts described later in this book, local-muscular endurance should develop at a satisfactory rate. The performance of stunts and exercises which tire or exhaust one or more groups of muscles or areas of the body but which do not cause rapid heavy breathing (do not cause the performer to become winded) will enhance the rapid development of local-muscular endurance, which appears to be a specific quality for each set or group of muscles.

Circulorespiratory Endurance

The efficient development of circulorespiratory endurance requires that the exerciser engage in physical activity that causes the heart to beat rapidly for several minutes (at twice the speed of its normal resting rate) and that force the exerciser to breathe heavily and rapidly for several minutes. An increase in circulorespiratory endurance is effectively promoted by successive bouncing (whether stunts are performed or not) for some time on a trampoline. The rapid performance of tumbling stunts combined into a routine as well as the rapid performance of free exercise will to some extent aid in developing circulorespiratory endurance.

However, the method almost universally used for the rapid development of circulorespiratory endurance is to run continuously, at a moderate pace, for distances of one-quarter to one and even two miles. For variety the exerciser can walk or jog a fixed distance such as one hundred yards and then sprint this distance. He then continues to alternate jogging and fast running for several minutes. This method of circulorespiratory endurance training causes the heart and the circulatory and respiratory systems to work at far above their resting or normal rates and therefore helps to develop rapidly this aspect of physical fitness. Distance swimming is effective as an exercise method for developing circulorespiratory endurance but because of the lack of a convenient and regular access to a swimming pool, and because of the inconveniences of this exercise medium, most gymnasts prefer to utilize running for this purpose.

Circulorespiratory training should be performed daily or at least five times a week while this aspect of physical fitness is being developed. Once a satisfactory level has been attained, training three times a week should be sufficient to preserve the attained state of endurance. Most gymnasts prefer to perform circulorespiratory endurance training at the completion of their gymnastics workout.

EXERCISES FOR IMPROVING GYMNASTICS FORM

The acquisition of the ideal gymnastics form—toes curled under, the feet pointed sharply and forming a continuation of the line made by the lower leg, the body stretched tall with only a slight suggestion of an arch, and the head in line with the trunk—is an important attribute toward which every gymnast should practice unceasingly as soon as he begins to practice gymnastics. In competitive gymnastics the judges make their decision on the number of points to award for the performance of a routine from the point of view of form, execution, control and difficulty. Because form in gymnastics is valued so highly, every gymnast should constantly strive to perfect his form while performing gymnastics stunts and routines. While learning a new gymnastics stunt or routine, the gymnast should be as conscious as possible of his form throughout his performance. When he has become sufficiently skilled that he is reasonably confident of successfully performing a stunt or routine, the gymnast should then devote his full attention to perfecting his form while performing the stunt or routine.

In order to accelerate his consciousness of and improvement in form, the aspiring gymnast should practice exercises specifically designed to aid this improvement. Because these exercises are not tiring they may be performed whenever a few minutes are available. In addition, they probably should be performed immediately before each gymnastics workout.

Toe Curls (Figure 3.17)

To perform this exercise the gymnast points his feet and vigorously curls his toes toward the soles of his feet; he holds the toe curl for several seconds.

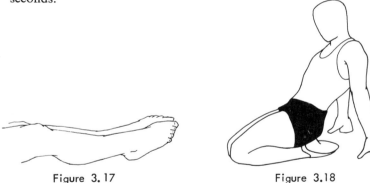

Figure 3. 17   Figure 3.18

Lean-Back on Feet (Figure 3.18)

The gymnast kneels on a mat and so points his feet backward that the top of his feet are resting on the mat. The gymnast sits back on his legs and feet, placing as much weight on his feet as possible while forcing them to a maximum degree of point. He holds this position for several seconds.

Leg Press and Extension (Figure 3.19)

The gymnast, while in a sitting, standing, supporting or hanging position, extends (straightens) his legs, feet, and toes to the maximum degree possible and at the same time squeezes his legs tightly against each other, making sure that his knees, ankles, and feet are tightly in contact with each other. He continues to hold this static or motionless position for from seven to twelve seconds, rests, and then repeats the exercise one or two additional times.

Figure 3.19

Figure 3.20

Stretch Tall (Figure 3.20)

The gymnast, while in a standing or preferably a supporting or hanging position, stretches his body to the maximum, forcing himself to be as tall as possible. His body should be slightly arched and his head and neck should be in line with the line formed by the long axis of his body. He holds this position for seven to twelve seconds and after a few seconds of rest repeats it one or two times.

SPECIAL PROBLEMS THAT MAY BE ENCOUNTERED IN GYMNASTICS TRAINING

Caloric Needs

A daily diet of approximately 2,400 calories is recommended for the average American adult male, weighing 154 pounds. Those who are moderately active need approximately 3,000 calories, and those doing heavy physical work need 4,500 calories. During their period of physical growth teenage boys need a daily diet of 3,800 or more calories in order to maintain activity and still grow physically. Athletes, because they often expend large amounts of energy in training for and playing their sport and because their training routine frequently increases their physical development, may need as many as 6,000 calories daily. Because training for and participating in gymnastics involves the expenditure of considerable energy, and hence calories, the novice gymnast who is still growing should probably consume 3,500 to 4,500 calories daily. Aspects of the daily diet other than its caloric value are also important and should be carefully considered.

What to Eat

The goal of a body-building diet should be to obtain a large number of calories from foods that are easily digestible. Food that is rich in calories and that is easily digestible such as milk, eggs, and dates should form a large share of the diet. Moist, well-cooked foods, including starch-rich foods such as breakfast cereals, potatoes, and bread should be consumed in large quantities as should plenty of fruit and sugar. Sugar is a valuable energy food but should not be eaten in a concentrated form when the stomach is empty. Foods that prove to be constipating, rich mixtures of food likely to cause indigestion, and condiments, relishes, and stimulants should usually be avoided. During serious training certain food items, particularly for the meal immediately preceding competition, should in large part be avoided. These include such vegetables as cabbage and turnips; and fatty meats, especially pork, because of the possible difficulty in digesting them, and pies, cakes, rich puddings, and confections, because of the danger of undue fermentation and gas formation caused by such rich mixtures.

High Calorie Diet

A well-rounded diet contains an adequate amount of the six basic food essentials: (1) proteins, (2) fats, (3) carbohydrates, (4) vitamins, (5) minerals, and (6) water. A well-rounded diet includes adequate amounts of different food groups, which for a person in training includes the following minimum daily amounts: (1) milk, three to four cups; (2) vegetables, one serving of green, leafy, or yellow vegetables; (3) fruits, two servings, one of which should be a citrus fruit; (4) meat, fish, poultry, cheese or beans, one serving; (5) whole or enriched grain bread or cereals, four servings; (6) butter or enriched oleomargarine, two tablespoons; and (7) potatoes, one serving.

The foods listed on page 43, which constitute a well-rounded diet, illustrate what foods might be utilized as the basis for a high-calorie diet of about 4,000 calories. In order that the reader may gain an idea of the size of serving of the various food required to comprise a 4,000 calorie diet, the size of each serving is listed. Naturally, the person undergoing gymnastics training may vary the size of the serving (as well as the food items in his daily diet) in order to obtain the number of calories needed for his individual desires and wants. Many may, for example, prefer to consume more than one pint of milk daily or eat more than a small serving of meat at the noon or evening meal.

Illustrations of a High Calorie Diet

This diet contains approximately 195 grams of carbohydrates, 162 grams of proteins, and 300 grams of fat—a total of 3,800–5,000 calories.

FOODS	HOUSEHOLD MEASURE	ESTIMATED NO. OF CALORIES
For Entire Day (1,175 calories)		
Cream—40% (heavy)	1 cup	900
Milk, whole	1 pint	275
Morning Meal (1,015–1,070 calories)		
Fruit	1 serving	40–70
Cooked cereal or	½ cup	65–90
Cornflakes or	1 cup	110
Shredded Wheat	1 biscuit	100
Eggs or	2	150
Egg and	1	75
Bacon	2 slices	75
Bread or toast	2 slices	150
Butter	1 tbsp.	100
Marmalade, jam, or jelly	2 tbsp.	150
Noon Meal (550–860 calories)		
Meat or fish or chicken	1 moderate serving (3 oz.)	100–150
Potato	1 medium	130–150
Vegetables	⅔ cup	30–110
Bread or toast	2 slices	150
Dessert	1 serving	40–200
Evening Meal (710–1,130 calories)		
Meat or fish or chicken	1 moderate serving (3 oz.)	100–150
Potato, rice, or macaroni	1 serving	90–150
Vegetable	⅔ cup	30–110
Bread or toast	2 slices	150
Butter	1 tbsp. (3 pats)	100
Dessert or	1 serving	100–200
Fruit and	1 serving	40–70
Cake	1 serving	190–200
Variables that may be eaten with the above meals or at other times		
Soup	1 cup	30–110
Salads with dressing	1 tbsp.	50–150
Dates or figs	1 serving	100
Nuts	1 cup	215
Raisins	1 cup	200
Vanilla Ice Cream	1 cup	400

Remarks. The male gymnast of average size, who requires a daily caloric intake of 3,000 calories, should gain nearly one quarter of a pound per day if he consumes 4,000 calories daily, which is about one-third more than the normal requirement.

When to Eat

The person who desires to gain weight or who cannot consume sufficient calories by eating three regular, well-balanced meals daily, should seriously consider eating one or two extra snacks during the day. These can be eaten during the middle of the morning, midafternoon, evening, or an hour or two before bedtime. A glass of milk or malted milk, a sandwich, fresh fruit, fruit juice, or breakfast cereal are all food items that are useful for this purpose.

Consumption of Water

Because of the body's constant need for water it is important that a minimum of several glasses of water be consumed each day. The internal medium of the body is literally bathed in water. Before food can be absorbed within the body, it must usually be converted into a solution or emulsion using water as a solvent. Therefore, water is essential for life. A large amount of water is expelled each day from the body through the skin pores, lungs, and kidneys. Therefore, it is necessary to take in an amount of water each day that is at least equal to the amount of water expelled. Four facts concerning water intake into the body should be noted by the gymnast who is in training.

(1) He may drink as much water as he wishes between meals.

(2) He should not drink more than one or two glasses of water at a meal; some authorities recommend that a minimum amount of water be consumed during eating.

(3) He should not drink water too freely immediately before and during exercising as it requires the stomach several minutes to empty itself.

(4) He should, during strenuous exercise, rinse out his mouth occasionally or take a few swallows of water if desired.

WEIGHT REDUCING

Need for Normal Body Weight

The possession of excess body weight in any degree is a great handicap to becoming proficient in gymnastics. Many aspiring gymnasts find that performing stunts on gymnastics apparatus is difficult because they have surplus body weight for their arm strength to handle. Although many of the elementary gymnastics stunts referred to in later chapters can be performed by almost everyone, advanced gymnastics stunts are quite difficult for most overweight persons to master. Because highly advanced artistic routines can be accomplished with ease only by the practitioner with the gymnastic image—powerful, well-developed forearms, upper arms, shoulders, chest, back, and abdomen, and with a high degree of flexibility in the neck, shoulders, spine, and hips—the potential gymnast should shed any surplus body weight. Fortunately, most high school and college men are not overweight and those who are usually need to lose only a few pounds in order to regain normal body weight. Consequently, before or concurrently with the first attempts at performing gymnastics exercises on the apparatus, the reduction of surplus body weight should be started.

Explanations for Obesity

The person who wishes to reduce weight in order to enhance his skills in gymnastics should realize that almost all cases of overweight occur for the very simple reason that the overweight person consumes more calories than he expends. Several studies of overweight children and youths have revealed that these people usually do not eat more food than their peers but rather that they perform far less physical activity, and that the onset of obesity was preceded by a period of inactivity, not by a sudden, large increase in food intake. On the other hand, many overweight people have acquired this condition in part because they have been trained from infancy in the eating habits of their parents who are overweight and accustomed to eating large meals and who become concerned if their children do not also eat large meals.

In recent years medical doctors, physiologists, and other researchers have discovered that a few people, mostly adults, are what is termed metabolically obese. In studying the blood chemistry of these people it was discovered that most of the food they ingested was converted to fat instead of sugar as is true of the vast majority of people. Because the utilization of an equal amount of fat yields more than twice as many calories as do either carbohydrates or protein, these people were utilizing their food very efficiently—a trait that would be most helpful in famine conditions but which, in our calorie-rich modern civilization, is a distinct handicap. This unusual pattern of food utilization was found to be broken by having such people fast at least twenty-four hours and then having them eat at least five small meals a day, in which situation they did not develop feelings of hunger. It should be emphasized that the metabolically obese person is quite rare and most cases of obesity are caused by eating too much food and performing too little physical activity. However, many people who diet eat only one meal a day, erroneously believing that by forsaking two meals they can eat all they wish at one large meal and still reduce. Consequently, these people, by following a one-meal-a-day practice, are doing the one thing that may be least apt to cause them to lose weight.

Attacking an Overweight Problem

The vast majority of young people who desire to lose surplus body weight, which is accumulated as adipose or fatty tissue in the body, need to employ a twofold attack on their problem: (1) perform at least one and preferably two hours of strenuous physical activity daily, and (2) reduce their daily food intake to a level below the amount of calories expended.

As noted earlier in this chapter, for the average-sized American male this amount is approximately 2,400 calories, and for those who are still growing this amount is around 3,000 calories.

Some foods are quite rich in calories and thus should be avoided or consumed only in small amounts if one wishes to lose weight.

(1) Fats, such as butter, fatty portions of meat, salad oil and especially cream.

(2) Starchy foods, especially potatoes, bread, breadstuffs and pastry.

(3) Sugar and sweets. The elimination of sugar from the diet will in the course of a few weeks represent a substantial equivalent of body fat and hence will permit increased use of foods that assist in balancing the diet such as milk, bread, cereals, and vegetables.

Recommended Foods for Reducing

The reducing diet should satisfy hunger and aid the dieter to avoid a sense of deprivation from food. The following foods should constitute the mainstay of the diet and can be eaten in moderation; however, they should not be cooked with fats or dressed with sugar.

(1) Soups
(2) Eggs
(3) Lean meats
(4) Green vegetables
(5) Fresh fruits
(6) Skimmed milk or buttermilk
(7) Cereals, bread, cake, and potatoes may be taken in restricted amounts.

Vegetables that grow above the ground rather than those that grow below the ground should be eaten by the dieting person. These include asparagus, Brussels sprouts, cabbage, cauliflower, celery, cucumbers, salad greens, mushrooms, radishes, and spinach. The following vegetables may be eaten occasionally: beets, carrots, onions, squash, and turnips. The dieter should especially avoid eating the following foods: barley, cakes, candy, cookies, crackers, gravies or fried foods, macaroni, mayonnaise, noodles, nuts, pies, rice, spaghetti, and sugar.

Diet for Reducing Body Weight

The diet presented below has for many years been utilized and proven beneficial at the Peter Bent Brigham Hospital in Boston, Massachusetts. This diet contains approximately 120 grams of carbohydrates, 70 grams of protein, 50 grams of fat, and totals slightly more than 1,200 calories.

FOODS	HOUSEHOLD MEASURE
Morning Meal	
Fresh fruit, without sugar (no bananas)	1 serving
Egg (not fried)	1
Bread or toast	1 slice

Butter	1 level teaspoon
Coffee or tea (no sugar or cream)	As desired
Milk	2 tablespoons

Noon Meal

Lean meat, fish, or chicken	1 medium serving
Potato	1 medium
Bread—slightly buttered	1 slice
Vegetables (see list)	2 saucers
Fresh fruit, without sugar (no bananas)	1 serving
Milk	1 glass

To supplement the above meals the following food items may be taken as desired: tea, coffee, lettuce, mineral oil, and chicken broth with all fat removed. If food is desired between meals, fresh fruit without sugar (no bananas) is recommended.

Between Meal Snacks

The purpose of a carefully planned dietary regime is defeated by eating extra meals or other food indulgences that the dieting person views as having no or little dietary significance. Actually, these indulgences often increase the daily caloric intake by a large percentage. Ice cream, ice cream sodas, candy, and nuts have high fuel value, and even a moderate indulgence in these sweets or fatty foods will offset abstinence during regular meals from substantial portions of butter, cream, bread, cereals, sugar, or other calorie-rich food.

Hints for Reducing

The person who is overweight should make every effort to become as active as possible in his general habits of life. Walking is an excellent mild exercise; if possible the overweight person should walk a minimum of two miles each day. The overweight person who starts an exercise program should begin with light exercise, and he should increase the amount and vigor of the exercise day by day. When exercising he should wear sufficient clothing and do sufficient work that he sweats profusely.

Many kinds and varieties of exercises are satisfactory for reducing. The flexibility, strength, and endurance exercises named and described earlier in this chapter will serve quite well as reducing exercises because their performance involves the expenditure of considerable energy and all parts of the body are exercised. Performing the gymnastics stunts described in Part II of this book will also be useful if one is not too overweight to handle his body when performing many of them. The markedly overweight person can usually obtain a vigorous workout in a short time by simply bouncing or performing simple stunts on the trampoline. Although no definite formal scientific evidence has been produced that specifically exercising the group of muscles or area of the body where the largest portion of fat is located will reduce the adipose tissue in this area, this method of area or spot exercising is sometimes recommended for the over-weight person. Vigorous physical activity of a general nature when combined with a well-planned diet for weight reducing should soon yield definite results in acquiring a more desirable body weight.

Group I Exercises

The first group of reducing exercises involves movements that are designed to increase the flexibility of the performer. These exercises should be executed while in a stride-stand position (feet spread apart—Figure 3.21) and should be performed at a moderate pace the first few exercise periods. After the preliminary stage of exercising, the pace and the number of repetitions of each exercise should be gradually increased. The names given to the exercises are descriptive names.

Bending sideward and downward (*Figure 3.22*). From a standing position, the performer bends downward and to his left and touches his left foot with both hands. He returns to an erect position and then bends downward and to his right and touches his right foot. Begin this exercise with eight repetitions.

Rotating the trunk (*Figure 3.23*). From an upright position with the arms spread sideward at shoulder level, the performer twists his trunk and head to his right as far as possible and then twists them to his left. Begin with twelve repetitions.

Kidney twist (*Figure 3.24*). Keeping his legs straight and spreading his arms sideward at his shoulders, the performer flexes his body forward until his trunk is parallel with the floor. While maintaining this flexed posture, he rotates his body until his left hand touches his right foot, and he then rotates in the other direction and touches his right hand to his left foot. Begin with eight repetitions.

Bobbing exercise (*Figure 3.25*). From a standing position, the performer flexes forward and with both hands touches his right foot. He raises his body about ten inches; then flexes forward, and touches both hands between his feet. He raises his body; then again flexes downward and touches both hands to his left foot. He returns to a standing position. Begin with four repetitions.

Sideward or lateral bending. With his arms straight and his hands clasped overhead, the performer flexes his trunk directly to the left as far as possible and then to the right. Begin with eight repetitions.

Forward and backward bending (*Figures 3.26 and 3.27*). Starting with his hands on his hips, the performer flexes forward as far as possible; returns to an erect position and next bends backward as far as possible. He then returns to the starting position. Begin with six repetitions.

Lateral bobbing (*Figure 3.28*). With his right hand on his hips and his left arm extended overhead, the performer bends to his right as far as possible and then bobs to his right three times. He returns his left hand to his hip and bobs to his left as far as possible three times. Begin with four repetitions.

Trunk rotations (*Figure 3.29*). With his hands positioned overhead and keeping his legs straight, the performer flexes his trunk forward as far as

Figure 3.21

Figure 3.22

Figure 3.23

Figure 3.24

Figure 3.25

Figure 3.26

Figure 3.27

Figure 3.28

Figure 3.29

possible. He then bends to his left; then backwards, and then to his right. Begin with six repetitions.

Group II Exercises

The first series of the second group of exercises are done while in the sitting position. These exercises should be performed at a moderate pace during the first few exercise sessions.

Jack and swan (*Figures 3.30 and 3.31*).   The performer bends forward **and** touches his toes, and then with the arms spread apart he returns to a sitting position. Begin with eight repetitions.

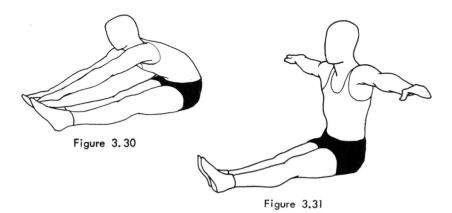

Figure 3.30

Figure 3.31

Football kick.   The performer alternately kicks each leg as high as possible, raising his hips off the floor on each kick. Begin with eight repetitions.

Jack and row (*Figures 3.32 and 3.33*).   The performer flexes forward and touches his toes; while returning to the sitting position he moves his arms in a rowing motion. Begin with eight repetitions.

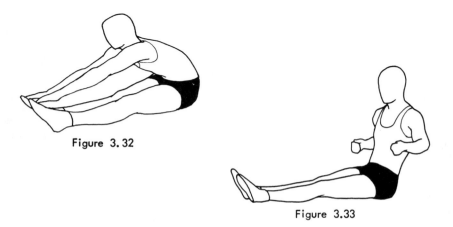

Figure 3.32

Figure 3.33

Raise and swing (Figure 3.34).   The performer spreads his legs and leaning on his left arm he raises his hips off the floor. He then twists his body and swings his right leg over his left shoulder. He next swings his left leg over his right shoulder. Begin with six repetitions.

Figure 3.34

Jack and extend (Figures 3.35 and 3.36).   The performer bends forward, touches his toes, and then raises his arms to an extended position overhead. Begin with eight repetitions.

The second series of the second group of exercises is done while lying on the back and with the hands placed under the hips. These exercises should be performed at a rapid pace.

Leg raising (Figure 3.37).   Keeping both legs straight and keeping his right leg on the floor, the performer raises his left leg as high as possible. He next raises his right leg as high as possible. Begin with six repetitions.

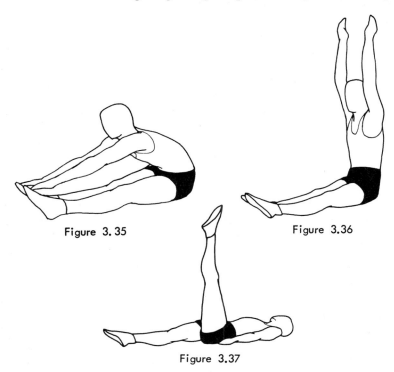

Figure 3. 35

Figure 3.36

Figure 3.37

Alternate leg raise (*Figure 3.38*). The performer raises both legs slightly above the floor and then alternately raises his right and left legs, keeping both legs straight. Begin with six repetitions.

Leg raise and spread (*Figure 3.39*). Keeping his legs extended, the performer raises both legs about ten inches above the floor. He next spreads his legs apart as wide as possible. He then brings them together and lowers them to the floor. Begin with six repetitions.

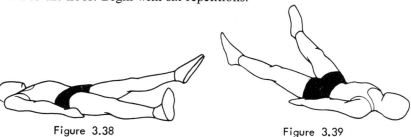

Figure 3.38   Figure 3.39

Alternate knee bending. The performer flexes his left leg and brings his left knee as close to the chest as possible. He returns his left leg to the floor and repeats this movement with his right leg. Begin with six repetitions.

PREPARING FOR GYMNASTICS PARTICIPATION

When to Exercise and Perform Gymnastics

Although a person should normally be capable of performing gymnastics at about any time other than the regular period of sleep, most gymnasts find that they feel most like performing gymnastics at one, or for some, perhaps, two specific periods during the day. Many gymnasts are most in the mood to practice gymnastics in the late afternoon for a number of reasons. (1) The late afternoon is a traditional time to practice sports. (2) Although some studies have indicated that eating a light meal immediately before swimming or running various distances has no adverse effect on performance, the gymnast, because he repeatedly manipulates his own body, should feel light and strong and hence his stomach should be empty of food. For psychological reasons, and perhaps because of tradition, many athletes do not feel capable of all-out exertions soon after eating. (3) The late afternoon marks the end of the work or school day and one is ready to relax and enjoy a change of pace; engaging in gymnastics activities aids in releasing stresses and tensions created while working or studying.

By varying the time during the day of the practice period, however, the gymnast can adapt to being forced to practice at whatever time gymnastics facilities are available and still be able to practice efficiently. This ability, if fully developed, can be extremely helpful to the skilled competitive gymnast who may be forced to compete during the morning, afternoon, or night. Many gymnasts who hope to place high in national competition often practice twice a day, usually in the morning and afternoon or afternoon and evening. Practicing gymnastics twice a day enables the gymnast to perform routines while fresh and unfatigued and also aids in increasing his physical fitness for gymnastics.

Length and Frequency of Practice Period

Research in psychology and motor learning has produced findings that suggest that the more complicated and involved are the skills practiced, the longer one may practice these particular skills with profit during a single period of practice. Conversely, the unskilled performer should practice the same skill for only short periods of time and should practice a variety of skills during a single practice session. For the unskilled gymnast the implications of these findings are that he should practice only a short time on one stunt or even on one apparatus but such practice should be at rather frequent intervals. As the gymnast improves his skills he may profitably spend increasingly longer periods of time practicing stunts and routines in only one gymnastics event.

For the most rapid learning of gymnastics stunts and routines, gymnastics practice should be done each weekday or at least every other day. New stunts should be learned and practiced only during class time or regular practice in order that an instructor, classmate, or team member may aid in spotting (and thus avoiding accidents) and offering suggestions for correcting a sloppy or an incorrect performance. Several different research studies lend support to practicing an entire stunt or routine (the largest whole possible) instead of breaking it into parts. The practice of a stunt or routine should be done at regular speed—the only time performing a stunt at slow speed seems to be helpful is during the initial learning stages. The tendency or desire to constantly learn new stunts and stunt combinations instead of working toward a routine should be avoided.

For the beginner, regular gymnastics workouts with progressively longer practice periods help to condition the skin on the palms of the hands. Whenever the skin on the hands feels tender and sore, practice should be discontinued because calluses are built up from the inside out and ripping the skin markedly delays this process. Those persons with tender skin should apply Tincture of Benzoine to the palms after practice in order to toughen their hands rapidly. The skin on the palms becomes toughened most rapidly if several different pieces of apparatus are used in practice. Carbonate of magnesium chalk should be liberally rubbed on the palms and fingers before working on metal or wooden bars or doing two-man balancing stunts. Powdered rosin should be dusted on leather-soled gym pumps when tumbling (this is not necessary if rubber-soled gymnastics slippers are worn).

The Warm Up

An effective warm up stimulates and prepares a person for additional activity of an increasingly vigorous nature and it helps to prevent pulled muscles and muscle strains. To remain in a warmed up state during the workout a sweatshirt and sweatpants should be worn between practice periods. The sweat that is produced by the body during exercise is a waste product and should be removed by showering immediately after the completion of the workout. When showering, a short, warm shower with soap followed by a cold shower for a few minutes is preferred by some. However, the water temperature of the shower should be whatever the individual finds most enjoyable.

The gymnast should first warm up at the beginning of the practice period and then use his practice time as efficiently as possible. He should particularly avoid the habit of sitting around too much and watching the other gymnasts perform. Several different gymnastics events should be practiced during the workout. The beginning gymnast should concentrate on one apparatus and practice stunts and routines in that event until fatigued or until little progress is being made; at this time he should move on to another event after taking a short rest. The workout should always include some work in tumbling, trampolining, or free exercise; some on a hanging apparatus (rings and high bar) and some on a supporting apparatus (parallel bars and side horse). The inexperienced gymnast should not practice difficult tricks until the practice is well underway and the performer is thoroughly warmed up and in the proper frame of mind to make an all-out effort to master the untried stunt.

Mental Practice

Recent studies conducted in several sports areas have yielded evidence that mental practice can be an efficient method of learning new sports skills and improving those previously learned. Because gymnastics stunts and routines can be rather easily practiced mentally, the aspiring gymnast who frequently mentally practices gymnastics stunts should considerably accelerate the learning process. Such mental practice should take into account all aspects of each stunt practiced and the separate movements should be realistically reviewed in their correct sequence. The mental practice of untried gymnastics stunts and routines should prove beneficial in gaining the confidence needed to attempt those ranging from the simple to the very complex and difficult.

Practicing for Form

A sharp foot-and-toe point often is the difference between a gymnast with average form and one with superior form. Therefore, the gymnast should practice foot and toe pointing several times each day when not practicing gymnastics. During practice he should do such toe pointing exercises as curling the toes of one foot as much as possible and then resting part of his weight on the backs of the bent-over toes in order to increase his toe point. An excellent foot pointing exercise is to extend the feet backward, kneel on a mat, and sit on the feet, pointing them backwards as far as possible by leaning the body backward, thus placing additional weight on the feet.

Self-Confidence

Success in the performance of a skill or sport normally generates pleasure and self-satisfaction. In gymnastics each success will probably motivate the student of gymnastics to continue gymnastics and to progress to gymnastics skills of increased difficulty. The self-confidence of the beginning gymnast should grow with the acquisition of each new and increasingly difficult gymnastics skill. The self-confidence.developed in mastering the intermediate gymnastics skills is needed in order to attempt advanced gymnastics skills. For example, it would be foolhardy to attempt to execute a double-back somersault on the trampoline unless the single-back somersault had first been successfully mastered. Thus self-confidence is a natural outcome of progression from simple to complex gymnastics skills.

Relaxation

Unnecessary muscular tension must be eliminated if the gymnast is to display rhythm and grace of movement while performing gymnastics stunts and routines. For many movements the beginner in any sport frequently contracts both the protagonistic (muscle aiding the movement) and antagonistic (muscles opposing the movement) muscle groups and thus fights his movements and decreases his coordination. The skilled performer, on the other hand, has learned to use only those muscle contractions that are essential and thus is very efficient in his movements and actions. Consequently, as skill and confidence increase, the antagonistic muscle groups relax more and more thus permitting smooth, coordinated movements. This is readily observed when a beginner bounces and attempts to perform stunts on the trampoline for the first time. The performer on the trampoline must react to the reaction of the rebound of his body from the trampoline bed by relaxing the muscles not used in controlling his lift from the bed or for maintaining the correct body position. The secret of success in performing gymnastics stunts and routines is to use only those muscles and muscle groups necessary for the accomplishment of the desired move.

Other Aspects of Training

Stimulants such as coffee and tea often excite the nervous system and accelerate the heart action, whereas alcoholic drinks normally depress and slow down mental and bodily activities. The gymnast who wishes to train seriously and who hopes to become a top level performer should carefully consider avoiding the intake of either stimulants or narcotics. The chief objection to coffee and tea is that their use tends to eliminate milk, which is nourishing, from the diet. Coffee and tea by themselves contain no nourishment.

The use of tobacco, which contains nicotine, is more and more being condemned because of its unhealthful effects, noted in a much increased incidence of lung cancer and heart disease. The ability of the tobacco smoker's blood to carry oxygen is thought to be reduced, and an abundant oxygen supply is vitally important to the athlete. Therefore, no athlete aspiring to maximum proficiency should smoke because this partly determines the amount of circulorespiratory endurance (wind) that he possesses.

The use of alcohol at any time by an athlete is universally condemned because its use can do nothing but contribute to athletic failure. Its detrimental effects become increasingly apparent over a long period of time. The imbibing of alcohol before an athletic performance can significantly affect the athlete's timing, coordination, and judgment. Even a small amount of alcohol can mean the difference between success and failure.

Practice Apparel

The following items of clothing are recommended when practicing gymnastics: (1) Shorts for tumbling and trampoline and free exercise (long pants with tight fitting legs for apparatus work); (2) T shirt (serves to protect the armpits for work on the parallel bars); (3) White socks (help fight athlete's foot); (4) Gymnastics slippers, low cut sneakers, or stocking feet can be used. (Gym pumps are best; they aid in pointing the toes, look good, and can be used for tumbling, trampolining, and two-man balancing); (5) Athletic supporter, and (6) Sweatshirt and sweatpants for wear when resting or inactive to help preserve body warmth.

The above articles should be worn only during the exercise period or gymnastics practice and the clothing should be laundered regularly. Hand straps help to protect the skin on the palms of the hands and may prevent blisters or ripping of this skin, especially when working on the horizontal bar.

4 THE MECHANICS OF GYMNASTICS

THE NEED FOR A KNOWLEDGE OF THE MECHANICS OF GYMNASTICS

It is not essential that the person who plans to be only an average gymnastics performer acquire a knowledge of the mechanics of gymnastics. This is true providing that he is taught by a competent instructor who knows these mechanics and thus does not permit him to utilize incorrect mechanics in learning or practicing gymnastics stunts. A knowledge of mechanics, however, is a necessity for anyone who aspires to be a champion gymnast. The correct mechanics involved in the performance of particular gymnastics stunts can be obtained if the gymnastics performer has an opportunity to study gymnastics books (such as this one) that directly or indirectly present the mechanics of each gymnastics stunt described in the book. The serious shortcoming in relying on a book description is that many performers do not actually do the actions, movements, and timing that they believe they are doing. An example of this is the fact that most people, when throwing a ball with an overhanded throw, believe that they release the ball well in front of their throwing shoulder. Slow motion films demonstrate that this is incorrect and that the ball is actually released directly above the throwing shoulder. The explanation for this erroneous impression is that the thrower probably retains for a short time a memory of grasping the ball after he has actually released it. Were he in fact to release the ball where he believes he does then it would probably strike the floor or ground a few feet in front of him.

In addition to an unawareness of or error in recalling actions and timing, one difficulty that has retarded progress in various sports in the past has been the tendency of many performers to copy the styles and techniques of national champions. In swimming, for example, many swimmers, without considering their type of body build, height or arm length, amount of buoyancy, and other important factors, have tended to copy the swimming stroke techniques of the current record holder, regardless of their physical differences. The reasoning behind such mass imitation is apt to be "He is the national champion; he must be right because he can swim faster than anyone else." What is correct technique for one person may not be equally as correct for everyone else.

These examples illustrate the need not only for a careful self-analysis but also for independent observations of one's gymnastics performance. On seeing a slow motion film of his own sports performance, the gymnast is almost invariably surprised that he does certain things as the film shows him doing them; he frequently has the impression that he does them quite differently.

The preceding information emphasizes some of the values (and limitations) of having a knowledge of the mechanics of gymnastics. This knowledge should increase the gymnastics performer's confidence because he will have increased confidence that he is learning or performing gymnastics stunts and skills correctly. A knowledge of the proper mechanics of gymnastics should also prove helpful to the gymnastics performer who appears to possess the necessary physical attributes for mastering a gymnastics skill but who continues to encounter difficulty in mastering the stunt. If he or someone else who is present has a knowledge of mechanics then he may quickly be helped past this sticking point. Therefore, although a knowledge of the mechanics of gymnastics may be of limited value to some gymnasts it is of great value to others.

DEFINITION OF TERMS USED IN MECHANICS

The main scientific principles involved in the skillful execution of gymnastics activities are those found in the subdivision of physics called mechanics. Mechanics is defined as that branch of physics dealing with the action of forces on material bodies. It is divided into two main divisions: the first is statics, which deals with the action of forces in producing rest or equilibrium, a condition created by forces that are in balance; and the second is dynamics, which deals with the action of forces in producing motion. A knowledge of statics can be helpful to the gymnast whenever he wishes to hold his body in a position of balance, and a knowledge of dynamics can be helpful whenever he performs any gymnastics stunt in which movement is involved. Dynamics is divided into two parts: kinematics and kinetics. Kinematics deals with motion apart from their causes. Kinetics deals with the study of motion and of the forces related to the motion.

What is meant by the mechanics of gymnastics? The body and its parts may be considered a machine; hence, the action of each part of the body in the production of a skill or stunt performed on the mats or apparatus knowingly or unknowingly involves the correct applications of mechanics at the proper times. The relationship between the body and the stunt during the motion continuum of the activity, the role that each body part must fulfill, and the forces that must be applied by each body member in the execution of a stunt are therefore deeply involved in the mechanics of gymnastics. Balancing, direction of movement, speed of movement, and increasing or decreasing the speed of movement are the mechanical factors that a person must be capable of analyzing if he is to expedite the development of correctly performed skills on the mats, trampoline, and apparatus.

It should be noted that in gymnastics the application of mechanics can be done in two ways. The external application of mechanics involves the dynamics (motion) of the human body that result from the propulsive and resistive forces exerted on it. The internal applications of mechanics include the statics involved with the holding of fixed body position by means of muscular forces in equilibrium, and the dynamics associated with the movement of body parts, acting as levers, that are caused by the exertion of muscular force. The external applications of mechanics will be the type considered in detail in this chapter because the internal applications also require a knowledge of anatomy and kinesiology.

The presentation of the mechanics of gymnastics that follows in this chapter is a review, together with examples and illustrations, of the mechanical principles that are associated with the performance of gymnastics in general. Only a few of these mechanical principles are applied to specific gymnastics stunts; instead, the information presented should allow the reader to understand how these mechanical principles may be utilized in the performance of a large variety of gymnastics stunts. Several research studies have been completed in which each phase of the performance of specific gymnastics stunts on apparatus, tumbling mats, or trampoline have been mechanically analyzed. But the authors believe that this approach would not be productive for many gymnastics stunts because in many cases the correct mechanical application is quite simple and is readily made. For example, shortening the radius of the tucked body by tucking tighter in order to rotate faster and therefore complete a somersault movement in less time involves the application of a specific mechanical principle but the knowledge of this principle is not needed to make the application. Therefore, various mechanical principles that apply to the correct performance of gymnastics will be presented without listing all the various gymnastics stunts to which the mechanical principle applies.

EXTERNAL APPLICATION OF MECHANICS

Mechanical Principles that Apply to Balancing Stunts

In applying mechanical principles to balancing stunts, the basic concern is with the changes of position that must take place in the body in order to keep its center of gravity (axes of the body intersect) in the proper position during the performance of a balancing stunt. The center of gravity of the body may be considered as the perpendicular axis around which, irrespective of body position, the body weight is in balance on all sides. This concept involves both the amount of weight located on all sides of the axis and the distances of the weight from the axis. (See Figure 4.1.) The center of body weight is that point of the performer's body at which the vertical, horizontal, and anterior-posterior axes meet. (See Figure 4.2.)

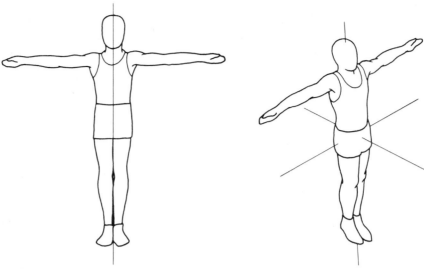

Figure 4.1
Perpendicular Axis of Center of Gravity of Body

Figure 4.2
Center of Body Weight

The center of gravity must rest over or under the place or base of support if the body is to be maintained in a position of balance. When a person is standing at attention (as depicted in Figure 4.3a) the center of gravity would, if observed from the front or back, divide his body along the spinal column, and the weight of the body to the right of the axis would be the same as the weight of the body to the left of the axis, providing these weights are equidistant from the axis. Although the body depicted in Figure 4.3b is flexed, it remains in a balanced position because its center of gravity lies within the base of support. In Figure 4.3c the balance of the body has been upset or lost because the center of gravity is located outside the base of support. In Figure 4.3d the body is supported on the head and in spite of the fact that the base of support is quite small, and hence very unstable, the body is balanced because its center of gravity lies above the middle of the head. In Figure 4.3e is illustrated the position of the center of gravity when the body is in a front-leaning-rest position. In Figure 4.3f is illustrated the location of the center of gravity during the performance of the one-hand handstand. The center of gravity is located directly above or below the area of support when the pike on the rings (Figure 4.3g), the feint on the side horse (Figure 4.3h), the shoulder stand on the parallel bars (Figure 4.3i), and the inverted hang on the rings (Figure 4.3j) are correctly performed.

Techniques for Maintaining Balance

When performing balancing stunts the gymnast may retain or regain his balance by any one or combination of the following balancing techniques: (1) by increasing the size of the supporting base, (2) by moving a part of the body and thus changing the position of the center of gravity

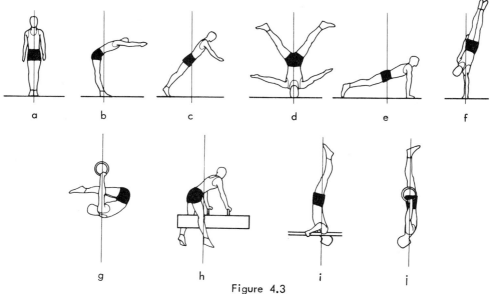

Figure 4.3
Center of Gravity of Body When in Various Positions

of the body in relationship to the base of support (oscillating or alternating movements may be employed for this purpose also), (3) by transferring or moving the center of gravity from above or below one place of support to another, (4) by supplementing through the use of other objects, or (5) by decreasing the height that the center of gravity of the body is located above its base of support.

Increasing the size of the supporting base. If the size of the base of support is increased, the center of gravity has an increased area within the boundaries of the supporting base in which it may be located and still allow the body to remain in balance. Walking on a windy day with the feet spread wide apart is an example of a use of this principle. The utilization of this principle comes into prominence when a head-and-hand stand is done with the hands widespread and distant from the head. This is one of the reasons why a head-and-hand stand is easier to hold than is a two-hand stand which is easier to hold than a one-hand handstand (the height of the center of gravity is also a factor).

Projection of a body part. Projecting a body part can be accomplished by extending the legs forward or flexing them backward, or by raising or lowering the arms for the sake of counter-balancing. If while standing a person starts to fall backward, quickly projecting the arms, head and upper body forward will help to re-establish the balance by realigning the center of gravity over one or both feet. This technique is employed whenever the amount of body arch is increased or decreased when a handstand is performed on the still rings. The arms and the legs are often projected as balancing aids when a free headstand (one done without touching the hands on the mat or floor) is performed. To hold a handstand with little muscular effort, the head must be extended and the back slightly arched. (See Figure 4.4.) During the performance of the one-half-inverted hang on the rings or parallel bars, the legs must be extended for the maintenance of proper balance. (See Figure 4.5.) During the performance of the scale in a free-exercise routine, the arm must be projected with the leg if proper body alignment and a stable balance are desired. (See Figure 4.6.) Oscillation or alternating movements as a balancing technique involves a rapid and repeated projection of one or more body parts. This technique involves an alternate muscular control of body position, either from front to rear, side to side, or in a circular motion. The performance on the still rings of a handstand (as depicted in Figure 4.7) requires the performer to keep the rings located in such a position under the body that his body's center of gravity is within the base of support provided by the rings. This may be accomplished by either repeatedly shifting with the hands the position of the rings, by moving the legs as needed, or by combining both actions. The performance of the two-handed handstand on one bar of the parallel bars as depicted in Figure 4.8 requires an oscillating movement from side to side in order to maintain the handstand. The free headstand illustrated

Figure 4.5
One-Half Inverted Hang

Figure 4.6
Front Horizontal Scale

Figure 4.4
Handstand

Figure 4.7

Figure 4.8
Two-Handed Handstand on One Bar

in Figure 4.9 is a balancing stunt that requires a very sensitive balance. During the performance of this stunt, the arms and the legs can be observed to raise and lower in oscillating movements. The one-hand handstand on one bar of the parallel bars, as illustrated in Figure 4.10, may require alternate movements of the legs to supplement the alternate contractions of the muscles of the forearm and shoulder of the supporting arm (an internal application of mechanics).

Figure 4.9
Free Handstand

Figure 4.10
One-Hand Handstand

Transferring or moving the center of gravity.   Walking on the hands demonstrates the principle of constantly transferring or shifting the center of gravity of the body from one hand (support) to the other. The performance of leg circles on the side horse illustrates the movement of the center of gravity that takes place and the consequent need to support the body with first one hand and arm and then the other. The transference of the center of gravity or body weight may be from below to above a piece of apparatus as illustrated in Figure 4.11. The transference of the center of gravity from below to above the parallel bars during the performance of the drop-kip is depicted in Figure 4.11.

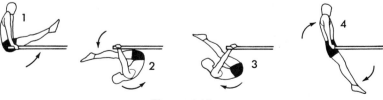

Figure 4.11
Drop-Kip on Parallel Bars

Supplementation. Supplementation involves adding, at the correct location, weight or resistance to an unbalanced body in order to restore it to equilibrium. The two-man balancing stunt depicted in Figure 4.12—the thigh stand—is an example of using supplementation to restore a position of balance. In this stunt the gravitational axis of the bottom man is outside his base of support (his feet) but he is in a position of balance when the body weight of the top man is resting on his thighs. In the performance of the three-man balancing stunt shown in Figure 4.13—The Three Jacksons—the common center of gravity must pass within the area of the feet of the bottom man if overall balance is to be maintained. The pyramid shown in Figure 4.14 would be destroyed if the center of gravity of the group were to move far enough to one side that it were outside the base of support.

Decreasing the height of the center of gravity. This technique is commonly employed whenever a person walking on a slippery surface starts to fall and squats to regain his balance. When under-balancing in a handstand the performer often flexes his arms and lowers his body in order to save his balance. This principle accounts for the reason why a squat handstand (frog stand or knee handstand) is so much easier to hold than is a regular handstand.

Figure 4.12
Thigh Stand

Figure 4.13
The Three Jacksons

Figure 4.14
Pyramid

Movement or Motion in Gymnastics

Momentum is the result of the application of a force or of unbalanced forces. Force is defined as "That which changes the state of rest or motion in matter" and is measured by the rate of change of momentum. The movement or motion in gymnastics stunts may be classified as angular or rotary motion, vertical linear motion, horizontal linear motion, and various combinations of these. Because the pull of gravity is always present and because during the performance of many gymnastics stunts the body, while in motion, is supported or suspended by the arms and hands, the body usually has more than one kind of movement. However, the primary or main type of movement can often be identified and for many stunts this single type of movement is the main concern of the gymnast.

Angular motion or momentum. Angular motion occurs when a body revolves around its horizontal (side-to-side), short (front-to-back), or vertical (head-to-feet) axis or around a point of support for the body such as the hands. Somersaults (airos), kips, handsprings, walk-overs, and forward and backward rolls demonstrate angular motion or rotation around the horizontal (cross or side-to-side) axis of the body or around the hands or shoulders. The use of angular motion is illustrated in Figures 4.15, 4.16, 4.17, and 4.18. During a regular cartwheel the rotation of the body

Figure 4.15
Back Somersault

Figure 4.16
Front Somersault

Figure 4.17
Neckspring from Rolled-up Mat

Figure 4.18
Front Handspring

is around the hands, and during the performance of an aerial or Arabian cartwheel the rotation of the body is initially around its short axis as illustrated in Figure 4.19. The performance of pirouettes involves the rotation of the body around its vertical (head-to-feet) axis. As illustrated in Figure 4.20, the performance of twisting airos (somersaults) not only involves the rotation of the body about its horizontal axis but also about its vertical axis, which results in a rotation of the body about a third (resultant) axis (Figure 4.21).

Figure 4.19
Arabian Cartwheel

Figure 4.20
Pirouette

Figure 4.21
Twisting Airo

The instant when force is either added or deducted is often the crucial point when applying force in performing a gymnastics stunt; this serves as the connecting link in gymnastics routines. Thus angular momentum may be obtained, at least in part, when (1) the horizontal run is converted into vertical lift as in the approach for the high jump, (2) vertical momentum is converted into horizontal momentum while performing the giant swing on the high bar, (3) vertical momentum is converted into angular momentum when initiating airos or somersaults from the tumbling mat as illustrated in Figure 4.22, (4) horizontal momentum is converted into angular momentum when handsprings or flyaways are initiated as illustrated in Figure 4.23, (5) angular momentum is converted into vertical movement in the descent when performing a flyaway from the rings as illustrated in Figure 4.23, (6) angular momentum is converted into horizontal momentum while performing a front airo over a piece of apparatus, Figure 4.24, and (7) angular momentum in a plane is converted into angular momentum in another plane when a twisting movement is combined with a turning movement. In these movements, force is applied at one end of the body after an initial momentum or velocity is attained.

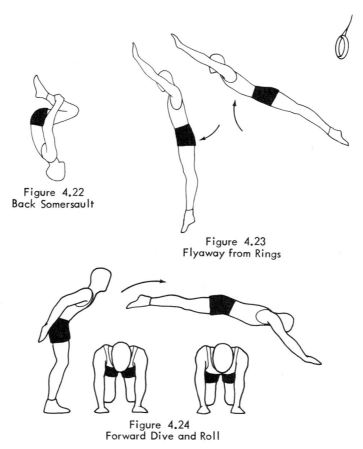

Figure 4.22
Back Somersault

Figure 4.23
Flyaway from Rings

Figure 4.24
Forward Dive and Roll

Rotation of Body Around One of its Axes

When performing gymnastics stunts in which the body revolves or rotates around one of its axes, the body should usually be completely flexed (tucked as tightly as possible) or completely extended. The force or forces that are used to assume these positions may also aid the body to turn, rotate, or twist. For the largest force to be applied, the distance of the moment of force (which causes the turning, twisting, or rotating action) should be as far as possible from the axis of rotation before the force is applied and it should be as close as possible to this axis after it is applied. This principle is illustrated in Figures 4.21 and 4.29. For some gymnastics stunts the smoothness of the rotation depends upon how evenly balanced is the weight on all sides of the rotating axis, particularly when the body is not airborne.

Linear motion. Movements against or with the pull of gravity such as the bounce on the trampoline (Figure 4.25), the drop or dismount off the rings, and high vaulting are examples of movement in gymnastics in which

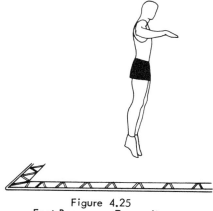

Figure 4.25
Feet Bounce on Trampoline

vertical linear motion is present. Movements that are perpendicular to the pull of gravity such as the forward dive in the dive and forward roll on the mats and vaulting over the long horse, Swedish box, or buck are examples of gymnastics movement in which horizontal linear motion takes place. In order to generate additional linear motion, the gymnast should utilize two different mechanical principles. One of these involves the transfer of momentum from a part to a whole and occurs when the arms are thrust forward in the dive and forward roll on the mats or when the arms are vigorously lifted during the upward phase of the trampoline bounce—in both of these the momentum of the arms is partially transferred to the entire body. The other principle involves adding an additional force when the velocity of the body, body part, or object is greatest and its acceleration is least. This principle is utilized when jumping on the trampoline by waiting to extend or push down with the balls of the feet only after the legs are almost straightened. Most golfers make use of this principle in their golf swing by not using wrist action until an instant before hitting the golf ball after first rotating their body and swinging their arms.

The Utilization of Velocity in Gymnastics

Velocity is defined as the time rate of motion, always in a specified direction. The magnitude of velocity is determined by dividing distance by time; hence the terms miles per hour and feet per second are expressions of the magnitude of velocity. The velocity (or rate of speed of the momentum or movement) at any given time during the performance of a gymnastics stunt depends upon several factors, all of which have a direct role in determining velocity: (1) the position of the body in motion, (2) the gravitational relationship, (3) the leverage involved, which is discussed in a later section, (4) the availability and application of forces, and (5) the method of initiation. Two indirect factors that are related somewhat to the velocity are the size of the body in motion and the coordination or summation of forces.

Position of the body in motion. The longer the radius of the body (approximately one-half the distance from one end to the far end of the body) the greater the force required to rotate this body and thus the slower the rotation; the shorter the radius of the body, the faster it will rotate when the same amount of force is applied at the same location. For this reason, somersaults are performed much faster in a tuck position than in a straight body position and hence are easier to learn and require less effort to perform when in a tucked position. The speed of revolution in the tuck position demonstrates the principle known as the radius of gyration adjustment—the shortening of the radius of gyration in rotary motion accelerates the angular movement and lengthening it decelerates the angular movement. Once a twisting movement is initiated, the speed at which the body twists (revolves) depends markedly on the position of the arms and legs. The closer the arms are held to the body and the closer together the legs (which should be straight), the faster is the speed of rotation of the body. This can easily be observed by noticing how the rotation of an ice skater increases when he brings his outstretched arms to his body while performing pirouettes.

Velocity and gravitational relationship. Ignoring air resistance, which plays an extremely minor role in gymnastics, the effect of the force of gravity is the same for all freely falling bodies. Gravity is ever present and always acts to pull the body toward the center of the earth. It affects the performances of all gymnastics stunts regardless of whether the body is swinging, hanging, balancing, or is free of support. Velocity and momentum depend upon many factors. One of the most important is the position of the center of gravity of the body in relation to the place of support—the farther the center of gravity is away from its point of support, the farther the fall of the body and the less able is the gymnast to exert effective force in resisting this effect of gravity. During the downswing on the rings, parallel bars, or horizontal bar the momentum of the body is assisted by the pull of gravity; during the upswing, the body's momentum is resisted by the pull of gravity. The proper utilization of this principle means that during the upswing on an apparatus the center of body weight should be brought near the place of support in order that the time during which the pull of gravity retards the upswing will be reduced. On the downswing, however, the center of body weight should be extended as far as possible from the point of support in order that the body's center of gravity will fall a greater distance and thus can obtain increased velocity. This principle is utilized when a giant swing on the horizontal bar is performed—during the upswing, particularly the last half, the gymnast flexes his body thus shifting his center of gravity nearer his hands and the bar; at the beginning of the downswing he extends or straightens his body to the maximum degree. Swinging stunts on the rings should usually be performed at the end of the upswing because at this time the pull of gravity has momentarily been neutralized and hence the performer needs to apply a minimum of force in order to successfully complete the stunt.

Sir Isaac Newton first formulated the three basic laws of gravity. The first law states that a body in motion will continue in uniform motion in a line unless compelled to change that motion by forces impressed upon it. If one end of a rotating or revolving body is anchored, the body will be forced to rotate around the stationary end. However, as soon as the anchored end is released, inertia will cause the center of gravity of the body to take the course of a straight line (uniform motion) unless the other forces (such as gravity) act upon it. This principle is illustrated by the direction of travel of the body when a flyaway is performed from a giant swing on the horizontal bar.

Availability and application of forces. The velocity attained during the movement depends upon the forces available and how they are applied. Several methods of making force available and applying it correctly may be utilized in gymnastics.

(1) During the execution of many advanced gymnastics skills, sufficient muscular strength must be available to exert the proper amount of force at the correct time. The strength exercises on the apparatus that are required in competition are included to test the performer's ability to perform a routine in which skills requiring maximum strength are included.

(2) The momentum of a part of the body in motion can be partially transferred to the entire body. The forward-upward throw of the arms and the backward extension of the head initiates the backward rotation of the body when performing a back airo or somersault. The right hand is thrown up and across the left shoulder to help rotate the body in performing a full-twisting back airo. The upward and forward extension of the legs in the execution of handsprings and walkovers on the tumbling mats or kips on the rings, parallel bars, or horizontal bar aids in raising the center of gravity of the entire body and thus allows additional time in which to complete the somersaulting motion of the body.

(3) When a flyaway is performed, inertia (a body at rest tends to remain at rest and a body in motion tends to continue that same motion unless

acted upon by an external force) carries the body away from the bar upon releasing the grasp on the horizontal bar. Inertia is also partially utilized when a gymnast executes a momentary handstand out of a free hip circle on the horizontal bar. Inertia (sometimes called centrifical force in such instances) helps to maintain the correct position of the legs when double leg circles are performed on the side horse.

(4) The gymnast makes use of the pull of gravity in the execution of many skills on the rings, horizontal bar, and parallel bars. The pull of gravity during the downswing is translated into angular motion and hence assists in the performance of stunts that are executed during the upswing.

Initiation of movement. The velocity of the movement depends mainly upon the method or technique used to initiate the movement and in part upon the amount of time during which velocity is generated. Movements may be initiated from, for example, a still or stationary position, a run-and-hurdle, a run-and-jump, a swing, a flyaway, a bounce, a fall, or a kip. Angular motion is used as the initiating movement of many skills. The function of the hurdle (or skip step) in tumbling is to help convert horizontal motion into angular (rotary) motion (as well as to get set for the somersaulting action) by allowing the tumbler to correctly time the raising of his arms and hands overhead in preparation for flinging his arms and upper body toward the mats.

Another common method of initiating the movements of a number of tumbling skills from a run is the use of the two-footed take-off, combined with the lift of the arms and shoulders. The momentum from the run enables the tumbler to jump higher and thus gives him increased time in which to complete the stunt. The purposes of the preliminary jump preparatory to the two-footed take-off are (1) to get the feet together in order to jump an increased height, (2) to obtain a symmetrical movement with its attendant increased ease of control, and (3) to help place the center of gravity of the body in front of the feet before lift-off in order that force is applied behind the body's center of gravity, causing the body to somersault. The two-footed stomp of the feet utilizes Newton's third law— "To every action, there is always opposed an equal reaction" (as the feet press down on the mat the mat presses up on the feet). As the jump from the mat is executed, both arms should be forcibly flung upward and forward in order that their momentum will help to lift the body off the floor in observance of the principle that "The momentum of a part (the arms) is transferred to the whole (the body)." As soon as the life from the mat is initiated, the arms, shoulders and head are flung forward and downward, the heels are brought to the hips, and the hips continue to be raised. These actions increase the speed of the rotation of the tucked body around its horizontal axis because they aid somewhat in transferring the momentum from a part to a whole and also shorten the radius of gyration.

Size of the body in motion. The heavier the body, the greater the forces required to move it or change its movements; however, equalizing this to a great extent is the fact that increased muscular tissue (and strength) is available to exert force.

Coordination or summation of forces. The effect achieved during the execution of a gymnastics stunt depends on how well all available forces are coordinated. This fact is demonstrated by the execution of the fundamental trampoline bounce in which the reaction of the bed, plus the push of the legs, plus the lift of the arms all contribute to lift the performer off the bed. The height of the resultant bounce depends upon how accurately coordinated are these forces and the timing of the addition of each new force. The force supplied by the apparatus upon which the gymnast performs is actually force stored there that was originally supplied by the performer. This stored force must be added at the correct time to the forces applied by the performer.

Utilization of Acceleration in Gymnastics

Acceleration is the time rate of change of velocity in either speed or direction and is measured in such terms as feet per second per second. To accelerate a body means to increase its velocity; therefore, any discussion of acceleration involves velocity. A body may be accelerated by (1) increasing or decreasing the applied forces, and (2) utilizing the radius of gyration adjustment.

Increasing the applied forces. This principle is easily demonstrated by checking the height of the bounce on the trampoline when the arms and hands are held at the side as compared to when the arms swing in a normal fashion. This principle is also demonstrated when a kip from the mats is first performed without the use of the hands and then when a push of the hands is applied to the mat at the beginning of the kip. The performance of a front handspring or a front airo from a stand and from a run is another example of increasing applied forces.

Radius of gyration adjustment. When the radius of a rotating body is decreased, its angular velocity will increase; when the radius of a rotating body is increased, its angular velocity will decrease. This principle is illustrated by contrasting the time required to perform the back airo or somersault when in a tuck position and when in a lay-out position. Lengthening the radius on the downswing and shortening it on the up-swing is another way that this principle is utilized.

INTERNAL APPLICATION OF MECHANICS

As stated at the beginning of the chapter, a knowledge of anatomy and kinesiology is needed for a full understanding of a comprehensive presentation of the internal application of mechanics. In addition, the practical uses of this information are limited. For these reasons the discussion in this section is minimal.

Levers and Lever Systems of the Body

The movements of the body and its components are produced through a system of levers. The bones act as the levers and they are acted upon by the contracting action of the muscles. The lever is a mechanical device that produces turning motion or torque. A lever consists of a fulcrum (a joint), which is the point of rotation or movement; a power arm (or force arm), which is the perpendicular distance from the fulcrum to the point where the force is applied, and a weight (or body part) upon which the force is acting or creating movement.

Levers are divided into three types according to the relative positions of the fulcrum (joint), the weight (body part being moved), and the application of force (muscular contraction). A first class lever is one in which the fulcrum is located between the weight and the force such as is seen in a teeter-totter. A second class lever is one in which the weight is located between the fulcrum and force such as is seen in a wheelbarrow. A third class lever is one in which the force is located between the fulcrum and the weight, such as occurs when a weight in the hand is lifted by contracting the biceps muscles with the elbow joint forming the fulcrum. Most of the body movements are produced through third class levers. Unless they are of the first class balancing type, levers create a mechanical advantage either by trading speed for increased force of movement (second class lever) or by exchanging strength for increased speed of movement (third class lever).

The longer the force arm, the greater is the moment of force that can be applied about the axis (fulcrum) but the shorter and slower is the resultant movement. The shorter the force arm, the smaller is the moment of force applied but the faster is the speed of the resultant action. In most of the levers in the body, the length of the force arm is relatively short; the speed of movement is fast but the force of the movement is relatively weak. For example, when the forearm is curled or flexed the force exerted by the biceps may be 250 pounds but the maximum weight that can be lifted in the hand by this action may be only 40 pounds. However, this loss of force results in a marked increase in the speed and distance that this weight is moved by the contraction of the biceps. Because in the body the force arm and the moment of force constantly change as the movement takes place around a joint, the resultant angle formed by the two is constantly changed. Both of these, however, can be controlled. In order to most easily overcome the moment of force (resistance or weight) or hold it to a minimum, the moment of force should be made as short as possible and the force arm as long as possible. If the moment of force can be positioned at the center of rotation (directly above or below the fulcrum) then there is no moment of force with which to contend and only a small force is needed in order to make the desired movement. This principle of reducing the moment arm to the minimum should be utilized when lifting a heavy weight. On the other hand, there are some situations in gymnastics in which gravity lends assistance and it is advantageous to increase the moment arm to the maximum possible.

Part II DESCRIPTIONS AND ILLUSTRATIONS OF GYMNASTICS SKILLS

ORGANIZATION AND USE OF GYMNASTICS SKILLS

Progressive Stunt Lists

In the chapters that follow the names of selected stunts or skills, the techniques of performing these stunts, and illustrations of the stunts appear for each gymnastics event. The stunts are arranged in a progressive order for eight gymnastics areas: tumbling, trampolining, balancing and flexibility, floor exercise, side horse, parallel bars, horizontal bar, and rings. For each event approximately twelve representative stunts are presented for each of three levels of skills—basic, elementary, and intermediate—a total of at least thirty stunts. With the exception of stunts that demand mainly strength for their correct performance, the stunts listed for each of the three skill levels are presented in their approximate order of difficulty.

Because only thirty to fifty stunts ranging from the beginning through the intermediate skill level are listed for each gymnastics event, the listing of stunts is by no means exhaustive of those belonging in these categories, but instead it is intended to be representative of the wide range of possible stunts that might have been included. Also a stunt described under one apparatus can often be performed on other pieces of apparatus. An example of this is the kip which may be performed on the horizontal bar, rings, parallel bars, tumbling mat, or floor. One reason why no attempt has been made to present all the possible stunts in each gymnastics event is that this complete a listing is likely to be more confusing than helpful for the average gymnast. A mastery of most or all of the stunts presented for an event should give the practicing gymnast an excellent basis for performing gymnastics routines and for proceeding to gymnastics stunts of an advanced level. In addition by this stage in his development he should be thoroughly prepared for participation in competitive gymnastics. Therefore, if possible, all the stunts in each stunt list should be mastered because even expert gymnasts at one time could perform only elementary stunts and had to first learn the fundamental gymnastics skills. If only limited time is available to the gymnast, then he needs to practice only the first half of the stunts from each group. The gymnast with limited gymnastics experience may wish to concentrate his initial efforts in mastering the stunts in the stunt group in which his present skills level on that piece of gymnastics apparatus is located.

The authors have attempted to list the most common name of each gymnastics stunt and to be consistent in naming the stunts for all pieces of apparatus. For many stunts that have another name that is popular or descriptive, a second name is also listed. This procedure is necessary because, at the present time, gymnastics terminology is at times confusing as it has arisen from several different sources; however, gymnastics terminology is becoming increasingly standardized.

For the sake of clarity and convenience and in order to avoid making each chapter quite lengthy, all stunts are presented as single stunts and not in combination with other stunts as would be done in composing various gymnastics routines. The reader who is at all interested in competitive gymnastics should remember that quite early in his training every effort should be made to combine stunts into routines in which one stunt after another is performed in continuity and without pause between stunts. As the gymnast increases his level of skill he should devote more of his practice time to routines and less of his time to individual stunts. In order to aid the beginning gymnast in constructing and practicing routines, at the end of each chapter some sample routines utilizing the stunts included in the chapter are listed. Routines on gymnastics apparatus begin with a mount onto the apparatus, some intermediary stunts are performed, and the routine ends with a dismount from the apparatus.

Simplified Points System

At the end of each chapter the stunts described for that chapter are listed on a chart. The practicing gymnast should use these charts to check his progress in acquiring gymnastics skills in the various areas. A point system is recommended for this purpose.

5 points—Perfect performance.

4 points—Satisfactory performance except for bent knees or unpointed toes.

3 points—Poor form, knees are bent and toes are not pointed.

2 points—No form, but there is knowledge of how to perform the stunt.

1 point—Mere ability to perform the stunt with extremely poor form and knowledge of the stunt.

0 points—Inability to perform the stunt.

Because it is extremely difficult to rate one's self when performing a gymnastics stunt, a qualified instructor or another gymnast should rate the performance of each gymnastics stunt. Improvement and progress in gymnastics are the key reasons for gymnastics practice; therefore, the gymnast should occasionally be rechecked or rerated on the same gymnastics stunts in order that he may keep a constant check on his progress in improving his form and mastering the stunts.

The check list at the end of each chapter for the gymnastics stunts should be helpful to the practicing gymnast in constantly evaluating the amount of gymnastics skill that is being acquired. Naturally, the subtotal of points and the total points for all the stunts listed for an activity should be maintained in pencil in order that a higher number of points can be written in the appropriate space whenever a higher score is awarded. This system of maintaining the total number of points awarded for each activity allows the prospective gymnast to appraise realistically his overall gymnastics skill level, his rate of progress, and his most skilled and least skilled areas of gymnastics.

Directions for Performing Gymnastics Stunts

For those stunts that may be performed in a right- or left-handed or a right- or left-footed direction, the instructions, unless otherwise specified, are given for a right-handed and right-footed performer.

5 SINGLE AND DUAL TUMBLING STUNTS

Tumbling may be defined as a series of controlled muscular movements of the body consisting of turns, twists, dives, springs, and kips that are performed on mats, the floor, or the ground. Man, particularly in childhood, has probably always engaged in some types of tumbling activity. Many gymnastics authorities believe tumbling to be the foundation of the gymnastics program because it is an excellent lead-up activity, can be successfully performed by young children requires little or no special equipment, can be performed in many places, and may be done with one or more partners. The practice of tumbling stunts on the wooden floor or free-exercise mat is excellent preparation for performing floor exercises. Tumbling stunts, which can be practiced at almost any time, are considered by many to be a basic gymnastics activity that serve as a foundation for learning other gymnastics skills. Practicing tumbling therefore is considered an excellent introduction to gymnastics.

OBJECTIVES OF TUMBLING

(1) To develop preventive falling or to learn how to fall safely.

(2) To become oriented to spaceability or to develop the kinesthetic sense (an awareness of the position of the body and its parts at all times).

(3) To help develop equilibrium.

(4) To help develop coordination, speed of movement, agility, flexibility, poise, and neuromuscular skills.

(5) To develop a time-direction-space association or sense; for example, to learn the time (and the direction of movement) required to perform a forward somersault, land on the feet, roll forward, and come to a standing position.

LEAD-UP DEVELOPMENTAL EXERCISES FOR TUMBLING

In the next portion of this chapter various exercises which serve several purposes are listed, described, and illustrated. The main purposes of these exercises are to strengthen the muscles that are commonly used when performing tumbling stunts, to improve the flexibility needed in tumbling, and to develop agility and balance. The general exercises contained in Chapter 2, Preparing for Gymnastics Participation, also serve these purposes; therefore, the exercises that follow are supplemental and engaging in them will aid the tumbler-to-be to rapidly develop these components to a high degree. Another purpose of these exercises is to prepare, both physically and mentally, the tumbler-to-be for participation in tumbling stunts. The performance of these exercises accustoms him to some of the body positions that are assumed when tumbling and helps him to develop self-confidence in his potential tumbling ability. Because the first level of tumbling stunts presented in this chapter is quite basic and is relatively simple to perform and because its performance leads or builds the tumbler toward performing tumbling stunts of increased difficulty, the performance of these lead-up developmental exercises is especially helpful to anyone who has experienced difficulty in mastering the beginning level of tumbling stunts. These exercises should only be performed at the completion of gymnastics (or tumbling) practice because they are quite fatiguing.

Animal Walks (For developing the muscles of the upper and lower body and the limbs)

These exercises should be performed for from five to ten minutes with no rest periods and may be done in any order desired.

Galloping dog run (Figure 5.1). The galloping dog run consists of running on all fours as depicted in the illustration.

Squirrel hops (Figure 5.2). Squirrel hops are performed by repeatedly diving to the hands and landing in a squat position as shown in the figure.

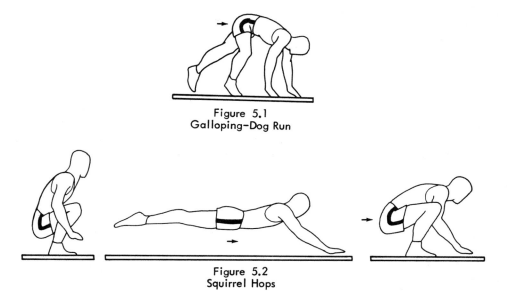

Figure 5.1
Galloping–Dog Run

Figure 5.2
Squirrel Hops

Forward or backward crab walk (Figure 5.3).   Crab walking is done by walking forward or backward on all fours with the back facing the floor and with the hips lifted as high as possible as illustrated.

Elephant walk (Figure 5.4).   The elephant walk is performed by keeping the legs straight and the feet spread apart as illustrated.

Wet cat walk (Figure 5.5).   The wet cat walk is performed by walking on the hands and one foot as illustrated. Shake the foot in the air.

Bear walk (Figure 5.6).   The bear walk is performed by keeping the legs straight and the feet together as shown.

Duck waddle (Figure 5.7).   The duck waddle is performed by maintaining a deep knee-bend position, placing the hands on the hips and walking as illustrated in the figure. Duck waddles are believed by some to be injurious to the knee joints and therefore should not be done by anyone who has a history of injury to the knee joints or by anyone with an unstable knee joint.

Rabbit hop (Figure 5.8).   The rabbit hop is performed by repeatedly diving forward to the hands, tucking the legs, and landing in a squat position. The legs are spread apart on alternate hops, and are kept together during the other hops. The rabbit hop is illustrated.

Figure 5.3
Forward or Backward Crab Walk

Figure 5.4
Elephant Walk

Figure 5.5
Wet–Cat Walk

Figure 5.6
Bear Walk

Figure 5.7
Duck Waddle

Figure 5.8
Rabbit Hop

Snail drag (Figure 5.9). The snail drag is performed by dragging the body forward with the arms while keeping the legs inactive as illustrated in the figure.

Gorilla hops (Figure 5.10). The gorilla hop is done by bouncing around on all fours (both hands and both feet) as illustrated.

Worm measure (Figure 5.11). The starting position for the worm measure is the front-leaning rest (prone-fall) position, which is the position assumed for beginning a push-up. From this position, keeping the legs straight, the feet walk forward up to the hands and then the hands walk forward away from the feet as depicted.

Figure 5.9
Snail Drag

Figure 5.10
Gorilla Hops

Figure 5.11
Worm Measure

Exercises for the Legs

The names of the leg exercises that follow are self-descriptive; therefore, no descriptions or illustrations of the exercises are given. These exercises should be performed for five to ten minutes with as few rest periods for as brief a time as possible. They may be performed in any order desired and only the number required to induce leg fatigue should be done.

(1) High stepping
(2) Forward jumps
(3) Sideward jumps

(4) Backward jumps

(5) Forward jumps with hands in back of neck

(6) Forward jumps in a zigzag fashion

(7) Forward jumps with a wiggle

(8) Backward jumps with a wiggle

(9) Forward jumps striking the knees with the hands

(10) Forward jumps striking the heels with the hands

(11) Forward jumps with one-half twist to the left (or right)

(12) Forward jumps with one full twist to the left (or right)

(13) Backward jumps, alternate spreading of feet and bringing them together

(14) Backward jumps striking the heels

(15) Backward jumps striking the knees

(16) Hop on the right foot while holding the left foot

(17) Hop on the left foot while holding the right foot

(18) Standing broad jumps

(19) Repetition hop, step, and jump

(20) Rope jumping

BEGINNING TUMBLING STUNTS

Spinal Rock (Figure 5.12)

From a supine position on the mat, the performer raises his head as high as possible, flexes his legs at the knees, and hips, and grasps his shins. He then rocks his body back and forth.

Figure 5.12
Spinal Rock

Forward Roll (Figure 5.13)

From a squat position, the performer reaches his hands forward and places them shoulder width apart on the mat and slightly in front of his shoulders. He tucks his chin on his chest while raising his hips and moving them forward, rounds his back, and as his weight moves forward, he momentarily supports his weight on his hands and lowers his body until his upper back and neck touch the mat. Keeping his body tightly tucked, he rolls forward until his body weight is resting on his feet at which time he comes to a standing position.

Figure 5.13
Forward Roll

Forward Roll to the Back (Figure 5.14)

The forward roll to the back is performed as described for the preceding stunt except that after the forward roll is initiated the performer's head and upper back continue to remain in contact with the mat and the performer finishes in a supine position on the mat in which position he is lying on his back. After his body passes over his head, the performer does not lift it but keeps the back of his head in contact with the mat.

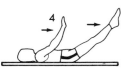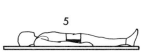

Figure 5.14
Forward Roll to the Back

Forward Roll—Arms Folded (Figure 5.15)

The forward roll is performed in the usual way except that the performer initially crosses his arms and they remain in this position resting on his chest during the entire stunt. This stunt requires extra care in correctly placing the top of the head on the mat before rolling forward and coming to the feet.

Figure 5.15
Forward Roll — Arms Folded

Forward Roll—Cross the Legs (Figure 5.16)

The regular forward roll is performed with the lower legs crossed, and as the performer comes to his feet he turns his body a one-half turn thus uncrossing his legs. He completes the stunt by facing in the opposite direction from which he started the stunt.

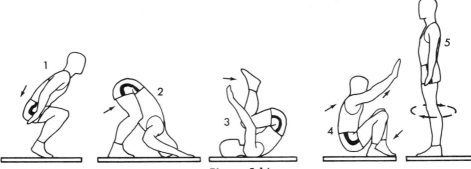

Figure 5.16
Forward Roll — Cross the Legs

Forward Roll While Holding the Toes (Figure 5.17)

From a deep knee bend position with his knees spread apart, the performer reaches between his knees and grasps his toes. He then places the top of his head on the mat and rolls forward while forcing his head and shoulder forward as vigorously as possible.

Figure 5.17
Forward Roll While Holding the Toes

Forward Roll—Hands Behind the Head (Figure 5.18)

From a squat position with his fingers laced together behind his head, the performer places the top of his head on the mat and performs a forward roll while maintaining his body in a tightly flexed position.

Figure 5.18
Forward Roll — Hands Behind the Head

Backward Roll Over One Shoulder (Figure 5.19)

The performer lies on his back on the mat, places his right hand alongside his right side, places his left arm to the left of his left shoulder, and rotates his head to the right. He then quickly raises his legs and knees up and over his left shoulder, pushes with his right hand, and lands on his knees. Follow the knees with the eyes.

Figure 5.19
Backward Roll Over One Shoulder

Backward Roll from a Jackknife Position (Figure 5.20)

The performer, while keeping his legs straight, flexes forward at his hips, positions his hands alongside his thighs, drops back to a straight-leg sitting position, raises his flexed legs, tucks his body, and rolls directly backward over his head while supporting his weight on his hands which are over his shoulders. He completes the stunt by coming to a squat position on his feet.

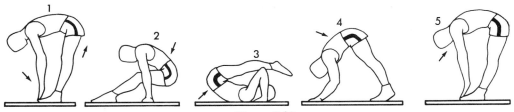

Figure 5.20
Backward Roll from a Jackknife Position

Football Roll (Shoulder Roll) (Figure 5.21)

The performer spreads his feet apart, bends over and places his left hand on the mat directly in front of his left shoulder. He then reaches under his left arm with his right arm and rests his weight on his right forearm and then on his right shoulder. He rolls simultaneously forward and sideward, rolling across his back from his right shoulder to his left hip. He next comes up on his left knee and then steps up onto his right foot.

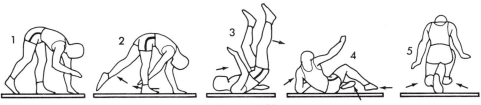

Figure 5.21
Football Roll

Side Roll (Figure 5.22)

The performer positions himself on his hands and knees in a sideward position on the mat. He then rolls to his right, placing his right hip and shoulder on the mat, then his back, then his left hip and shoulder and finally returns to the starting position. With practice this stunt can be performed with a run from which the performer jumps to a sideward position, lands on his right hand and foot and then quickly does a side roll and comes to a standing position.

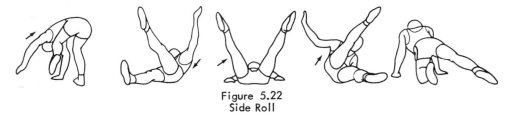

Figure 5.22
Side Roll

ELEMENTARY TUMBLING STUNTS

Cartwheel (Figure 5.23)

The right-handed and right-footed performer assumes a position on the center of the mat in which his right side faces the length of the mat. Spreading his legs and holding his arms overhead, he flexes at his waist and whips his right arm and shoulder down and to his right and, keeping his arms and legs stiff, places his right hand approximately eighteen inches to the right of his right foot. He then places his left hand to the right of his right hand and at least shoulder-width distance from his right arm. He then flexes his legs over his hips and to his right and places his left foot on the mat and comes to a standing position with his legs spread apart. During the cartwheel the body is slightly arched and the head somewhat back, similar to the body position during a handstand. With practice, successive

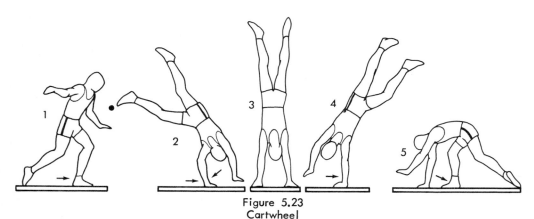

Figure 5.23
Cartwheel

cartwheels can be performed and the first cartwheel may be performed after taking a short run and hopping on the left foot and doing a one-quarter twist counterclockwise before the take-off.

Back to Back Pullover

The performer and his partner stand back to back, stretch their arms sideward, and interlock their elbows. The bottom man squats slightly and positions his hips directly under the top man's hips. On the count of three the bottom man pulls hard against the top man's arms while flexing vigorously and sharply forward at his hips until his back is parallel with the mat. As soon as the bottom man begins his pull the top man pikes his legs, flexes his head forward, and rides on the bottom man's back until his feet are on the mat. At this time the two release each other's arms. With practice the top man can obtain sufficient snap that he may safely disengage the bottom man's arms while still upside down.

Backward Extension Roll (Figure 5.24)

The performer performs either a regular or a jackknife backward roll and when his weight is on his shoulders he quickly extends (shoots) his legs toward the ceiling and slightly behind him and at the same time he extends his head backward and looks at his hands as he forcefully extends his arms in order that he attains a momentary handstand. He then flexes his legs at his hips and comes to a standing position by vigorously pushing off the mat with his hands.

Figure 5.24
Backward Extension Roll

Backward Extension Roll to Chest Roll (Fish Flop) (Figure 5.25)

The performer initiates a regular backward extension roll and comes to a momentary handstand position in which he is slightly off balance backward. Keeping his neck flexed and his head forward he arches his body to the maximum and lowers his body until his weight is resting on his chest. He then rocks backward to his hips, thighs, and legs. Should the performer overbalance forward when performing this stunt he should tuck his head toward his chest, tuck his body and lower himself until his weight is on the back of his shoulders and upper back. From this position he does a tucked forward roll. A chest roll can be quickly learned by kicking up to almost a handstand, simultaneously arching the body and lowering the chest to the mat, and rocking backward toward the feet, partially supporting the body with the hands to avoid forcing the body into too great an arch.

Figure 5.25
Chest Roll

Backward Roll to Head and Handstand (Figure 5.26)

The performer does a backward extension roll in which he lifts his body only several inches high and as soon as possible he very quickly extends his head backward. Keeping his hips and legs overhead, he then lowers his forehead to the mat and holds a head- and handstand (head balance). The performer must place his hands at least several inches in front of and to the sides of his head.

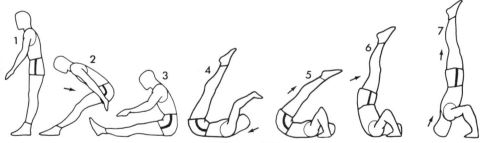

Figure 5.26

Dive and Roll Over Three Men (Figure 5.27)

The performer should first master the simple dive and roll and then practice the dive and roll, gradually increasing the distance and height of the dive. In performing the dive and roll it is essential that when the hands touch the mat the hips are directly overhead and the performer is looking at the mat. He then quickly tucks his head and body (which is already semitucked or semipiked) and rapidly lowers his upper back to the mat and completes a fast forward roll to his feet. In performing a dive and roll over three men, the performer takes a short run and on his last step, hops on one foot and lands on both feet in order to utilize a two-footed take-off. Keeping his head up, he lands first on his hands, and then ducks his head, tucks his body tightly and rolls forward to his feet. During the performance of the dive it is essential that the performer do a relatively high dive so that he has adequate time in which to absorb the force of the dive by giving with his arms, and to duck his head and roll.

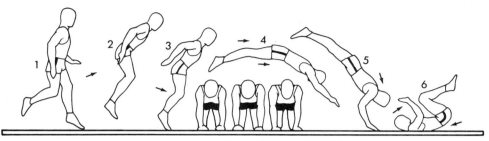

Figure 5.27
Dive and Roll Over Three Men

Double Rolls—Forward and Backward (Two-Man Rolls) (Figure 5.28)

To assume the starting position, one partner lies on his back and pikes his legs. The other partner stands in a position in which his feet are located immediately behind his partner's shoulders. They then grasp each other's ankles. To do two-man rolls forward the standing partner leans forward and does a forward dive and roll, placing his partner's feet next to his hips—this partner must be certain that his knees and feet are spread hip width apart. The partner doing the dive and roll then pulls vigorously forward with his legs and the other partner rapidly curls his trunk forward and comes to a semitucked standing position by allowing the pull of his partner's legs to assist him to a standing position. Without any pause these actions are repeated and a series of forward double rolls are performed. For this stunt it is essential that the partners somewhat relax their legs and permit the top man to position them.

From this same starting position two-man backward rolls are initiated by the standing partner who squats and quickly rolls backward pulling his partner's feet backward as strongly as possible and positioning his partner's feet just behind his shoulders. In turn the partner who started in the down position performs the same actions as those required to complete a backward extension roll. Without pausing the partners continue these actions and perform several double backward rolls in succession.

Figure 5.28
Double Roll

Triple Roll (Figure 5.29)

The three performers needed for this stunt lie face down and side by side on the mat. The middle man rolls to his left (and to the outside) and simultaneously the man on the left springs upward and to his right from his hands, knees, and feet (toward the middle), passing over the middle man and landing in the center. The middle man continues moving to his right (the outside) by executing one side roll and comes to rest on his hands and knees. The original left-hand man then rolls to his right while the right-hand man springs over him. The pattern is for the outside man to spring to the middle (passing over the middle man who does a side roll) and upon landing on his hands, knees, and feet to roll sideward from the middle to the outside. The middle man always does a simple side roll to the outside. Only two men at any one time are in movement. This stunt may also be performed by having the outside man dive and roll toward the middle while the middle man does a tightly tucked forward roll underneath him and toward the outside.

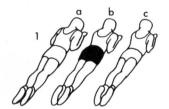 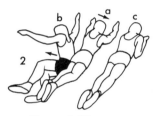 

Figure 5.29

Shoulder-Knee Handspring (Figure 5.30)

The bottom man lies on the mat on his back and places his heels next to his hips with his knees about shoulder width apart. His arms are fully extended above his shoulders. The performer takes two or three steps, hops on one foot and quickly flexes his body forward, placing his hands on the bottom man's knees. Leaning far forward in order that his shoulders are above the bottom man's shoulders, the top man kicks his free leg upward in a splitting movement followed by his other leg. As soon as the top man's shoulders are within range the bottom man grasps them and keeps his arms extended while supporting them. The top man, who attempts to look at his partner's face as long as possible, pushes vigorously against the bottom man's knees in order to continue his handspring movement and as he falls behind the bottom man he tucks his body somewhat while the bottom man pushes upward on his shoulders. The top man lands in a semisquat position behind the bottom man. This stunt is easy to perform if the bottom man is competent and experienced. Little danger is involved in this stunt as long as the top man avoids the tendency to duck his head between his partner's knees; hence, failing to get his shoulders and weight forward over his partner's shoulders. A variation of this trick is for the top man to place his hand alongside the bottom man's side and near his shoulders. In this version the bottom man keeps his legs extended and on the mat.

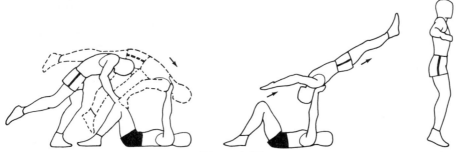

Figure 5.30
Shoulder Knee Handspring

Kip Over Rolled-Up Mat (Neckspring on Mat) (Figure 5.31)

By performing this stunt from the rolled-up mat, the center of gravity of the body is raised several inches, enabling the performer to rotate his body a one-half rotation forward with increased ease and thus get his feet under him in sufficient time. To learn this stunt the performer should place his neck on the mat and then so flex his body at the hips that his extended legs are at right angles to his body. The performer then overbalances and just as his balance is lost, he vigorously kicks his legs forward and downward and pushes hard with his hands, coming to his feet in a squat position. With practice this stunt can be done from a walk or run and without the use of a rolled-up mat.

Figure 5.31
Kip Over Rolled-Up Mat

Handspring from Mat (Figure 5.32)

Once the handspring movement is initiated the mechanics and actions of this stunt are identical to those of the headspring. This stunt may be done with the arms straight or bent. With his arms overhead, the performer takes a step (or short run) and hops once on his right foot. He then stomps his raised left foot to the mat and quickly brings his hands to the mat several inches in front of his left foot. He next kicks his right leg vigorously upward behind him and then raises his left leg. He continues to look downward at his hands until his hands leave the mat He then snaps both legs forward and downward and arches his body in order to maintain his hips in as high a position as possible, coming to an upright position. When learning this stunt, the performer may have to flex his legs at the knees and land in a squat position. With practice a straight-leg landing is possible. The secret of performing this stunt is a fast snap down of the arms and then a vigorous push with the shoulders just before the hands leave the mat. When performing this and similar stunts in which the performer runs forward and hops to initiate the stunt, it is essential that the performer execute the feet stomp with a minimum of knee flexion in order that his body will receive the full benefit of the reaction from the push off the mat. As his hands contact the mat, the arms should be held fully extended in order to keep his center of gravity as high as possible and in order that the kick of his legs will transfer as much momentum to his body as possible.

Figure 5.32
Handspring from Mat

INTERMEDIATE TUMBLING STUNTS

Round-Off (Figure 5.33)

Holding his arms overhead, the performer takes a short run, hops on his right foot, and then stomps his raised left foot to the mat. Keeping his arms fully extended, he sharply flexes his body forward and whips his left and then his right hand down to the mat. His left hand has a quarter turn and is placed twelve to eighteen inches directly in front of his left foot, and his right hand has a half turn and is placed directly in front of the left hand. He kicks his right leg and then his left leg upward. Then piking his legs vigorously downward the performer gives a strong push with his hands and shoulders and snaps both feet to the mat. He lands facing the direction from which he started. The above actions are all continuous and occur in rapid order—they are separated only to aid in understanding and comprehending them. The performer should complete the round-off by leaping upward as high as possible after landing.

Figure 5.33
Round-Off

Mule Kick (Bucking Bronco or Snap-Down) (Figure 5.34)

This stunt prepares the performer for the back handspring because the action in this stunt is identical to that performed in the last half of a back handspring. The performer starts the mule kick from a momentary handstand in which the legs and the arms are slightly bent. As he falls toward his stomach and feet, the performer snaps his legs downward by flexing his hips and pushes hard with his arms and shoulders as illustrated in the figure. The correct landing position for this stunt is one in which the body is bent forward, the arms are reaching backward and upward, and the legs are flexed. Upon landing on his feet the performer immediately reverses his arm movement and jumps back into the momentary handstand position, keeping his head down during the jump. In this stunt the goal is to be able to snap down from the handstand position to an almost upright standing position.

Figure 5.34
Mule Kick

Arabian Cartwheel (Figure 5.35)

The performer takes a short run, does a low hop, and from a two-footed take-off does a high forward dive about five feet in length, landing in an upside-down cartwheel position. He then completes a regular cartwheel.

Figure 5.35
Arabian Cartwheel

Kip From Mat (Snap-Up) (Figure 5.36)

The performer lies on his back on the mat, places his hands on the floor directly above his shoulders, and with his legs tucked he rolls back until his weight is resting on the back of his head, shoulders, and upper back. As his body begins to roll forward he shoots his legs upward and forward and pushes hard with his hands. He then flexes his legs, curls his head forward, and lands in a squat position on the mat. A variation of this stunt is the rollover kip from the mat, which is begun as a forward roll and as soon as the shoulders contact the mat or floor, a kip is performed. With practice the performer can do this stunt without placing his hands on the mat but instead as he kips he pushes against the mat with the back of his head and quickly thrusts his hands to his knees and pushes against them.

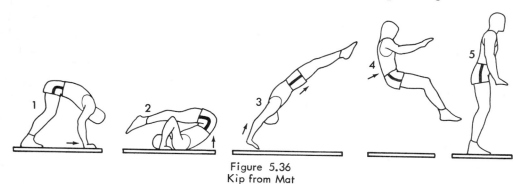

Figure 5.36
Kip from Mat

Pitch From Belly (Figure 5.37)

In this stunt the top man performs a front handspring with the assistance of the bottom man. The bottom man lies on his back on the mat and raises his slightly flexed legs to a position over his hips. His feet are held in a V position with the heels together and the balls of the feet spread apart. The top man faces the bottom man and stands next to his hips. He leans forward and places his stomach against the bottom man's feet. The bottom man pulls the top man forward, and as he feels all the top man's weight, he pulls the top man's upper body to him and then pushes hard with his feet by forcefully extending his legs. As the top man's weight passes behind the bottom man, the bottom man pushes with his hands and the top man, with his chin on his chest and looking forward, lands in a semisquat position. The assistance of at least one spotter during the learning process is essential. The spotter, who stands to one side of the top man, must be especially ready to give assistance, by grasping the top man's upper arm, in case the top man overthrows the front handspring.

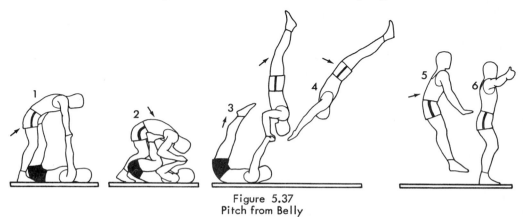

Figure 5.37
Pitch from Belly

Wheelbarrow Pitch (Figure 5.38)

The top man spreads his legs and assumes a push-up position on the mat. The bottom man stands between the top man's feet and grasps his ankles. Doing a slight dip with each count the bottom man counts to three and on the count of three he forcefully lifts the top man's legs as high as possible. As this lift begins the top man, who is looking forward, vigorously pikes his hips upward and forward and as his hips pass overhead he pushes against the mat with his hands, and at the same time he flexes his head

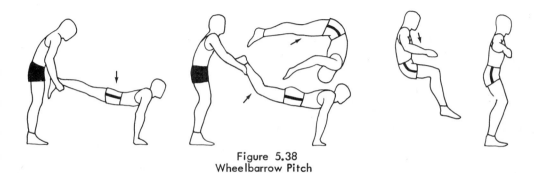

Figure 5.38
Wheelbarrow Pitch

forward. He then quickly tucks his body and lands in a semisquat position. As for the preceding stunt, a spotter should be ready to give assistance during the learning stages.

Headspring

The performer places the top of his head on the mat and his hands just forward of his head. He does a headstand, pikes his legs, and as his body falls off balance backward to a position where it rolls past the point of balance, the performer kicks his legs vigorously forward and downward (as when performing the kip) and pushes hard with his hands. He lands in a squat position on the mat. With practice the headspring can be performed from a short run and it is possible for the performer to land in an arched standing position.

Front Handspring (Figure 5.39)

The performer takes a short run, hops on his right foot, stomps his left foot on the mat, and whips his hands to the mat. He kicks his right leg forcefully backward and upward and pushes hard with his other foot. He keeps his arms extended and his head up as long as possible. As his legs pass overhead, the performer whips his legs forward and downward and then flexes them, flexes at his waist, and lands in a squat position on his feet. Again with additional practice and skill the performer can land in a standing position.

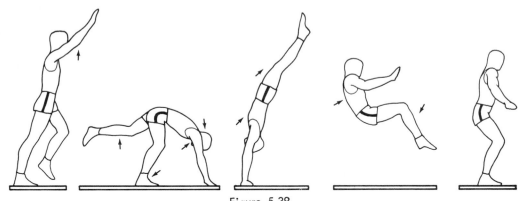

Figure 5.39
Front Handspring

Hands Between Legs Pitch to Front Airo (Figure 5.40)

With his back to the bottom man, the standing performer spreads his legs and flexes forward, positioning his wrists and hands between and behind his legs. The bottom man faces the performer and stands immediately behind him and grasps the performer's wrists. On the count of three the performer, keeping his legs spread wide, jumps upward and rotates his body forward while the bottom man lifts the top man's wrists vigorously. The performer keeps his chin on his chest and lands in a

Figure 5.40
Hands Between Legs to Front Airo

semisquat position while the bottom man retains his grasp on the performer's wrists. This stunt allows the performer to experience with safety the rotation of a complete forward somersault. Because the bottom man supplies most of the lift and rotation, it does not have the feeling of a regular front airo.

Front Airo (Front Somersault) (Figure 5.41)

This stunt can be performed in a number of different ways. One of the most effective methods is the use of the backward-upward two-arm lift technique in which the performer takes a short run and hops to a two-footed take-off from which he jumps upward vigorously. As the two-footed take-off is made, the head and upper body are flexed forward and downward and the arms are, in the order given, thrown forward, downward, backward, and upward, and the body is tucked tightly by lifting the hips and heels high. The performer tucks his body tightly and keeps his chin on his chest, and keeps his eyes open and focused on seeing the mat. When he sees the mat he extends his legs and lands in a semisquat position with his feet slightly in front of his hips. The fundamentals of this stunt may be quickly learned by piling several mats on top of one another, standing on them, and with the flexed arms over the forehead, throwing the arms, head, shoulders, and trunk forward and downward while

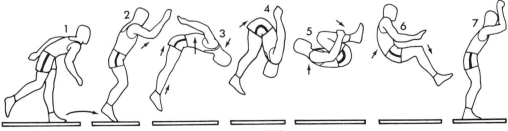

Figure 5.41
Front Airo

jumping the hips upward. Using this technique the beginner should easily rotate far enough in the air to land on his back. With increased effort and better timing, he can proceed to the point of landing on his hips and feet, while in a squat position. He next takes a run and performs a front airo as described.

Side Leg Pitch Back Airo (Figure 5.42)

The performer stands with his back facing the length of the mat. He raises his right leg forward until it is parallel with the mat. The bottom man stands directly to the right of the performer and places his left hand under the performer's hips and grasps the performer's right heel with his right hand. On the count of three the bottom man lifts the performer's hips and right leg. Dipping with each count the performer jumps up at the count of three and at the same time raises from his sides his flexed arms forward and upward to an overhead position. At this time he moves his head backward and looks for the mat and lands in a semisquat position. When learning this stunt a spotter should stand on the other side of the performer and grasp his belt or top of his shorts and with the other hand grasp the performer's upper arm in order to guide his somersaulting action and insure that he does not over-rotate the somersault.

Figure 5.42

Pitch Back Airo (Figure 5.43)

The pitch back airo should not be attempted unless the top man is spotted. The top man stands on the palms of the bottom man, who is sitting on the mat and facing the top man. On the count of three, while leaning slightly off balance backward, the top man throws his arms forward and upward as far as possible and simultaneously jumps upward and slightly backward with all his strength. The top man then throws his head back and quickly raises his tucked legs to his chest in order to accelerate his rotation. As the top man jumps, the bottom man forcibly lifts his feet upward and then may lie back in order to avoid any possibility of being kicked in the face. Because the assistance rendered by the bottom man may cause the top man to overthrow his somersault and land in a sitting position, the top man needs to be spotted by a hand spot or in a safety belt. If a hand spot is employed, the spotter stands to one side of the top man, grasps his shorts at the waist (or a belt) with one hand and prepares to assist the top man's somersault by grasping his upper arm, shoulder, or back of his neck and assisting the somersault motion by applying force to that part of the top man's body. The spotter must be especially watchful as the top man lands because he must lift vigorously on his shorts if the top man underthrows or overthrows the somersault.

Figure 5.43
Pitch Back Airo

Back Airo (Back Somersault) (Figure 5.44)

From a standing position and with his arms spread shoulder width and outstretched in front of his shoulders, the back airo performer lowers his arms and flexes his body to about a one-quarter knee bend position. When his arms are lowered in a natural action to a position alongside his thighs, he throws his arms forward and overhead as fast as possible and, leaning slightly backward, he jumps upward vigorously. He immediately throws his head back, brings his knees to his chest and tucks his body. When he sees the mat he extends his legs and lands with his feet under-

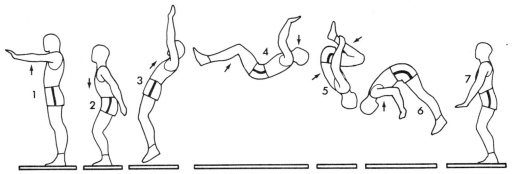

Figure 5.44
Back Airo

neath his hips. In learning the back airo, a spotter or an overhead mechanic (safety belt) should be used at all times.

Back Flip-Flop (Back Handspring) (Figure 5.45)

The correct performance of the back flip-flop begins with an action that is similar to sitting down on a chair. Keeping his back straight and his feet flat on the floor, the performer starts to sit back and at the same time vigorously swings his outstretched arms down and back until they pass to the side of and slightly behind his thighs. As his body is falling off balance backward, keeping his hands no more than shoulder width apart, the performer whips his arms overhead and backward as far as possible and vigorously throws his head backward. As the arms are thrown back, he reaches forcefully for the floor behind him and throws his hips toward the ceiling, landing in a fast moving handstand position with an extreme arch and with his hands and fingers pointing down the mat behind him. He then snaps his feet to the mat while pushing with his hands and shoulders in a manner identical to that used in the mule kick. The performer should be spotted by hand or in a safety belt until he has fully mastered the back flip-flop. Some teachers and coaches prefer to teach the back flip-flop before teaching the back airo whereas others reverse this order. Because learning one first somewhat inhibits at first the learning of the other, the authors, because of safety reasons, believe the back airo should be learned first.

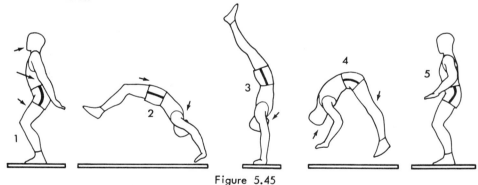

Figure 5.45
Back Flip-Flop

TUMBLING ROUTINES

Routine Composed of Beginning Tumbling Stunts

Football roll, forward roll; forward roll—arms folded; forward roll—cross the legs; backward roll from a jackknife position; backward roll over one shoulder.

Routine Composed of Elementary Tumbling Stunts

Handspring, dive and roll with legs crossed, backward extension roll, backward extension roll to chest roll, regain feet, jump one-half turn, cartwheel.

Routine Composed of Intermediate Tumbling Stunts

Arabian cartwheel, round-off, back extension roll, jump one-half twist, headspring, kip from mat, mule kick, back flip-flop.

CHART FOR RATING TUMBLING SKILLS

Beginning Tumbling Stunts	Rating of Stunt Performance*				
	1	2	3	4	5
Spinal Rock					
Forward Roll					
Forward Roll to the Back					
Forward Roll — Arms Folded					
Forward Roll — Cross the Legs					
Forward Roll While Holding the Toes					
Forward Roll — Hands Behind the Head					
Backward Roll Over One Shoulder					
Backward Roll from a Jackknife Position					
Football Roll					
Side Roll					
Sub-Total					

Elementary Tumbling Stunts	1	2	3	4	5
Cartwheel					
Back to Back Pullover					
Backward Extension Roll					
Backward Extension Roll to Chest Roll					
Backward Roll to Head and Handstand					
Dive and Roll Over Three Men					
Double Rolls — Forward and Backward					
Triple Roll					
Shoulder-Knee Handspring					
Headsnap Over Rolled-Up Mat					
Handspring from Mat					
Sub-Total					

Intermediate Tumbling Stunts	1	2	3	4	5
Round-Off					
Mule Kick					
Arabian Cartwheel					
Kip from Mat					
Pitch from Belly					
Wheelbarrow Pitch					
Headspring					
Handspring					
Hands Between Legs Pitch to Front Airo					
Front Airo					
Side-Leg Pitch Back Airo					
Pitch Back Airo					
Back Airo					
Back Flip-Flop					
Sub-Total					
Grand Total					

*The Simplified Points System containing the description of the five categories of ratings appear on pages 76-77.

(Figure 5.46)

6 TRAMPOLINE (REBOUND TUMBLING) STUNTS

THE TRAMPOLINE

The tramp consists of a sturdily constructed metal frame within which is attached, by means of elastic shock cords or metal springs, a solid canvas or nylon bed or a webbed nylon bed.

During the Middle Ages a French circus acrobat named du Trampoline, as a result of skill acquired in performing on the springboard and leaping board, visualized the possibility of doing tumbling stunts on the large safety net suspended under flying trapeze acts. From this beginning the trampoline gradually evolved and in order to reduce its size and add to its portability and rebounding capability the net was suspended to a frame by means of springs. For many years trampolines were used only in circuses and were handmade by the performers.

Joe E. Brown, before he became famous as a film comedian, was a noted trampolinist and was among the first ever to perform a triple back somersault on the trampoline. George Nissen and Larry Griswold were probably the first to commercially manufacture trampolines on a large scale, beginning in the 1930's.

The trampoline was first accepted as a competitive gymnastics event in the colleges in 1946, hence it is the most recent piece of competitive gymnastics apparatus. At first, competitive trampolinists attempted to perform a few difficult trampoline stunts with several bounces or breaks between each. Now the stress is on proper form and continuity of stunts; however, the difficulty of the stunts performed has also increased. As a result of this development many authorities credit the introduction of the trampoline with bringing about a revival in artistic gymnastics throughout the United States.

The youth of today who feel a desire for action are attracted to the trampoline because of its many challenges—to go high, to turn fast, and to turn and twist in many different ways and with a variety of stunt combinations. Difficult trampoline stunts such as double-front somersaults with a one-half twist, double-back somersaults, one and one-half twisting front somersaults, and double-twisting-back somersaults are commonplace and are easily performed by high school and college trampolinists. Such stunts as the double-front airo with one and one-half twists, double-back airos with a double twist, or a back somersault with a triple twist are often seen in college gymnastics meets.

Many values may be derived from practicing regularly on the trampoline. Not only is trampolining fun but such transferable skills as front and back somersault motions and twisting actions are perfected. The mechanics of these skills can be applied to tumbling, apparatus work, and a number of other activities such as diving, dancing, and skating. Increased agility, alertness, balance, coordination, courage, endurance, perseverance, self-confidence, self-control, and will power are all potential byproducts of trampoline training. Trampolining develops a sense of the position of the body and its parts—the kinesthetic sense—to a greater extent than does any other piece of apparatus. As a training device for developing these important qualities, trampoline tumbling was used extensively in Naval Aviation Training during World War II. In fact the Naval Aviation Program in gymnastics and trampolining helped to create and spread the popularity of trampolining.

How dangerous is the trampoline? It is no more dangerous than any other piece of apparatus if it is properly supervised and if the performers have a knowledge of the stunts that they practice and are not foolhardy. All beginners should first learn the basic or fundamental trampoline stunts in proper sequence, have well-qualified spotters in place, and proceed only as they can master the trampoline stunts in a regular progression of difficulty. Two of the main reasons that most trampoline centers did not long survive were (1) a lack of instruction thereby preventing the trampoline center users from progressing much past the fundamental skills of trampolining, and (2) a lack of supervision thereby allowing the users to attempt stunts that were beyond their skill levels and resulting in some accidents; but even here a small percentage of accidents occurred.

When practicing on the trampoline the performer should always have a clear understanding of how to perform all aspects of each stunt or routine that he attempts. If he is unable to visualize the method of performance, he is not ready to attempt the stunt unassisted but should instead make use of an overhead safety belt or, for many elementary stunts, a hand safety belt—making sure that the person handling the safety belt is competent and understands how the stunt being attempted should be performed. Once he begins a stunt the trampolinist should never change his mind but instead should always complete the stunt attempted. The trampolinist must remember that despite occasional advice to relax completely, he makes use of controlled relaxation and especially when landing and rebounding from the trampoline bed, he must tense those muscles involved in resisting the effects of gravity such as the muscles of the neck that hold the head erect or slightly back during a front drop. Especially during the learning stages, the trampoline performer is well advised to wear sweatpants and a sweatshirt in order to prevent scraping his skin, particularly at the knees and elbows.

The special spotting techniques that should be employed for a particular stunt are explained under the description of such stunts. There are six important general spotting techniques and principles for the trampoline.

(1) As a normal procedure, especially for the unskilled trampolinist, four spotters should be stationed, two at either side and two at either end of the trampoline. If an overhead safety belt is used, these spotters are unnecessary.

(2) The spotters should always know what stunt or routine the trampolinist intends to perform.

(3) The spotter must remain alert and next to the trampoline; he should never shy away if the performer starts to bounce or fall toward him.

(4) Should the performer bounce or fall toward a spotter, the spotter should attempt to forcefully push the performer toward the middle of the trampoline bed while he is still in midair.

(5) If the performer starts to fall off the trampoline, the spotter should attempt to catch and support his upper body by grasping his upper arm, neck, shoulder, or upper back.

(6) If the performer starts to fall off the trampoline he should depend on the spotter to catch him—the performer should not try to grasp the spotter but should instead relax when the spotter contacts him.

Because the trampoline performer should early learn to combine trampoline stunts into routines, several simple routines are listed in the stunts presented in this section.

BEGINNING TRAMPOLINE STUNTS

Feet Bounce (Figure 6.1)

With his feet spread shoulder width apart, the performer, facing one end of the trampoline, stands in the center of the trampoline bed. He

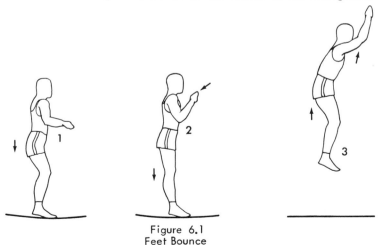

Figure 6.1
Feet Bounce

flexes his legs slightly and jumps, and at the same time he swings his arms forward and upward. As he descends toward the bed he swings his arms sideward and downward. He continues to bounce on his feet and during each take-off he forcefully extends his feet at the ankles just before leaving the bed. At the top of his bounce he holds his extended arms in front of and above his shoulders and he pikes his body slightly. The duration of the pause of the arm swing at the top of the bounce depends mainly on the height of the bounce; the pause should be such that at the bottom of the bounce the extended arms are swinging from slightly behind to down beside and in front of the thighs in order that as the body begins to rise the arms are beginning to swing forward and upward. While bouncing the performer looks at the end of the trampoline frame or beyond it in order to best retain his balance and to keep his head in line with his body. At all times when bouncing the performer should try to stay in the center of the trampoline bed.

Check Bounce (Kill Bounce) (Figure 6.2)

The trampoline performer should, as a safety measure, immediately learn how to stop his bounce at any time because if he is leaning off balance as he lands, his next bounce may carry him entirely off the trampoline bed, causing an accident. To kill his bounce the performer should, at the instant he starts to rise from the bed, quickly lower his body by flexing at his hips and knees in order that his trunk does not rise at all. This skill should be so throughly learned that anytime the performer lands off balance he instinctly ends his bounce.

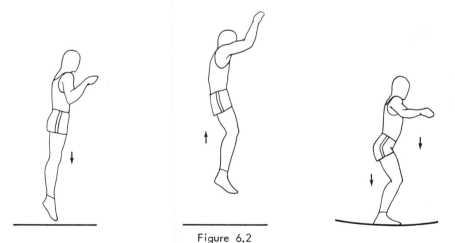

Figure 6.2

Routine

Six consecutive feet bounces with the body straight, three consecutive feet bounces tucking the body at the height of each bounce, check bounce. In performing this routine the performer should attempt to land on the center of the trampoline bed after each bounce.

Knee Drop (Figure 6.3)

As the performer rises from the bed from a feet bounce he slowly flexes his lower legs until they are parallel to the trampoline bed and at right angles to his thighs. Keeping his back and hips in a straight line from the knees up, the performer lands on the bed on his knees, shins, and insteps; landing on his knees in the spot that his feet contacted during the take-off. In order to obtain added lift for the take-off from the knee drop landing his arm swing is the same as when doing the feet bounce. If he wishes, he may glance down at the landing spot during the knee drop landing but as he bounces upward he should look forward again. With practice successive knee drops or alternate knee drops and feet bounces may be performed.

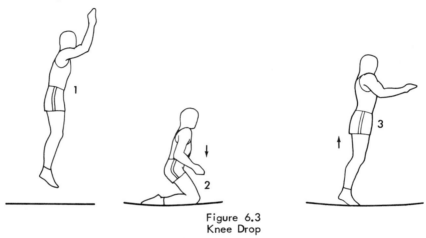

Figure 6.3
Knee Drop

Seat Drop (Figure 6.4)

As the performer leaves the bed from a feet bounce, he brings his legs together and flexes his hips, slowly lifting his extended legs until just

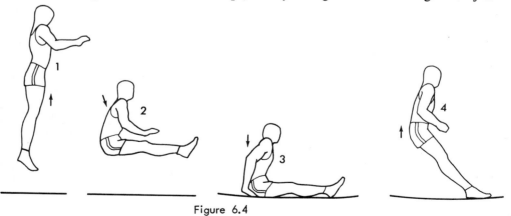

Figure 6.4
Seat Drop

before he lands they are parallel to the trampoline bed. Leaning slightly forward for the seat landing, he lands on his hips and backs of his thighs and calves and places his hands on the bed alongside his hips, fingers pointing forward, to push with as he rebounds off the bed. He then flexes his head and trunk forward, tucks his legs under him and comes to a standing position. With practice the performer can do alternate seat drops and feet bounces.

Routine

The performer does three knee drops in succession alternated with feet bounces, three seat drops in succession alternated with feet bounces, check bounce.

Knee Drop—Seat Drop Combination (Figure 6.5)

The knee drop and the seat drop are performed as for the single stunts except that after the knee drop is performed, the performer immediately performs a seat drop without first bouncing on his feet. He then performs a knee drop from the seat drop and continues to alternate the two stunts until each one has been done three times. He concludes the routine with a check bounce.

Figure 6.5
Knee Drop — Seat Drop Combination

All-Fours Drop (Hand and Knee Drop) (Figure 6.6)

The performer executes a low knee drop and as he rebounds from the bed he looks down and slowly curls his trunk forward and lands simultaneously on his hands and knees with his body parallel to the trampoline bed, his hands positioned directly under his shoulders and his knees directly under his hips. An excellent way to learn this position is, without bouncing, to assume an all-fours position on the trampoline bed. From this position the performer hunches his body, drives his hands and knees downward and attempts to develop an all-fours bounce. This should be practiced until it can be done to the point where the hands and knees always contact the bed at the same time and the body does not angle or tilt at all after each bounce.

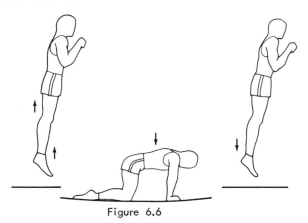

Figure 6.6

Front Drop (Belly Drop) (Figure 6.7)

When first attempting the front drop, the performer, in order to mini-mize the risk of injuries, should perform it from an all-fours drop, which is described in the preceding paragraph. When the front drop from an all-fours drop is mastered, the performer then practices the front drop from a low feet bounce take-off, and as his feet leave the bed he pikes his body and slowly raises his legs and curls his trunk forward. He should never dive forward as this causes the skin to be abraded by the bed during the landing, and could result in a back injury if the body is not parallel to the bed during the landing. The performer should never raise his knees higher than his chest. In landing, the chest, stomach, thighs, and inside of the arms should all simultaneously contact the bed. To recover to his feet, the performer pushes hard with his hands, lifts his head, and tucks his legs and feet.

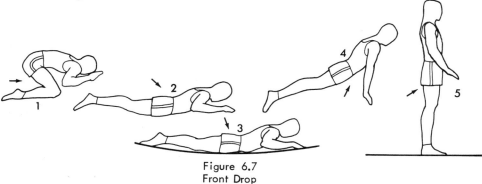

Figure 6.7
Front Drop

Routine

Three front drops are alternated with feet bounces, check bounce, all-fours drop, front drop, all-fours drop, knee drop, and check bounce.

Combination Front Drops, Knee Drops, Seat Drops and Feet Bounces

The performer should now be ready to practice various combinations of front drops, knee drops, seat drops, and feet bounces. Going from a front drop to a seat drop requires a forceful arm push on the bed and a forward thrust of the thighs as the legs are tucked, while the performance of a seat drop to a front drop requires the performer to push forcefully with his hands and to lean sharply forward as he rises from the trampoline bed; he then quickly extends his legs behind him.

Routine

Seat drop, proceed to front drop, knee drop, front drop, seat drop, front drop, and check bounce.

Feet Bounce, Half-Twist, Front Drop (Figure 6.8)

The performer does a few low feet bounces and as he leaves the bed on the last feet bounce he slowly extends both legs forward and thrusts his chest, stomach, and hips toward the ceiling, keeping his head above them. As he approaches the top of his bounce he rotates his head, shoulders, and arms, causing his body to complete a one-half twist. He then lands in a front drop position on the bed. The secret for performing this stunt is to do the twist without rushing and to look for the trampoline bed when the head is first rotated.

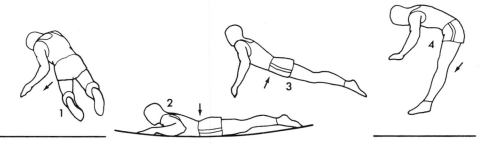

Figure 6.8
Feet Bounce, Half-Twist, Front Drop

Routine

Half-twist, front drop, seat drop, half-twisting front drop, and knee drop, ended by the check bounce. The new move in this combination is the half-twist to a front drop from the seat drop, which is accomplished by taking the lift from the bed and when in the air turning as when doing the half-twist to a front drop from the feet.

Front Drop, Feet, Half-Twist to Front Drop, Feet (Figure 6.9)

The performer, while performing this combination of stunts, should work to retain sufficient height at all times by using his arms to lift and by pushing off his toes during the take-off. This and other combinations of stunts should be practiced with the aim of developing maximum lift, control, and form.

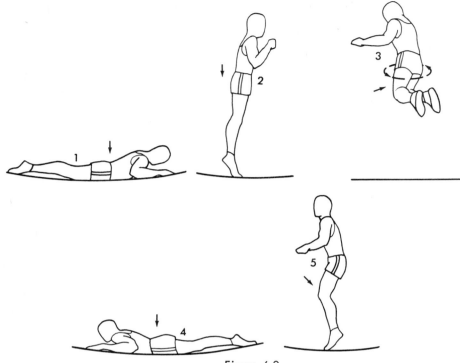

Figure 6.9
Front Drop, Feet, Half-Twist to Front Drop, Feet

Back Drop (Figure 6.10)

When first attempting the back drop on the trampoline many beginners find that they have to overcome a fear of falling backward. This fear often inhibits them when attempting the back drop, causing them to pike their bodies as they fall backward and resulting in a landing on the hips with the body held in a V position in which both the legs and back are several inches above the trampoline bed. This off-balance landing position often causes the performer to bounce from a hip landing to an upper back and back of the head landing which is discomforting. In order to avoid this difficulty and to learn a back drop easily, quickly, and safely, the performer should start from a stationary standing position. He places his arms and hands alongside his thighs, arches his back slightly, tucks his chin on his chest and keeps it there throughout the stunt. The performer then flexes his legs slightly, leans backward, and as he starts to fall backward he lifts one extended leg as high as possible with a kicking action while attempting to keep his other foot on the bed (this leg is tucked as the performer falls backward). The action of lifting one leg until it points toward the ceiling will cause the performer to land in the desired position on his back with his head and legs raised. As he rebounds from the bed he kicks (kips) both legs forward, tucks his body, and comes to a squat landing position on his feet.

When this technique has been mastered, the performer next stands in a slightly crouched position, leans backward, and as he falls back he lifts both legs, landing on his upper back. After mastering this technique the performer does a back drop from a low bounce initiating the stunt just as he bounces off the bed.

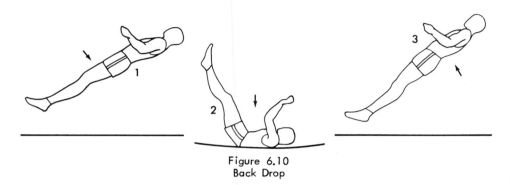

Figure 6.10
Back Drop

Routine

Three back drops are alternated with a feet bounce between each.

Front Drop, One-Half Back Somersault, Back Drop (Figure 6.11)

The performer, in order to accomplish successfully the one-half somersault required to move from a front drop to a back drop, must, as he leaves the bed, push hard with his hands, extend his head backward, and bring his knees to his chest while flexing his legs. This stunt should be learned from a medium-high bounce, and with practice the flexible performer can arch his body and perform the one-half backward turn while in a layout position. As the performer is moving from the front drop to the back drop he should watch the trampoline bed, looking slightly to one

Figure 6.11
Front Drop, One-Half Back Somersault, Back Drop

side in order to judge how much to tuck or extend his body in order to land in a correct back drop position. The somersault action used in performing this stunt is almost identical to that used in performing a back drop from a feet bounce, except that the action is more vigorous and the tucked position is held for an increased length of time.

Front Drop, Feet Bounce, Back Drop, Feet Bounce (Figure 6.12)

This routine of stunts combines front and back drops and aids the performer in gaining additional mastery of them. When the body turns (rotates) forward, the head is flexed forward and the legs are tucked, and when the body turns (rotates) backward, the head is extended backward and the legs are tucked. This combination of stunts should be repeated until the performer is well oriented in controlling the forward and backward rotation of his body.

Figure 6.12
Front Drop, Feet Bounce, Back Drop, Feet Bounce

Front Drop, Knee Drop, Seat Drop, Back Drop, Feet (Figure 6.13)

This combination of stunts contains only one new move—the seat drop to a back drop combination. To perform this combination the performer, as he leaves the bed from the seat drop landing just lays back, extends his head backward, and lifts his tucked legs to his chest, opening his body in time to make the back drop landing. Whenever combinations of stunts are performed, the performer should attempt to obtain maximum lift from the bed after each landing in order to maintain sufficient height to perform the next stunt.

Seat Drop, Half-Twist to Front Drop, Knee Drop, Back Drop, Feet (Figure 6.14)

The movements and combinations contained in this series of stunts have been explained. The performer should again work for control, height, and form as this combination of stunts is performed.

Figure 6.13
Front Drop, Knee Drop, Seat Drop, Back Drop, Feet

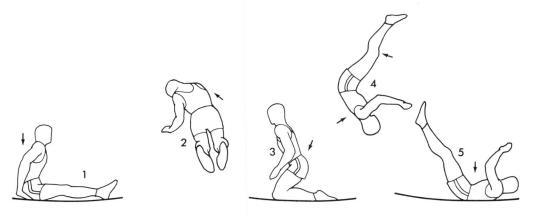

Figure 6.14
Seat Drop, Half-Twist to Front Drop, Knee Drop, Back Drop, Feet

Back Drop, Front Drop, Knee Drop, Seat Drop, Back Drop, Front Drop, Feet (Figure 6.15)

The performer should execute this routine with plenty of height and correct form.

Figure 6.15
Back Drop, Front Drop, Knee Drop, Seat Drop, Back Drop, Front Drop, Feet

ELEMENTARY TRAMPOLINE STUNTS

Back Drop, Half-Twist, Front Drop (Figure 6.16)

Before attempting this stunt the performer should first master a back drop. When doing a back drop, half twist, front drop, the performer executes a back drop, holding his upper arms extended from his shoulders and his forearms flexed. As he rises from the bed he swings one arm across his chest, the other elbow underneath its shoulder, and rotates his head in the direction in which he throws his arms, and looks for the trampoline bed. This action causes his body to do a one-half twist, during which time his body and legs should be extended and his legs held together. When he is in a front drop position he extends his arms and continues to watch the trampoline bed until he lands in a front drop.

After the performer has mastered this stunt he may proceed to performing a full-twist between landings by keeping his body straight and continuing to pull his arms across and under his body and turning his head until he is facing the ceiling. He then opens up and lands in a back drop. With additional practice a one-and-one-half or even a double twist can be performed in a like manner providing a high bounce is obtained. The performer must, however, avoid performing the twisting action until he is leaving the bed because if he starts it too early he will be thrown to the side of the trampoline. This twisting action is an excellent lead-up because it is identical to that used when performing back somersaults with twists.

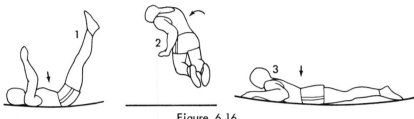

Figure 6.16
Back Drop, Half-Twist, Front Drop

Front Drop, Half-Twist, Back Drop (Figure 6.17)

This stunt is quite similar to the preceding stunt except that the one-half twist is initiated from a front drop landing. The twisting action is identical and the performer looks for the ceiling, landing in a back drop position.

After this stunt has been mastered, the performer, by taking a high bounce and initiating the twisting action with increased force and holding it longer, can perform a full twist to a front drop landing or a one and one-half twist to a back drop landing. This twisting action is similar to that used with twisting forward somersaults.

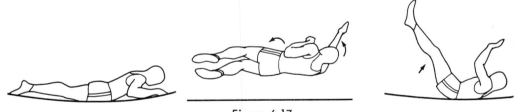

Figure 6.17

One-Half Turn-Table (Figure 6.18)

When performing this stunt the performer turns or revolves in a manner similar to the revolution made by a spinning table top or a piano stool. When doing this stunt, the performer should do a high front drop and as he leaves the bed he pulls with his right hand and pushes with his left hand to his right and pulls to the right with his head. He quickly tucks his body and revolves his body until a one-half revolution has been completed. At this time he extends his body and lands in a front drop position. When performing this stunt the performer must use care to avoid pushing his body upward when he pushes sideward with his hands because this would create a back somersaulting action. When a one-half turn-table has been mastered, the performer should proceed to the practice of a full turn-table. This is accomplished primarily by holding the tucked body position for an increased time until a full revolution of the body has been completed. The performer will also probably find it necessary to increase the height of his front drop and the force of his sideward arm push and pull and head pull. Because this is a safe stunt to perform, those who show aptitude for this stunt may wish to attempt a one and one-half or even a double turn-table. The only danger that may arise in performing this stunt occurs if the performer pushes and pulls his hands sideward before his body leaves the trampoline bed as this may cause him to travel to the side frame of the trampoline bed.

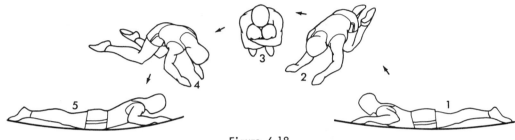

Figure 6.18
One-Half Turn-Table

Seat Drop, Half-Twist, Seat Drop (Swivel Hips) (Figure 6.19)

The performer, from a high feet bounce, does a regular seat drop and as he rebounds from the bed he comes to a vertical position with his body completely straight. At the same time he swings his extended arms forward, overhead, and behind him and he swings his legs downward directly under-

Figure 6.19

neath his hips and behind him. As his arms and legs start to move behind him he rotates his head 180 degrees, facing the opposite direction, and also cat twists his body a one-half twist while it is in a vertical straight position. He then lifts his legs and lands in a seat drop position.

When performing this stunt it is essential that the performer does not rush his twisting motion nor attempt to circle his legs around to one side of his hips. An excellent lead-up stunt is to do a seat drop to an upright feet landing but just before landing, the arms are swung overhead and behind and the body and head are rotated a one-half twist in order that the performer lands facing the opposite direction from which he started.

Seat Drop, Full Twist, Seat Drop (Figure 6.20)

From a medium to high bounce the performer does a seat drop and as he leaves the bed he leans his upper body back and raises his hips in order that his body forms a straight line with his feet at the lowest point. He then throws his right arm across his chest, vigorously pushes his left elbow behind his left shoulder and quickly brings his chin to his left shoulder. Keeping his body completely extended, he continues to pull with his arms and head until his body has completed a full twist and he can see the trampoline bed beyond his feet. He then lands in a seat drop. While twisting the performer must keep his body completely extended. He must not begin the twisting action before he leaves the trampoline bed because too early an initiation will cause him to revolve in a circular revolution similar to that of a one-half turn-table, causing him to land facing the side of the trampoline.

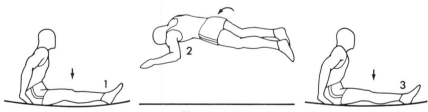

Figure 6.20
Seat Drop, Full Twist, Seat Drop

Knee Drop, Front Airo to Seat Drop (Figure 6.21)

In order to perform this stunt a true front somersault action must be employed. The performer, from a medium high bounce, lands in a knee drop position with his body and head erect and his hands held over his shoulder and slightly higher than the top of his head. As he starts to bounce upward, he throws his arms, head, and chest forward and downward, and continues his arm motion until he can loosely tuck his hands around his knees. At the same time he lifts his hips upward. Looking down his chest and slightly to one side of his legs, the performer extends his legs and comes to a piked position shortly before he lands in a regular seat drop position on the trampoline bed. If the performer does not initiate the front turn correctly or with sufficient force, by tucking tightly he can still somersault forward to a back drop position but because this landing, if uncontrolled, has an element of danger, the seat drop landing is recommended. If the performer overthrows or overspins his somersault he should, just before landing, almost completely extend his legs and as he lands give by flexing his knees and hips in the same manner as a check bounce is performed.

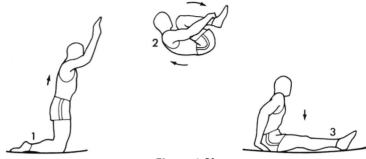

Figure 6.21
Knee Drop, Front Airo to Seat Drop

Front Drop, Half Forward Somersault, Back Drop (One-Half Front Cody) (Figure 6.22)

This stunt begins the front cody series and although it is quite safe to practice, it can alarm the performer during his first few efforts because his body rotates so slowly and because he lands blindly (can not see his landing). The performer does a front drop from a high bounce and as he begins to rebound from the trampoline bed he lifts his hips upward as high as possible, tucks his legs upward, and throws his arms downward and toward his hips and curls his head downward. He then holds this tucked position until he lands on his back. If he can see the trampoline bed a short time after the stunt is started, he is short and needs only to extend his arms down to the bed thus coming to a handstand position. The performer must be careful to swing his arms down the center of the trampoline and to not look sideward, otherwise he may get a side somersault motion. With practice this stunt can be done to a seat drop or even a feet landing.

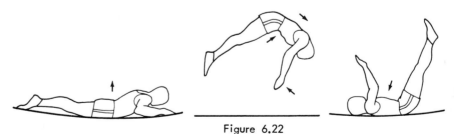

Figure 6.22

Back Drop, Three-Fourths Airo Backward, Feet Drop (Figure 6.23)

This stunt utilizes the same action employed in back somersaults and back codys. The performer should first learn the back extension roll on the mats before attempting this stunt. The back drop executed preparatory to doing the back turn (back somersault) must be one in which the performer lands on his hips and lower back as this landing position places the center of gravity in front of the contact with the trampoline bed thus causing the lift of the bed to assist in a back (instead of a front) somersaulting motion. Therefore the performer should never land only on the upper part of his back and shoulders when performing this stunt. From a medium high bounce on the forward half of the trampoline, the performer lands in a back drop position with his legs in a semitucked position. Upon landing he immediately thrusts his legs behind him forcefully and at a slight upward angle. As he completes this action he vigorously extends his head backward in order to see the trampoline bed. At the same time he tucks his body and at the proper time extends his legs beneath him, landing in a semitucked position and checking his bounce upon landing. When first learning this stunt the performer should quickly snap his head backward and extend his arms behind and under his shoulders as if he were performing a backward roll. In the event he loses his back somersaulting action by landing on his upper back or extending his legs directly upward, this technique will prevent neck injuries that might occur if he landed on his head. A variation of this technique in which the reaction of the trampoline bed furnishes the impetus for the back somersault action is to land in a backward-leaning seat drop position with the body tucked and the hands grasping the shins. By thrusting his legs with increased force and holding his tucked position longer the performer can do a complete back somersault to a back drop landing. By extending his legs, arms, and body as soon as he sees the trampoline bed, the performer can do a one-half back somersault to a front drop landing.

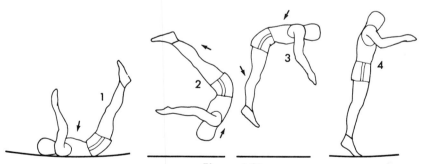

Figure 6.23
Back Drop, Three-Fourths Airo Backward, Feet

Back Drop, Half Forward Somersault with Half-Twist, Back Drop (Cradle) (Figure 6.24)

The performer should first learn to do with ease a back drop, half forward somersault, front drop. He then repeats the somersault movement from a back drop and just before his body is in a front drop position he does a half twist by throwing his left arm across his right shoulder, his right elbow under and beneath his right shoulder, and rotates his head to his right as far as possible. When he has completed a one-half twist he extends his arms sideward and lands in a back drop position. The common error to be avoided in this stunt is to twist too early. Wait until well past a vertical position. With practice and increased height, the performer can maintain his twisting actions for an increased time and lands in a front drop position after doing a full twist. The next step is to complete a one and one-half twist, landing in a back drop position; this twisting action is highly similar to that used in doing a one and one-half twisting front somersault to the feet. When twisting, the performer's body should be fully extended.

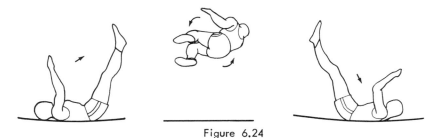

Figure 6.24

Back Drop, Forward Somersault, Back Drop (Cannonball) (Figure 6.25)

Before attempting this stunt the performer should have fully mastered the back drop, one-half forward somersault, front drop. From a high bounce on the back half of the trampoline the performer does a back drop landing on the upper portion of his back and with his legs in a semitucked

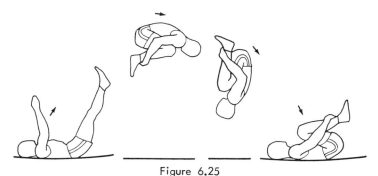

Figure 6.25

position. As he begins to rebound upward, he forcefully extends his legs forward and upward, immediately curls his trunk and head forward, and swings his arms forward and downward, tucking his body. He holds this tuck until he lands in a back drop. When performing this stunt the performer should keep his eyes open and watch the bed, making certain that he is somersaulting beyond a head drop landing (if he is short he should kick out to a handstand and do a dive roll or, if too short, a mule kick). With practice a one and one-fourth forward somersault to a feet landing can be done or even a one and one-half somersault to a front drop landing.

INTERMEDIATE TRAMPOLINE STUNTS

Knee Drop, Forward Somersault, Feet Drop (Front Somersault from Knees) (Figure 6.26)

This stunt is performed as is a knee drop, three-quarter front turn to seat drop except that increased height and somersaulting action are utilized. As the performer lifts off the bed he throws his arms, head, and chest forward and downward and lifts his hips and tucks his legs and body. He must use care during his landing and must be watching for the bed to appear in front of or beside his legs. This means that the performer must keep his eyes open as he performs the stunt but he should concentrate only on seeing the trampoline bed. If the performer overthrows this stunt he should kill his bounce during his landing and if he somersaults past a front drop position he may make an all-fours landing. Spotters, particularly at each end of the trampoline, should be present when this stunt is performed.

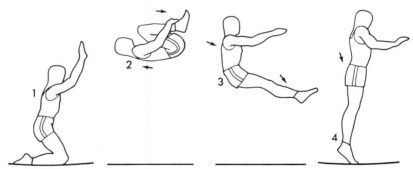

Figure 6.26
Knee Drop, Forward Somersault, Feet

Forward Somersault (Front Airo) (Figure 6.27)

This stunt is executed with the same action as that used for the front somersault from a knee drop. As the performer begins to rebound from the bed, in one integrated movement he throws his arms forward and downward from their overhead position, flexes his head forward to his chest, throws his chest forward and downward, lifts his hips behind him, and tucks his heels to his buttocks. He tucks briefly until he sees the bed in front of or to one side of his legs and then extends his legs and positions his feet under his hips, flexing his knees and hips as he lands. This stunt may be learned in a mechanic, with the assistance of another person, or else it may be developed from the forward somersault from the knee drop.

An efficient and quick method of learning the forward somersault is for the performer to do some fast forward rolls on the trampoline bed. He next progresses to a starting position in which his arms are overhead and he quickly swings his arms, head, and chest forward and downward; he forcefully pushes against the bed by extending his feet and simultaneously lifting his hips. With the proper timing these movements will produce a sufficient forward somersaulting action that the performer will not need to or even be able to touch his hands to the bed and he will somersault over to a tucked back drop position. In the next stage the performer assumes the same starting position and rises up and down on his toes in time with the lift of the trampoline bed. Just as he starts to rise on his toes the performer initiates the forward somersaulting action with his arms, head, and chest; pushes against the bed with the toes, lifts his hips, and somersaults forward to either a tucked back drop or a piked seat drop landing position. The performer should not travel forward on the trampoline bed more than about three feet.

When this phase is mastered and the performer can control his landing and can always see the trampoline bed before landing, he is ready to proceed to the final phase. In this phase the performer repeats the above actions with the same timing except that he does a low to medium feet bounce. The performer should, immediately before landing, extend his tucked body and head and also extend his tucked legs somewhat and unless he lands in a balanced position on his feet he should kill his bounce by

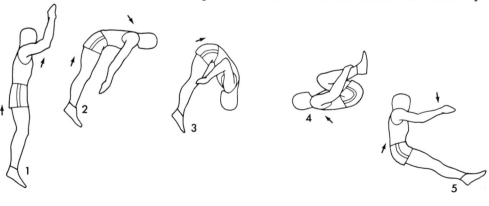

Figure 6.27
Forward Somersault

quickly flexing his knees and hips partway. After he acquires control and awareness of his landing position the performer may increase the height of his take-off bounce and thus have increased time in which to complete the forward somersault and get into position for the landing. This latter method is simple, safe, and allows the performer to progress to the front somersault from feet to feet at whatever rate of progress that he desires. By the use of this method, many beginners who have a background in the basic trampoline stunts master the forward somersault in one workout.

When the performer has complete control of his landings he may wish to try a second forward somersault from the landing of the first somersault thus performing swingtime airos. By increasing the height of his bounce, initiating the somersaulting actions with increased force, tucking his body into a more compact position, and/or holding his tucked position for an increased length of time, the performer can somersault just past a feet landing and then extend his body and legs and land in a front drop position thus completing a forward one and one-quarter somersault. After this stunt has been mastered the performer may, after he partially extends his body, do a one-half twist and land in a back drop position hence doing a one and one-quarter somersault with a half twist.

Backward Somersault (Back Airo) With Assistance (Figure 6.28)

The safest and most convenient method of spotting a performer who is learning a back somersault on the trampoline is through the use of the overhead suspension safety belt or spotting mechanic. However, this and other stunts can be spotted by a spotter (or two spotters) standing on the bed to one side of and behind the performer. If the spotter stands to the

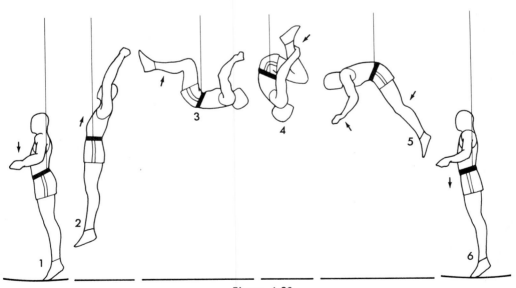

Figure 6.28
Backward Somersault with Assistance

right of the performer, he holds the performer's belt with his left hand and uses his right to grasp the performer's right upper arm and rotate and guide him to a safe landing. When standing on the trampoline bed the spotter(s) must time the performer's feet bounces and bounce with him in order not to kill the performer's height. Some spotters hand-spot this stunt by standing on the frame of the bed and moving to the performer as soon as he starts the back somersault, grasping his upper arm with both hands. In order that the spotter(s) will know when the back somersault will be attempted, the performer should count with each bounce and on the third bounce—the count of three—he does a back somersault.

When performing the back somersault the performer should take a few (three to five, usually) bounces in order to perform the stunt from normal height but he should not take too many bounces as this may fatigue him. While bouncing he should land on or near the center of the bed after he bounces as this indicates control on his part because he should not lean backward on his take-off. As he leaves the bed on the selected bounce, he looks straight ahead, swings his extended arms forward and upward until they are almost directly above his shoulders and as his arms rise above his head he lifts his tucked legs to his chest, attempting to lift his knees to his overhead hand position where he grasps his knees. Just prior to this instant he shifts his gaze from looking straight ahead to his knees in order to watch his hands grasp his knees. He then immediately extends his head backward and looks for the center of the trampoline bed. At the proper time he then so extends his legs and body that his feet land on the bed directly underneath his body. He should do a check bounce landing whenever he lands off balance.

Backward Somersault (Back Airo)

Whenever the performer has the feel of a back airo and believes that he can do it without assistance, he should attempt one without assistance. For most performers this stage is achieved after they have gone through the preliminary steps of preparation of being spotted while in an overhead safety belt or by a spotter standing on the bed.

The actions and techniques described for the assisted backward somersault apply to this stunt. When the performer can consistently land in good balance he may attempt two (or more) successive backward somersaults in swingtime. He may wish to also work on a piked and a layout back airo. The performer should soon develop the height and control to enable him to hold his tucked position past his feet and land in a seat drop or back drop position, thus performing a one and one-quarter backward somersault. By keeping his body in a semilayout (extended) position throughout the stunt, the performer may look backward immediately after initiating the back somersault movement and do a three-quarter somersault, landing in a front drop position.

Knee Drop, Round-Off, Knee Drop (Figure 6.29)

The modified round-off on the trampoline prepares the performer for the baroni (brandy) and can be valuable in aiding him to acquire insight into the correct feel of the actions utilized in performing a baroni. Practice of this lead-up stunt can often enable the novice trampolinist to master the baroni in twenty to thirty minutes. To perform a modified round-off on the trampoline the performer does a knee drop from medium height, landing with his arms extended overhead. As he rebounds from the bed, he whips his extended arms forward and downward and whips his hips and legs up and directly over his head at the same time. He places both hands on the bed slightly in front of the position in which he landed on his knees, coming to an overbalanced handstand position. He quickly does a half twist and pikes his knees to the bed as in the mule kick, landing on his knees and facing in the opposite direction from which he started. Throughout this stunt the performer keeps his eyes on the bed at all times; if he should duck his head his body will turn around its horizontal axis thus causing him to do a forward somersault. Instead his body should rotate around both its vertical and horizontal axes in which a one-half somersault is completed around the horizontal axis (or the hands if they support the body) and when in an upside down position his body does a one-half twist on its vertical axis. After this phase of the stunt is mastered, the performer, while watching the bed at all times, initiates the stunt as if he were going to do a front somersault from a knee drop. When almost upside down, without his hands touching the bed, and while still watching the bed he does a half-twist by bringing one arm and shoulder to the outside of his body and the other arm and shoulder to the inside of his body. He then lands in a knee drop. With increased height and force of throw he should be able to land on his feet. From this phase a baroni from feet to feet should be easily mastered, provided the twisting action is not started too early.

Figure 6.29
Knee Drop, Round-Off, Knee Drop

Knee Drop, One-Half Twist to Front Drop (Three-Fourths Baroni with Half-Twist) (Figure 6.30)

The performer takes a high bounce and lands on his knees in a position to throw a front somersault. As he leaves the bed, he throws his arms, head and chest downward and lifts his hips and legs. When upside down and while still watching the middle of the bed he does a one-half twist, keeping his body stretched in an extended position. Then, without prematurely touching his hands to the bed, he lands in a front drop position. The performer must wait until he is almost upside down before twisting and he should keep his body in a layout position after initiating the stunt. A variation of this stunt is to, just before landing, do another half twist and land in a back drop position.

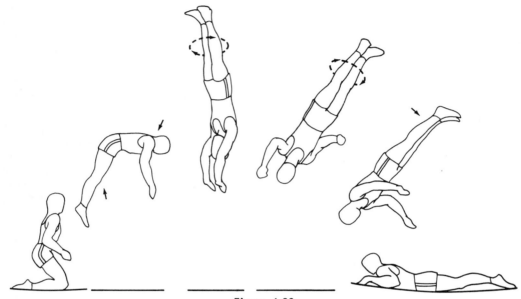

Figure 6.30

Baroni to Knees (Figure 6.31)

The baroni to the knees is an easy progression to follow after practicing the preceding stunt. When doing this stunt the performer whips his legs upward hard and fast to an overhead position. He twists and lands in a knee drop position. Again during the learning stages spotters should be located on both sides and ends of the trampoline.

Baroni (Figure 6.32)

With increased height, throw, and/or body pike, the performer can proceed to a baroni from feet to feet.

Back Cody (Figure 6.33)

Because being short on this stunt may involve landing on the head, it is absolutely essential that an overhead or hand safety belt or a hand spot be used until the back cody is mastered. Because this stunt calls for a complete back somersault, it involves no new elements of somersaulting motion to be learned. The new skill to be developed is initiating a back somersault from a front drop position in which the performer lands flat

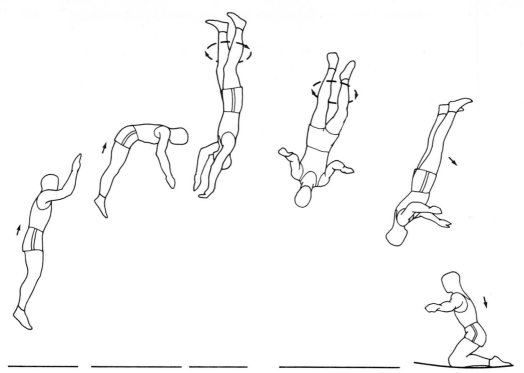

Figure 6.31

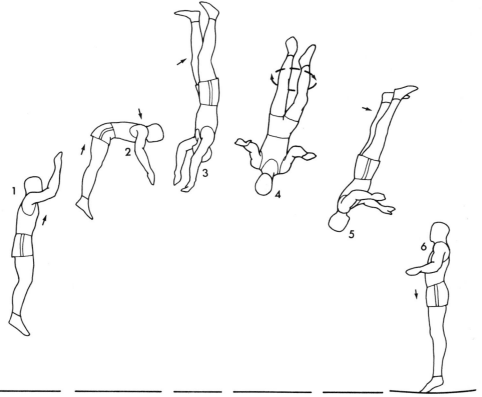

Figure 6.32
Baroni

on the bed with his lower legs flexed at his knees and with his hands beside his shoulders. As he begins to rebound from the bed, he gives a powerful push with his hands as if doing a fast push-up and at the same time he throws his head backward. Immediately after this and as early as possible he forcefully whips his knees forward under his hips and to his chest. He then grasps his knees in a tucked position and continues to extend his head backward while looking for the bed. When he is almost parallel to the bed he extends his legs and lands in a front drop position. With practice he can hold his tucked body position until he rotates to where he can land on his feet. The performer must be certain that he does a flat front drop, landing on his thighs, stomach, chest, and hands simultaneously. If he lands otherwise he should not attempt a back cody from that imperfect front drop.

Figure 6.33

Back Somersault With One-Half Twist (Half Twisting Back Airo) (Figure 6.34)

The performer throws a back somersault in a layout or semilayout position. He waits until he can see the trampoline bed and then does a half twist by throwing both hands and the chin to one shoulder. When learning this stunt it is best to slightly underthrow the somersault. A variation of this technique is to do a quick half twist on the take-off while raising the arms overhead and leaning backward slightly. The performer then throws a regular forward somersault action, landing on his feet.

Full Twisting Back Somersault (Figure 6.35)

Before attempting this stunt the performer should learn to do a layout back somersault in which he thrusts his hips forward during the take-off and lands near his take-off spot. When doing a full twisting back somersault the performer initiates a layout back airo as described. Keeping his

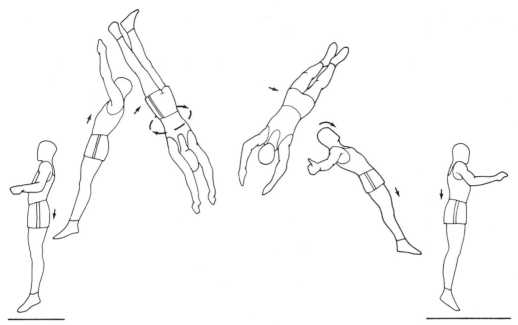

Figure 6.34

head back he waits to start the twisting action until he can see the trampoline bed. At this time his arms are whipped from a position above head level and to the front and sides of each shoulder to a clasping position on the left shoulder and at the same time his head is sharply rotated to his left. This action will cause him to twist and he should continue to hold this position with his body extended and watch the trampoline bed rotate or spin two times (two half revolutions). At this instant he extends his arms sideways and pikes his semitucked legs to the bed under his hips. In order

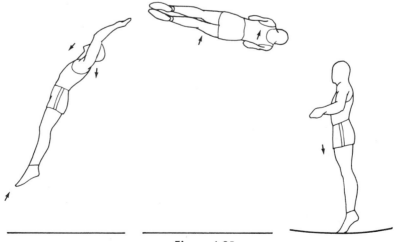

Figure 6.35

to perform this stunt successfully the performer must see the bed at all times and he must not start his twist until he can see the bed. The common error that most beginners make is that they try to twist before they do their somersault action and thus they never are able to complete the somersault. In order to avoid rushing the twist some performers prefer to look forward on the take-off until their chest lifts to their line of sight. They then look backward and start their twist. This stunt is best learned in a twisting safety belt fastened to an overhead mechanic.

Forward One-and-Three-Quarter Somersault (Figure 6.36)

Before attempting this stunt the performer should be able to do a forward one-and-one-quarter somersault, finishing the somersault at a considerable height above the trampoline bed. When this is achieved, the completion of the other one-half is a simple matter of keeping the body tightly tucked and the eyes open and seeing the bed apparently pass by. At this instant the performer loosens his tuck and lands in a back drop position. With a high take-off and a tight tuck the performer can easily somersault to a seat drop landing. Although this stunt can be done blind by closing the eyes after initiating it and holding the tuck until landing, the performer should always look for the bed to come around the second time; he should not attempt to see anything but the bed.

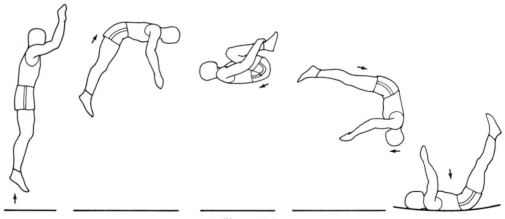

Figure 6.36

One-and-One-Half Twisting Front Somersault (Rudolph) (Figure 6.37)

Before attempting this stunt the performer should master a layout front somersault because this is the somersault position used when doing a rudolph. This is accomplished by the performer taking a high bounce and on the take-off forcefully throwing his arms, head and chest downward toward his feet and vigorously lifting his hips and legs, coming to an extended body position as quickly as possible and before he is upsidedown. He then holds the layout position and arches to a feet landing.

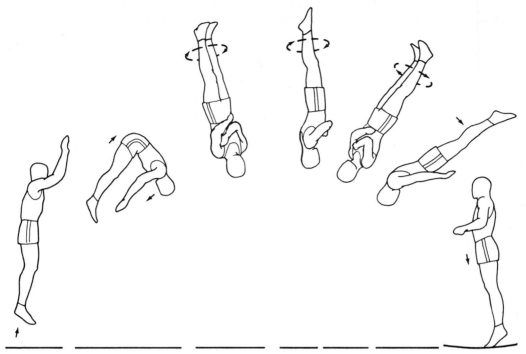

Figure 6.37

To do a rudolph the performer initiates the forward somersault as described in which he emphasizes the hip and leg lift behind him. As soon as his body is extended, the performer, watching the trampoline bed at all times, throws his right arm across his chest and to his left armpit, pulls his left elbow behind his left shoulder, and rotates his chin (and head) to his left shoulder. Holding this position he does one and one half twists (the bed will appear to spin around three times—three half rotations) and then pikes his legs and lands with his feet under his hips.

As with other twisting stunts the performer must be careful to avoid starting his twisting action too early. The twisting safety belt with an overhead mechanic should be worn until this stunt has been learned. Because the performer can see his landing in the rudolph at all times, it is safer than and probably as easy to do as the forward somersault with a full twist.

TRAMPOLINE ROUTINES

Routine Composed of Elementary Trampoline Stunts

Front airo from knees to seat drop; swivel hips; feet drop; front drop, half twist; feet; back drop, half twist; one-half turn-table; feet; back drop; cradle; check bounce.

Routine Composed of Intermediate Trampoline Stunts

Back airo, feet drop, front airo, feet drop, back airo, baroni, feet drop, half twisting back airo.

CHART FOR RATING TRAMPOLINE SKILLS

Beginning Trampoline Stunts	Rating of Stunt Performance*				
	1	2	3	4	5
Check Bounce					
Knee Drop					
Seat Drop					
All–Fours Drop					
Front Drop					
Half Twisting Front Drop					
Back Drop					
Half Back Airo from Front Drop					
Sub-Total					

Elementary Trampoline Stunts	1	2	3	4	5
Back Drop, Half Twist					
Front Drop, Half Twist					
One–Half Turn–Table					
Swivel Hips					
Full Twisting Seat Drop					
Front Airo from Knees to Seat Drop					
One–Half Front Cody					
Back Drop, Three–Fourths Back Airo					
Cradle					
Cannonball					
Sub-Total					

Intermediate Trampoline Stunts	1	2	3	4	5
Front Airo from Knees					
Front Airo					
Spotted Back Airo					
Back Airo					
Knees, Round–Off, Knees					
Knees, Half Twisting Three–Quarters Baroni					
Baroni to Knees					
Baroni					
Back Cody					
Half Twisting Back Airo					
Full Twisting Back Airo					
Forward One–and Three–Quarters Airo					
Rudolph					
Sub-Total					
Grand Total					

*The Simplified Points System containing the description of the five categories of ratings appears on pages 76–77.

(Figure 6.38)

7 BALANCING AND FLEXIBILITY STUNTS

Floor exercises are composed in large part of balancing and flexibility stunts and tumbling stunts; therefore, a mastery of most of the stunts contained in this chapter and Chapter 5 will be a large step forward in becoming a proficient floor exercise performer.

Single and two-man balancing stunts and flexibility stunts require no special equipment on which to perform, although during the learning stages a tumbling or floor exercise mat will absorb most of the force of any fall. Because they can be performed almost anywhere at any time convenient, they are valuable activities to perform as a way of maintaining a desired degree of physical fitness and they are capable of holding one's interest for many years. Whereas balancing stunts involve manipulating one's body (or a partner's) strength is developed and maintained at a high level.

Although the stunts contained in this chapter are, in general, listed in their approximate order of difficulty, the difficulty of each particular stunt is largely dependent upon the amount of strength, balance, and flexibility that one possesses. When practicing these stunts the performer should at all times strive to maintain as high a degree of good gymnastics form as possible, including an extended foot and toe point, legs even with one another and squeezed together when appropriate, the body stretched or extended unless otherwise indicated, and fingers and thumb of each hand extended and together unless the hand is supporting part of the body weight.

When learning the doubles balancing stunts in the position of the top man, it is wise to have a strong, skilled performer act as the bottom man. In checking the doubles balancing stunts off on the check list at the end of the chapter, only the top man receives credit.

BEGINNING SINGLE STUNTS

Squat Headstand (Frog Stand) (Figure 7.1)

The performer squats and so places his forehead and hands on the mat that they form an equilateral triangle with the distance of each side about eighteen inches. His forearms are positioned at right angles to his upper arms. The performer slowly places his knees, one at a time or simultaneously, on his upper arms just above his elbows and holds the squat headstand position as steadily as possible while pointing his feet and toes a maximum amount.

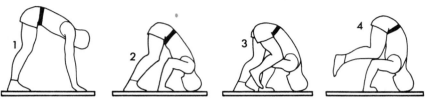

Figure 7.1
Squat Headstand

Squat Handstand (Figure 7.2)

The performer repeats the squat headstand and after securing his balance he slowly lifts his forehead from the mat and looks forward. He then may move his head about in order to study the effect of head position on maintaining a position of balance. If he begins to overbalance he presses with his finger tips and if he begins to underbalance he lowers his body slightly by bending his arms.

Figure 7.2
Squat Handstand

Headstand (Head and Hand Balance) (Figure 7.3)

The performer squats and so positions his forehead and hands on the mat that they form an equilateral triangle with each side 18–20 inches in

Figure 7.3
Headstand

distance. Keeping his legs tucked he raises his hips and legs slowly overhead and then extends his body, maintaining his balance in a slight underbalance at all times. A variation of this technique is to pike the legs and
slowly raise the hips first and then raise the legs. Once the headstand position has been attained the performer arches his body slightly, straightens
his legs completely and squeezes them tightly against each other, and points
his feet and toes as much as possible. Should the performer begin to fall
backward (toward his back), he tucks his body and rolls forward. Should
he begin to fall forward (toward his stomach), he pushes vigorously with
his hands and fingers to save his balance; if this action does not retain his
balance then he pikes his legs and brings his feet to the mat.

Two-Arm Planche (Figure 7.4)

The performer kneels on the mat and squeezes his elbows against his
sides just above his hips. He then leans forward and places his hands,
fingers pointing outward, directly under his hips and about twelve inches
apart. He continues to lean forward until his upper body is parallel to the
mat and his body is balanced on his elbows. He then slowly raises his legs,
arches his body slightly, and holds his body on balance in a horizontal
position. He must squeeze his elbows toward each other and against his
sides at all times. The two-arm planche can be performed with increased
ease by some beginners by doing it on one bar of a set of low parallel bars.

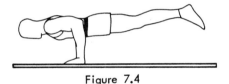

Figure 7.4

BEGINNING DOUBLE STUNTS

Sitting Balance (Figure 7.5)

The bottom man lies on the mat and positions his legs at a forty-five
degree angle. The top man stands just in front of the bottom man's hips and

Figure 7.5

faces the same direction. The top man places the soles of the bottom man's feet against the bottom of his upper thighs and then grasps the bottom man's ankles. With a small spring the top man jumps to a sitting position on the feet of the bottom man, who then straightens his legs. When the top man has his balance he releases the bottom man's ankles and extends his arms sideward. A spotter may stand beside the top man when he is first attempting this stunt.

Thigh Stand (Figure 7.6)

The top man spreads his legs and stands on the mat with his back to the bottom man. The bottom man squats and places his head between the top man's thighs. On the count of three the top man springs slightly and the bottom man stands erect, and grasps the top man's shins, flexes his legs slightly, and then shifts his grasp to just directly above the top man's knees. The top man places his feet on top of the thighs of the bottom man and stands up while the bottom man withdraws his head from between the bottom man's thighs. The top man then leans forward and the bottom man leans backward an equal amount. The bottom man pulls back on the top man's thighs and the top man extends his arms and arches his body. The bottom man can completely straighten his legs at this stage. A variation in mounting for this stunt is to have the bottom man stand directly behind the top man and grasp his waist. The top man grasps the bottom man's wrists and then steps up, one foot at a time, (or jumps up) on the bottom man's thighs.

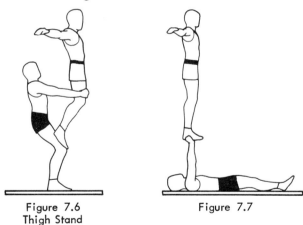

Figure 7.6
Thigh Stand

Figure 7.7

Foot-to-Hand Stand (Figure 7.7)

The bottom man lies down and pikes his extended legs to a 90 degree angle. The top man, facing the bottom man, stands on the bottom man's hands which are positioned just behind his shoulders. The top man then grasps the bottom man's feet. On the count of three the top man jumps straight upward and the bottom man presses vigorously against the top man's feet, completely extending his arms. When the top man is in a position of balance, he releases his grasp, stands erect, and extends his arms sideward. Throughout this stunt the top man looks straight ahead, not downward. At all times the bottom man only must maintain the top man in proper balance, and the top man must keep his body erect and firm. With practice the bottom man keeps his legs on the mat, the top man stands erect, and on the count of three he jumps up to a foot-and-hand stand.

Flying Angel (Swan) (Figure 7.8)

The bottom man lies on his back and positions his feet directly over his hips and the top man stands in front of the bottom man, facing him. The bottom man grasps the top man's hands, places his feet on each side of the pelvic girdle of the top man and slowly pulls the top man above his hips. The top man then arches his back and raises his head, and when he has a secure balance, he releases the bottom man's hands and extends his arms sideward from his shoulders.

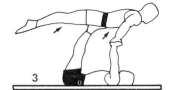

Figure 7.8
Flying Angel

Chest Stand on Partner (Figure 7.9)

The top man kneels and extends his head beyond the far side of the back of the bottom man, who is in an all-fours position. The top man places his chest on the back of the bottom man, grasps the upper arm and thigh of the bottom man, and kicks into a chest stand position. The top man arches his back, and holds tightly to the bottom man, moving his head up and down as necessary in order to help maintain his balance. The bottom man has his arms and legs spread apart and tries to maintain as solid a position as possible.

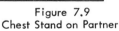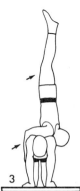

Figure 7.9
Chest Stand on Partner

ELEMENTARY SINGLE STUNTS

Front Scale (Figure 7.10)

The standing performer flexes his trunk forward until it is parallel with the floor. He then raises one extended leg to the rear, raising his foot until it is higher than his hips and as high as his head. At the same time he arches his back and looks forward while extending his arms sideward, holding them parallel with the floor and at right angles to his body. He holds this position several seconds, attempting to hold a steady, balanced position and not shift his supporting foot at all. During the learning stages the form of the performer should be frequently checked for correctness by another person.

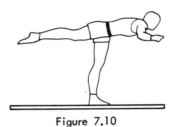

Figure 7.10

Supported Handstand (Figure 7.11)

The performer bends forward and places his hands shoulder width apart on the mat, points his fingers straight ahead, and 12–18 inches in front of his left foot. Keeping his head extended backward by looking forward down the mat, he kicks his right leg upward and then pushes off his left leg. Standing to one side to avoid the possibility of being kicked by the handstander, the spotter catches the handstander's lower legs when they reach a vertical position. The catcher should give the handstander only minimum help in order that the handstander may develop control of his

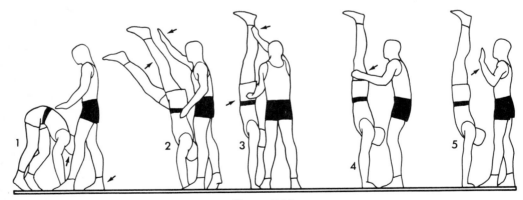

Figure 7.11
Supported Handstand

handstand as rapidly as possible. If the handstander begins to over-balance he presses vigorously with his fingertips, and if this fails he steps forward with one or both hands. If he underbalances he increases the arch of his body and if this fails he flexes his arms as much as is necessary.

Back Bend (Figure 7.12)

The performer stands on the mat with feet, toes out, spread about shoulder width apart. He raises his arms overhead and as far back as possible, extends his head backward, and flexes his legs slightly. He then slowly bends backward, bending all portions of his back, particularly his lower back. Keeping his balance at all times he continues to bend backward until his hands touch the mat and he is in a high bridge position. While acquiring the flexibility necessary to perform the back bend, the performer should practice this stunt by bending toward a wall and walking down the wall with his hands. A horizontal bar upright may also be used in this manner. A spotter should stand near the performer when he first does an unassisted back bend in case he should lose his balance. The attainment of the degree of flexibility needed to do a back bend normally requires a considerable amount of practice over a long period of time.

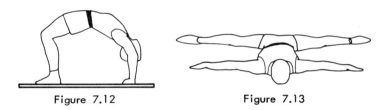

Figure 7.12   Figure 7.13

Forehead Touch from Straddle Sit (Figure 7.13)

The performer sits on the mat and spreads his extended legs as far apart as possible. He then leans forward, grasps his ankles, and pulls his trunk forward and downward until his forehead touches the mat. Again a long period of time is required before the average person can achieve the flexibility needed to perform this stunt. Another practice method is to grasp one ankle with both hands and, keeping the legs straight, then touch the forehead to the shin of the leg grasped.

ELEMENTARY DOUBLES STUNTS

Assisted Handstand on Knees (Figure 7.14)

The bottom man sits on the mat with his legs spread a comfortable distance apart. Facing the bottom man, the top man stands between the bottom man's feet, leans forward, and grasps his legs just above his knees. The top man then kicks into a handstand and as he comes to a vertical position the bottom man grasps his waist and steadies him.

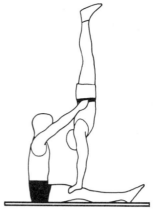

Figure 7.14

Two-High Shoulder Mount and Stand (Figure 7.15)

The right-handed top man stands facing the right-handed bottom man and both place the backs of their right hand on their foreheads with their palms facing each other. They grasp (palm to palm) each other's right hand at head level and each other's left hand at waist level in a position similar to the one used when shaking hands. Standing somewhat to the right of the bottom man, the top man places his left foot, with the toe pointing toward the middle of the bottom man's body, on the bottom man's left thigh and next to his hip. On the count of three the bottom man pulls upward directly overhead with his right hand and upward and around his head with his left hand, while the top man keeps his arms as straight as possible and steps with his right foot on the bottom man's right shoulder and then places his left foot on the bottom man's left shoulder. The top man keeps his legs close together and braces his shins against the back of

Figure 7.15
Two-High Shoulder Mount and Stand

the head of the bottom man who grasps the calves of the legs of the top man and pulls down and forward on them. The top man looks straight ahead and keeps his body straight in order that the bottom man may maintain the balance of the top man.

An alternate method of mounting is for the top man to place his left foot in the left hand of the bottom man, which is held just below his waist, and to place his left hand on top of the bottom man's head. The mount is then performed as described above. By "feeling" the top man's balance, the bottom man can easily walk and turn with him.

Knee-Shoulder Balance (Figure 7.16)

The bottom man lies on his back and so positions his feet on the mat that his thighs and lower legs form a 90 degree angle. His knees are about eighteen inches apart. The top man straddles one of the bottom man's feet, places his hand on the bottom man's knees and leans forward in order that the bottom man may grasp his upper arms or shoulders. The top man's shoulders are now directly above the bottom man's shoulders, where they remain at all times. The top man kicks one leg and then the other one upward and comes to a position of balance in which his weight is mainly supported by the bottom man's arms. The top man slightly underbalances and controls his balance by retaining his grasp on the bottom man's knees. If he overbalances, the top man twists thus rounding off to his feet beside the bottom man's shoulders. A spotter may be used the first few times this stunt is attempted. A variation of this stunt is for the top man to shift his grasp to the bottom man's upper arms and thus go from a knee-shoulder handstand to a low shoulder-to-shoulder balance.

Low Shoulder-to-Shoulder Balance (Figure 7.17)

The bottom man lies on his back and extends his arms upward. The top man straddles him, leans over, and they grasp each other's upper arms. The top man then kicks one leg upward and comes to a low shoulder-to-shoulder balance in which the bottom man is responsible for maintaining

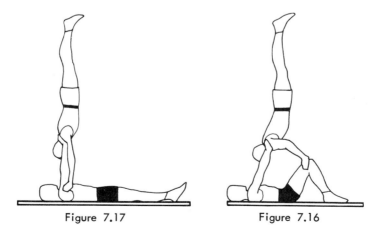

Figure 7.17   Figure 7.16

the balance while the top man looks at him and keeps his body extended. If he wishes the top man may come to the position of balance by tucking his legs, raising his hips, and then extending his legs upward.

INTERMEDIATE SINGLES STUNTS

Forearm Stand (Tiger Stand) (Figure 7.18)

Kneeling on the mat the performer places his forearms on the mat shoulder width apart, palms down, and forearms parallel to each other. Attempting to keep his upper arms almost vertical to the floor, the performer kicks up slowly to a balanced position. The performer may control his balance by moving his head up or down as needed or he may move his upper arms or body at the shoulders as needed.

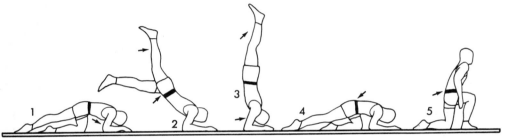

Figure 7.18
Forearm Stand

Head-in-Hands Balance (Figure 7.19)

The performer kneels and places his forehead in his hands and his forearms on the mat with his elbows spread shoulder width apart. He may then slowly kick one leg upward at a time as for the handstand or he may tuck his body, raise his hips overhead, and then slowly extend his legs. When performing this stunt the performer has a small base of support and therefore he should be cautious in his movements in order to avoid losing his balance.

Figure 7.19
Head-in-Hands Balance

Fifteen-Second Handstand (Figure 7.20)

In doing the handstand with a support, the performer kicks one leg upward at a time, coming into a good hand balancing position. Upon attaining this position, he keeps his head up and presses on the mat or floor with the fingers. He should point his feet and toes and tighten his muscles through the hips. The amount of press with the fingers, the use of the shoulder muscles, and up and down movements of the head can all be used to aid in maintaining the stationary handstand position.

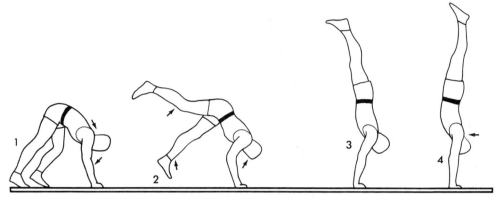

Figure 7.20
Fifteen-Second Handstand

Handstand Press from Headstand (Figure 7.21)

From a headstand position the performer underbalances until most of his weight is supported on his hands. He then quickly extends his arms, pressing up to a handstand position, and as soon as possible he extends his head backward and looks at his hands. He attempts to hold the handstand position. If the performer has insufficient strength to do a regular handstand press he should first tuck his legs and then vigorously kick them upward as he presses to a handstand.

Figure 7.21

Squat Handstand Press to Handstand (Figure 7.22)

From a squat handstand position the performer slightly overbalances and then quickly presses to a handstand.

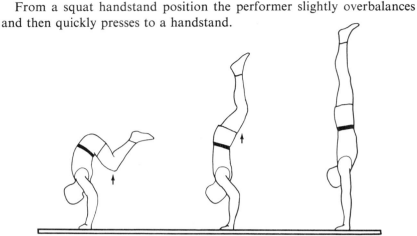

Figure 7.22

Chest Roll to Headstand (Figure 7.23)

The performer kneels on the mat, arches his body and rocks forward into a chest roll. He quickly places his hands on the mat beside his hips and as he rocks forward past his hips, he presses vigorously with his hands as he continues to arch his body and lift his legs. His pressing action should almost momentarily support his entire body weight and at this instant he ducks his forehead to the mat, and he continues to press his body until he comes to a headstand position. When learning this stunt the performer may find it helpful to rock back and forth on his arched body a few times before pressing to a headstand.

Figure 7.23

Back Extension Roll to Headstand (Figure 7.24)

The performer does a short back extension roll in which he kicks his feet just short of the vertical position. He quickly shifts his head from a forward flexed position to a backward extended position and places his forehead on the mat. He presses with his arms in order to avoid overthrowing the headstand. The direction in which the legs are thrust is the primary factor in mastering this stunt, and the speed of the back extension roll is another factor of importance.

Figure 7.24

Forward Roll to Straddle Stand (Figure 7.25)

The standing performer leans forward and pushes off (or does a small dive) into a fast tucked forward roll. When his body weight is on his upper back he extends his legs and splits them as wide apart as possible. As he rolls to his hips he drives his heels to the mat and curls his body forward, placing his hands on the mat immediately in front of his crotch. As his momentum carries him to his feet he pushes vigorously with his hands while continuing to lean forward. Keeping his legs straight, he comes to a straddle stand position and extends his arms sideward.

Figure 7.25

Headspring to Straddle Seat (Figure 7.26)

The performer leans forward, places his head and hands on the mat and initiates a regular headspring by placing his body in a piked position and then overbalancing. As he falls forward he spreads his legs and extends them, hitting the mat with his heels and legs and coming to a straddle sitting position.

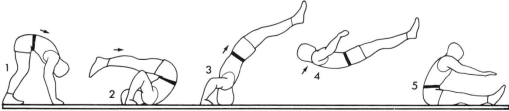

Figure 7.26

Side Scale (Figure 7.27)

The standing performer leans to his right side and lifts his left leg until it is in line with his body and both his left leg and body are parallel with the floor. Keeping his right leg straight he then extends his right arm so that it points away from his left leg, leans his head against his right arm, and places his left arm against his side and thigh.

Figure 7.27   Figure 7.28

Half Lever on Floor (L Position) (Figure 7.28)

The performer sits on the floor or a mat and places his hands on the floor beside his hips. Contracting his abdominal and hip flexor muscles and pointing his feet and toes, the performer pushes with his arm and shoulder muscles and lifts his hips, legs, and feet off the floor. He looks straight ahead and holds this position for several seconds.

Front Split (Figure 7.29)

The standing performer slides one foot forward and one foot backward thus lowering his body until his crotch touches or almost touches the floor. When first assuming this position he rests part of his weight on his hands as he lowers himself to a split position. When this is performed correctly the performer should then extend his arms sideward. As with most flexibility stunts the front split requires considerable practice and even then some gymnasts are unable to perform a deep split. An excellent front split exercise is to lower the body to a near front split position, place the hands on the floor on either side of the hips, and gently bounce the hips up and down.

Figure 7.29
Front Split

Figure 7.30
Side Split

Side Split (Figure 7.30)

The standing performer slides each foot directly to each side and slowly lowers his body until his crotch touches or almost touches the floor. After reaching the position the performer moves his hands from in front of his hips and extends them horizontally to each side.

CHART FOR RATING BALANCING AND FLEXIBILITY SKILLS

Beginning Balancing and Flexibility Stunts	1	2	3	4	5
Squat Headstand					
Squat Handstand					
Headstand					
Two-Arm Planche					
Sitting Balance					
Thigh Stand					
Foot-to-Hand Stand					
Flying Angel					
Chest Stand on Partner					
Sub-Total					

Elementary Balancing and Flexibility Stunts	1	2	3	4	5
Front Scale					
Supported Handstand					
Back Bend					
Forehead Touch from Straddle Sit					
Assisted Handstand on Knees					
Two-High Shoulder Mount and Stand					
Knee-Shoulder Balance					
Low Shoulder-to-Shoulder Balance					
Sub-Total					

Intermediate Balancing and Flexibility Stunts	1	2	3	4	5
Forearm Stand					
Head-in-Hands Balance					
Fifteen-Second Handstand					
Handstand Press from Headstand					
Squat Handstand Press to Handstand					
Chest Roll to Headstand					
Back Extension Roll to Headstand					
Forward Roll to Straddle Stand					
Headspring to Straddle Seat					
Side Scale					
Half-Lever on Floor					
Front Split					
Side Split					
Sub-Total					
Grand Total					

*The Simplified Points System containing the description of the five categories of ratings appears on pages 76-77.

(Figure 7.31)

8 FLOOR EXERCISE

Floor exercise is one of the most recent competitive events to appear in American gymnastics, and in many gymnastics meets it has replaced tumbling as an event. Floor exercises are performed on a defined area of the floor 12 by 12 meters (39 feet and 4.44 inches square) in size or on a thin mat especially made for this purpose. The term free exercise is often applied to this event because it is performed without the use of any apparatus and normally the performer is free to select the stunts of which his routine is composed. The names of free calisthenics and free-standing exercises are also sometimes used to describe this event.

The values derived from regularly practicing floor exercise include those that may be obtained from participating in tumbling and balancing; consequently, the development of agility, strength and power, sense of balance, flexibility, timing, neuromuscular skill and coordination, and creativity in constructing routines are outcomes that may be expected to accrue to the floor exercise performer.

A floor exercise routine for men should include a smooth, rhythmical flow of stunts involving primarily the elements of tumbling, balance, flexibility, agility, and strength whereas one for girls generally includes also ballet and acrobatic moves and de-emphasizes strength stunts. The floor exercise routine should cover most of the area, including a series of movements along one or two sides of the area and/or one or two series of movements diagonally across the area. The floor exercise should be one to one and one-half minutes in duration. Many of the tumbling stunts listed in Chapter 5 and many of the balance and flexibility stunts listed in Chapter 7 may be utilized in composing a floor exercise routine because stunts of these types comprise the major portion of the free exercise routine.

Sample Floor Exercise Routine

This routine is part of the Novice Grade Compulsory Exercise for Men that appears in the *A.A.U. Official 1965–66 Gymnastics Guide and Handbook*, which is published by the Amateur Athletic Union of the United States, New York, N.Y. The routine was prepared by the Men's Technical Committee of the National A.A.U. Gymnastics Committee.

148

1. Rise on toes raising arms fore-upward, step forward with right leg, arms lowering sideward, and hop forward on right foot swinging left leg and arms forward, step forward with left foot and with ¼ turn right execute cartwheel left. As right foot touches floor execute ¼ turn left, step out on left foot and dive to forward roll to squat stand.

2. Jump in place with ½ turn left or right swinging arms fore-upward bend body forward to front horizontal scale on right leg, arms sideward—*HOLD*.

3. Bend trunk forward and placing hands on floor rise to handstand—*HOLD*.

4. Lower body, half bent, to neck and kip to stand arms upward.

5. Lower arms forward bending trunk and drop backward executing back roll through momentary handstand to front leaning rest position, with supple movement.

6. Bend right leg and place right foot between hands and circle left leg under left hand under right hand and under right leg, again, under left hand while pivoting ¼ turn right, execute ½ turn left to front leaning rest position with legs joined.

9 SIDE HORSE STUNTS

Although different types of construction are employed in building side horses, all types follow a basic design that is composed of three main parts: the body, the covering, and the base. The body is constructed of wood, padded with felt, and covered with vinyl or leather. It is 62 inches long and 15 inches wide and its height may be adjusted from 36 to 57 inches by means of a hand crank. The body is supported by a column and base that may be cast in one or two pieces. Swivel casters that may be raised or lowered are ordinarily attached to the base in order that the side horse may be easily moved. Rubber or leather pads attached to the bottom of the base protect against floor damage. On top of the body are attached two pommels constructed of either laminated wood or iron covered with rubber or leather. On some side horses the pommels are adjustable in width from $14\frac{1}{2}$ to $20\frac{1}{2}$ inches.

The side horse is believed to have been originated by the ancient Romans who used it as an exercising device for their soldiers. During the Middle Ages, knights in heavy full armor practiced mounting and dismounting from a side horse in order to be able to do this from their horses. The side horse was a popular exercise apparatus in the German physical education (gymnastics) playground of Frederich Jahn during the early nineteenth century and it has been used as a gymnastics apparatus since that time.

Practice on the side horse involves many of the muscles of the body, and the muscles of the arms, shoulders, chest, back, abdomen and hips in particular are strongly exercised.

A mastery of all but the elementary skills on the side horse normally requires considerable practice, and because progress on the side horse is often slow, some gymnasts find that it is a discouraging gymnastics apparatus on which to work. This feeling is often intensified because for the beginner falls are common because it is at first difficult to maintain a balanced position while practicing many of the stunts performed on the side horse. Although these falls are not dangerous if mats are in place on the floor around the side horse, their occurrence can cause the novice performer on the side horse to become disheartened. However, as some proficiency is acquired on this apparatus, the performer loses his balance much less frequently and when he does he is often able to retain his grasp on the side horse pommels and thus prevent a fall. Therefore, the possession of a large amount of patience is an important attribute for the performer who desires to become an expert on the side horse.

One important technique that must be utilized if skill in performing side horse stunts is to be rapidly acquired is to keep the body's center of gravity within and above the base of support (the hands). Unlike many balancing stunts in which this techique is applied, the center of gravity of the body is usually moving; consequently, the side horse performer must take this into account, particularly when he is supporting himself with only one hand and has an extremely small area as his base of support. However, the fact that the center of gravity is shifting allows him to momentarily be off balance, providing his center of gravity is soon moved within his base of support. Many of the long, sweeping, circular motions used in performing side horse skills such as double leg circles require that the performer's center of gravity be revolved around a relatively unstable area of support in which the performer may frequently momentarily lose and then regain his balance.

Most champion performers on the side horse possess a long, lean body with relatively light legs; apparently this body type is an advantage when side horse routines are performed and it also presents a graceful appearance during the performance.

A mastery of the vaulting stunts presented in this chapter, which are not performed on the side horse during competition, is advantageous in many ways. Their practice allows the novice to make rapid progress and achieve a sense of accomplishment on the side horse. Skill in performing such vaults enables the performer to better save himself if he should start to fall while practicing on the side horse. And the performance of vaulting stunts on the long horse is closely akin to many of the vaulting stunts performed on the side horse thus enabling a transfer of training to be made to long horse vaulting. In addition vaulting stunts are easier and safer to learn on the side horse than on the long horse.

The directions for performing those stunts that involve movement to a side are given for right-handed performers; these directions may be reversed for the left-handed performer.

BEGINNING SIDE HORSE STUNTS

Developmental Exercise (Figure 9.1)

The developmental exercise on the side horse, which prepares the performer to do stunts and skills of increased difficulty on the side horse, is performed by jumping forward and upward, pushing with the arms and raising the hips.

Squat Vault (Figure 9.2)

Grasping the pommels and using a two-footed take-off the performer lifts his hips high and tucks his legs as he vaults up and forward. Keeping his head up he passes over the horse with his knees between his arms and

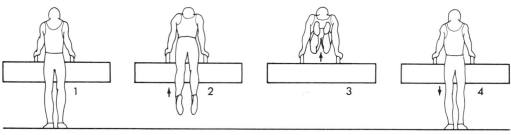

Figure 9.1
Developmental Exercise

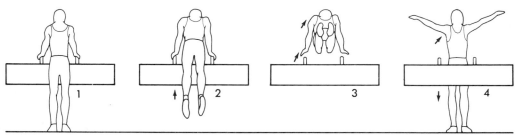

Figure 9.2
Squat Vault

then extends his legs and pushes back with his hands, landing on the mat with his back to the horse. When first learning this stunt the performer may benefit by jumping to a squat stand on top of the horse with his feet between the pommels, retaining his grasp on the pommels. He may practice the second part of the squat vault by jumping forward from this squat stand position and making a regular landing in which he extends his arms sideward and does a slight squatting movement in order to absorb the force of his landing.

Flank Vault (Side Vault) (Figure 9.3)

In first performing a vault of any type, the performer should start from a standing position immediately behind the side horse. When he has

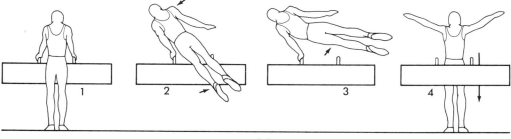

Figure 9.3
Flank Vault

acquired a knowledge of how to perform the vault he may then take a short run in order to gain horizontal momentum before vaulting—this momentum is partially transferred to vertical momentum during the take-off. For most vaults a two-legged take-off is used.

To do a flank vault the performer takes a two-footed take-off, and while grasping both pommels and first pulling and pushing with his hands, he vaults upward and forward. One side passes over the top of the side horse. As he starts to pass over the top of the side horse, the hand grasping the pommel closest to his feet is lifted from the pommel. As he lands with his back toward the side horse, the performer quickly does a partial knee bend to absorb the force of his landing and extends his arms sideward as an aid in maintaining his balance. A right-handed performer usually vaults to his right thus keeping his left hand on the left pommel throughout the vault. During the entire vault the performer's legs are extended and his feet and toes are pointed. The performer attempts to keep his entire body, including his legs, in as straight a line as possible during the vault. At all times he tries to avoid flexing at his hips.

The spotter should stand in front of (or behind) and to the left of the horse. If he wishes he may grasp the upper left arm of the performer during the vault.

Rear Vault (Figure 9.4)

The right-handed vaulter will normally perform a rear vault to the right in which his body makes a one-quarter turn to the right (clockwise) and the back of his body passes over the horse during the vault. As his body passes over the horse, the vaulter releases the right pommel with his right hand and just before landing he regrasps the right pommel with his right hand and extends his left arm sideward. The illustrations show a rear vault to the right. This stunt is termed a rear vault because the rear or back of the body passes over the top of the horse.

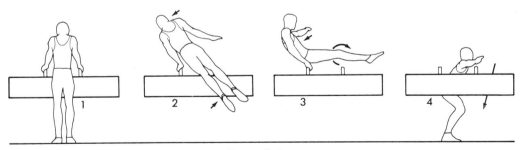

Figure 9.4
Rear Vault

Front Vault (Face Vault) (Figure 9.5)

The right-handed performer initiates a regular two-footed take-off and lifts his legs and hips vigorously to his right. Immediately after starting the vault he performs a one-quarter body twist so that his body faces the horse

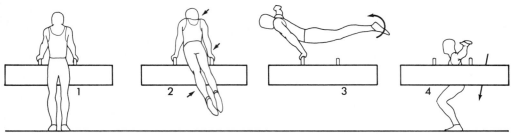

Figure 9.5
Front Vault

as he passes above it. He lands with his left side facing the horse and with his left hand on the left pommel and with his right arm extended horizontally from his shoulder.

Feint—Left or Right (Figure 9.6)

From a front-support position on the side horse the performer swings one leg to the outside of the horse and up and over the end of the horse (either the right end of the horse which is called the croup or the left end which is called the neck). If the right leg is moved around the right end of the horse, the performer turns his face to his left; if his left leg passes around and over the left end of the horse, he turns his face to his right. After passing his leg over the horse, the performer, in a reverse movement, returns his leg to its original position. Throughout the performance of a feint the performer keeps his arms fully extended, his legs straight, and his feet and toes pointed. He retains his grasp on both pommels throughout the performance of the feint.

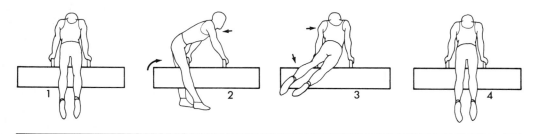

Figure 9.6
Feint

Five Sets of Feints

Once a single feint has been mastered, the performer should practice consecutive feints, alternating the leg being feinted in smooth, rhythmical movements and keeping the center of gravity near the hand around which the feint is being made. As his leg is returned from a feint to one side the performer continues to shift his hips toward the other side as he circles the other end of the horse with his other leg.

Wolf Vault (Figure 9.7)

The performer makes a regular take-off from either a stand or a run and as he passes above the side horse he performs a flank vault with the inside leg tucked—a combination flank and squat vault. If his vault is to his right, he keeps his right leg extended and flexes his left leg under his left hip. He lands with his back to the horse, arms extended.

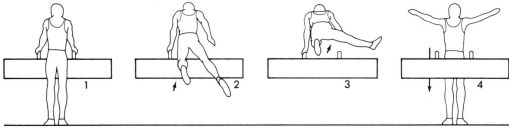

Figure 9.7
Wolf Vault

Straddle Mount (Figure 9.8)

Before attempting a straddle vault the vaulter should first practice only the first half of the vault by leaping up and placing one foot on each end of the horse, straddling his legs as widely apart as possible and keeping his legs straight. Throughout this mount the performer retains his grasp on the pommels.

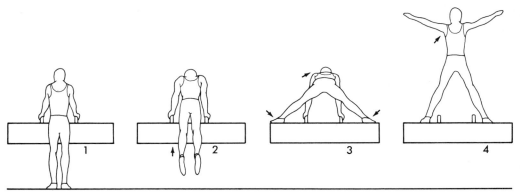

Figure 9.8
Straddle Mount

Straddle Vault (Figure 9.9)

When once mastered, this vault is fairly easy to perform. During the learning stage, however, one or two spotters should stand on the far side and at the ends of the horse in order to be in the best position in which to closely spot the vaulter. In initiating the straddle vault the performer must powerfully jump and vigorously lift his hips while simultaneously thrusting with his hands strongly downward and forward on the pommels. As the performer begins his vault he spreads his legs as far apart as possible but attempts to keep them straight and his feet and toes pointed. After his body, legs, and feet have completely passed above and beyond the side horse the performer brings his legs together and lands in the usual vaulting landing position with his arms outstretched. Throughout the vault, the vaulter should keep his head up and should look forward and downward. During the early and middle portion of the vault the vaulter should pike his body.

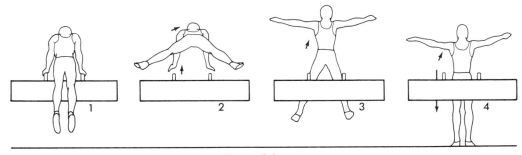

Figure 9.9
Straddle Vault

Knee Vault (Courage Vault) (Figure 9.10)

The performer jumps to a kneestand mount. He then releases his grasp, leans forward slightly, and jumps upward and forward from his knees, throwing his arms forward and upward and pushing against the horse with his shins. He lands in a partial knee-bend position with his arms extended sideward. A spotter should be positioned on the far side of the side horse during the learning stages of this vault.

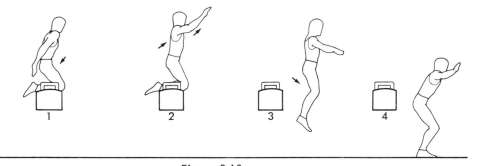

Figure 9.10
Knee Vault

Cut Left or Right (Figure 9.11)

From a front-support position the performer swings one leg toward the right end of the side horse, passing it over the end and under one hand. During this action the weight of his body is supported by the opposite hand. By moving the same leg in the opposite path, the performer returns to the starting position.

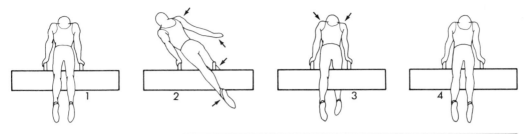

Figure 9.11
Cut

Four Sets of Cuts

The performer moves one leg to the right side and cuts it forward, and as it completes the movement back to the starting position the other leg is cut around the horse and back to a support position. This action is continued until four complete cuts have been executed. While performing the cuts the performer shifts his body weight smoothly from arm to arm.

ELEMENTARY SIDE HORSE STUNTS

Squat Vault to Rear Support (Figure 9.12)

The performer takes a regular two-footed take-off and over the top of the side horse executes the first part of a squat vault, lifting his hips high but keeping his center of gravity directly above the horse in order that, after his legs have passed over the saddle, he may come to a rear-support position with his body arched. He should attempt to maintain good form during and after the completion of the vaulting part of the movement.

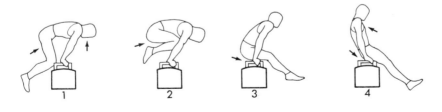

Figure 9.12
Squat Vault to Rear Support

Flank Vault to Rear Support (Figure 9.13)

The performer executes the first part of a flank vault but as soon as his body passes over the horse he regrasps the pommel and comes to rest in a rear-support position. Again it is essential that the performer maintains correct form throughout the performance of this stunt.

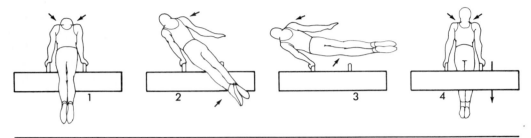

Figure 9.13
Flank Vault to Rear Support

Chest Stand (Figure 9.14)

The chest stand is performed with the arms bent as depicted in the figure. Facing the horse, the performer bends over it and from the outside grasps the pommels. Keeping his head back and looking at the mat, the performer tucks his legs and raises his hips above his shoulders. He then extends his legs toward the ceiling and holds a chest-stand position. When ready to return to a standing position, the performer reverses his movements, tucking his legs downward and coming to a stand. During the learning stages the performer should be spotted closely; the spotter must be especially watchful that during the stunt the performer does not lose his grasp and fall head first toward the mat.

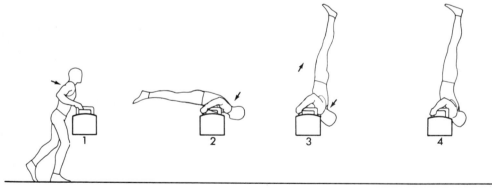

Figure 9.14
Chest Stand

Seat Hops

The performer straddle sits on one end of the horse and places his hands on the pommel nearest his body. He then pushes hard with his arms and raises his body over the pommel, travels forward, and drops to a sitting position on the saddle. He then repeats this movement over the next pommel. By reversing the direction in which he is facing the performer can then do seat hops to travel to the other end of the side horse.

High Front Vault (High Face Vault) (Figure 9.15)

The performer takes a short run and, using a two-footed take-off, pushes vigorously with his arms and attempts to raise his hips and legs to shoulder height. As he begins to pass over the horse he performs a one-quarter twist of his body in order that his face, chest and stomach face the horse during the vault. During his landing he retains one hand on the pommel, extends the other arm to the side, and does a partial knee bend as he lands.

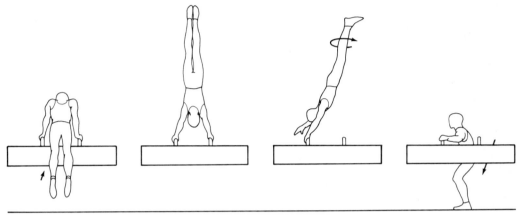

Figure 9.15
High Front Vault

Corkscrew Vault (Figure 9.16)

To perform the corkscrew vault, the vaulter executes a front vault and as his body passes over the side horse in the front vault position he executes an additional one-half twist in the same direction as his initial one-quarter twist. Consequently, the twisting action is in the opposite direction from the one done in the rear vault. The performer, if right-handed, twists in a counter-clockwise direction and lands with his right side facing the horse and with his right hand grasping the right pommel and his left arm extended to the side.

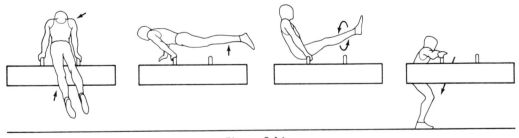

Figure 9.16
Corkscrew Vault

Thief Vault (Figure 9.17)

The thief vault resembles the movement used by track and field athletes when running over a hurdle except that use is made of the pommels. For this vault the vaulter does a one-footed take-off, kicking the extended non-take-off leg up and over the saddle, and he brings his tucked take-off leg under his body and above the saddle. He then places both hands on the pommels, supporting himself as depicted in the second figure, from which position he pushes with his hands and drops to a normal landing.

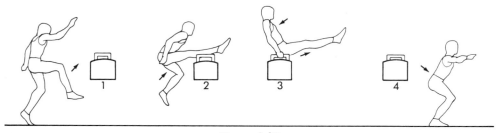

Figure 9.17
Thief Vault

INTERMEDIATE SIDE HORSE STUNTS

Flank Vault Right to Rear Support; Reverse Flank Vault Left to Front Support (Figure 9.18)

If the weight is kept over the horse as the flank vault is performed, the catch to the rear support is not difficult. To perform the reverse flank vault, the weight is supported on the right arm. The secret of the vaults and catches is proper weight distribution.

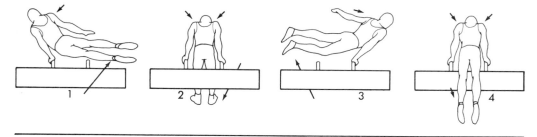

Figure 9.18
Flank Vault Right to Rear Support;
Reverse Flank Vault Left to Front Support

Neckspring Vault (Figure 9.19)

Before attempting the neckspring vault from the side horse, the performer should first master the neckspring and headspring from the floor or a rolled mat. When executing a neckspring vault, the performer tucks his legs and raises his hips high on the take-off. When his weight is positioned over the saddle of the horse, the performer ducks his head, pikes his body, and momentarily holds a balanced position atop the side horse as depicted in the second figure. The performer allows his body to fall forward partially off balance and then does a kipping action when his upper body is at approximately a 45 degree angle from a horizontal position. As the kipping action is made the performer pushes vigorously against the pommels with his hands. He lands in a partial knee bend with his body arched and his arms extended sideward. The two essential actions in performing this stunt are the ability to jump into a balanced kipping position on the saddle of the horse and the correct timing of applying the kipping action as the body rolls forward. A spotter, located on the far side of the horse, should always be present when this stunt is being learned, and he must be alert to aid the vaulter if he overthrows (overspins) the neckspring and is in danger of landing on his stomach and face. If the kipping action is applied too early the spotter must prevent the vaulter from landing on his back on the saddle—this can be prevented by grasping his upper arm and pulling him forward while lifting him—or from landing on his feet off balance backward and then falling backward onto the side horse.

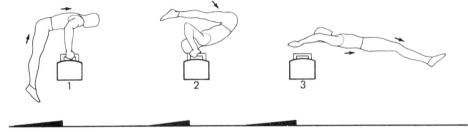

Figure 9.19
Neckspring Vault

Single Leg Circles (Figure 9.20)

Single leg circles on the side horse can be initiated from a front-support or a rear-support position, and they may be done in a clockwise or counter-clockwise direction. If a leg feint is first made, the performer can easily obtain the momentum needed to perform a single circle with little effort. If the single leg circle is started to the right, the weight is shifted to the left arm and the right leg is passed over the right end of the horse and under the right hand. The right hand then regrasps the right pommel and the weight is shifted to the right hand while the right leg passes under the left hand and over the left end (neck) of the horse and the starting position is again taken. By going in the opposite direction, a single leg circle with the left leg may be performed. The reverse right single leg circle is performed by circling the right leg clockwise around the horse and under both hands. The reverse left single leg circle is executed by circling the left leg counter clockwise around the horse and under both hands. For all single leg circles it is important to shift the weight from one arm to the other at the correct time. When one single leg circle can be performed the performer should practice consecutive single leg circles striving to maintain a smooth, rhythmical movement.

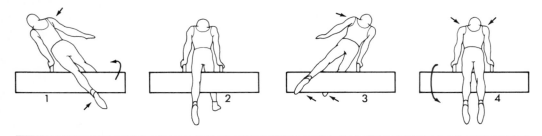

Figure 9.20
Single Leg Circle

Regular Scissors (Figure 9.21)

From a position in which he straddles the saddle of the horse and grasps each pommel with his arms extended, the performer develops a swinging motion from his shoulders while keeping his legs extended and feet and toes pointed. As the performer swings sideward (the direction in which his chest, stomach, and hips are facing), he raises his hips and legs as high as possible, releases his grasp on the right pommel, crosses (scissors) his legs thus rotating his hips a one-half turn, regrasps the pommel, and returns to his starting position except that he is now facing the opposite end of the horse. With practice the performer should be able to do consecutive scissors by maintaining a steady, rhythmical swinging movement of the hips and legs. It is important to raise the hips and legs as high as possible when performing scissor movements. A spotter is ordinarily not required for this stunt; if the performer misses his regrasp of the pommel he should immediately squeeze his legs against the sides of the horse and thus avoid a fall. The illustration depicts a scissors vault.

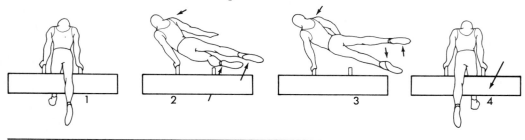

Figure 9.21
Regular Scissors

Reverse Scissors (Figure 9.22)

The reverse scissor movement is performed in a similar manner to the regular scissors movement except that the scissor movement of the legs is performed at the height of the back swing instead of the front swing. Because it is impossible to pike the legs at the hips, the successful performance of reverse scissors is considerably more difficult than is the regular scissors movement. For this reason it is necessary that a large swinging movement be obtained and that the hips and legs be raised as high as possible. For all scissors movements the performer must have almost all his weight centered over the supporting hand when the scissors movement is executed.

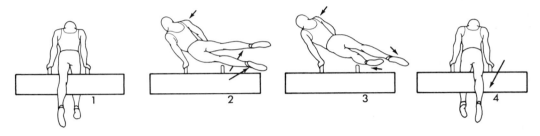

Figure 9.22
Reverse Scissors

Double Leg Circles (Giant Hip Circles) (Figure 9.23)

Although double leg circles may be initiated from either a front- or a rear-support position, the beginner should start from a feint position. The right-handed performer will probably prefer to begin this stunt from a front-support position in which the extended left leg is brought around the left end of the horse and placed above the horse and just outside the left arm and pommel. From this starting position the performer swings his hips to the right and at the same time swings his extended left leg around the left end of the side horse. As the left leg approaches the right leg the hips begin to swing to the right and both legs, while held together, continue to swing to the right and circle around the right end of the horse. The legs and hips then swing to the left, passing past a rear-support position, and circle the left end of the horse thus enabling the performer to completely circle the horse in a counter clockwise direction and return to a front-support position. As the performer circles the horse he must first release

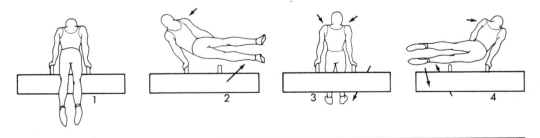

Figure 9.23
Double Leg Circle

his right hand as his hips near it and then he quickly regrasps the right pommel with his right hand, releases the left pommel before the left hip hits the left arm and then quickly regrasps the left pommel. When one double-leg circle in a counter-clockwise direction has been mastered, a double-leg circle in a clockwise direction, from a right leg feint, should be mastered. Next the performer should practice doing as many consecutive double-leg circles, in both directions, as possible. Again he must maintain a rhythmical hip movement originating at the shoulders and he must keep his arms extended at all times.

CHART FOR RATING SIDE HORSE SKILLS

Beginning Side Horse Stunts	Rating of Stunt Performance*				
	1	2	3	4	5
Developmental Exercise					
Squat Vault					
Flank Vault					
Rear Vault					
Front Vault					
Feint					
Five Sets of Feints					
Wolf Vault					
Straddle Mount					
Straddle Vault					
Knee Vault					
Cut					
Four Sets of Cuts					
Sub-Total					

Elementary Side Horse Stunts	1	2	3	4	5
Squat Vault to Rear Support					
Flank Vault to Rear Support					
Chest Stand					
Seat Hops					
High Front Vault					
Corkscrew Vault					
Sub-Total					

Intermediate Side Horse Stunts	1	2	3	4	5
Flank Vault Right to Rear Support; Reverse Flank Vault Left to Front Support					
Neckspring Vault					
Single Leg Circle					
Regular Scissors					
Reverse Scissors					
Double Leg Circle					
Sub-Total					
Grand Total					

*The Simplified Points System containing the description of the five categories of ratings appears on pages 76-77.

(Figure 9.24)

SIDE HORSE ROUTINE

Routine of Side Horse Stunts

Flank vault right to rear support, full single left leg circle left, half double leg circle left to front support, half single right leg circle right to straddle, regular scissors left, regular scissors right, half single right leg circle left, feint; right rear vault dismount to the left.

10 STUNTS ON THE PARALLEL BARS

INTRODUCTION

The parallel bars were developed in 1812 by Frederick Jahn of Germany and used on his playground. They have been utilized in German gymnastics since that time. Modern parallel bars are so designed that they may be adjustable in height and width in order to provide the best fit to the individual performer. The design of most parallel bars is such that they are rigid and secure and the uprights are usually connected to a base composed of convex steel rails, which design eliminates dangerous projections on the uprights and base. To the top end of the uprights are fastened, by flexible machine-fitted joints, hand rails made of the finest grain hickory wood and ranging in length from 10 feet to 11 feet and six inches. The telescoping section of the upright is brass-on-steel tubing. Most of the adjustable parallel bars range from approximately three feet to five feet and three inches in height. The majority of parallel bars may be adjusted from a width of 13 inches to 20 inches in the low position and from a width of nine and one-half inches to 22 inches in the high position.

When learning the stunts described in this chapter the performer should, if possible, so adjust the parallel bars that they are shoulder width or slightly wider and their height for each stunt should be such that he may practice the stunt with the lowest part of his body only a few inches above the mat lying on the floor under the parallel bars. All areas of the base of the parallel bars and the floor around it should be covered with mats. Low parallel bars (about 12 inches in height) are safest for learning balancing stunts.

Regular work on the parallel bars should particularly help to develop the muscles of the arms, shoulder, chest, and back.

BEGINNING PARALLEL BARS STUNTS

Handwalking Exercise with Legs Motionless (Figure 10.1)

To perform successfully and with ease handwalking on the parallel bars, the performer must alternately lean from left to right (transfer most of his weight from the left bar to the right bar and move his left hand and vice versa). He must keep his arms fully extended throughout the exercise.

The spotter, who stands alongside one of the bars, should be alert in case the performer is unable to keep his support arm straight and thus collapses and falls. In such an event the spotter should grasp the performer's upper arm and give him support and keep his body positioned between the bars. The performer may practice handwalking backward after he has mastered handwalking forward on the parallel bars.

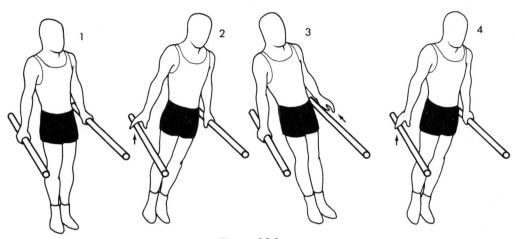

Figure 10.1
Handwalking Exercise with Legs Motionless

Handwalking Exercise with High Knee Lift (Figure 10.2)

With each forward hand movement the performer lifts as high as possible the knee of the leg that is next to the hand moving forward. After the performer is accomplished in this handwalking technique he should practice lifting the opposite knee with each hand movement. These two techniques may also be employed when hand-walking backward.

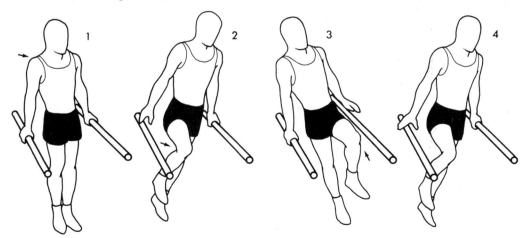

Figure 10.2
Handwalking Exercise with High Knee Lift

Handwalking Exercise while Striding (Figure 10.3)

The handwalking exercise while striding is quite similar to the previous exercise except that the legs are straight and with each hand walk movement are spread far apart front and back in a stride position. As before, this stunt may be done with either leg moving forward as one of the hands walks forward and the handwalk may also be in a backward direction.

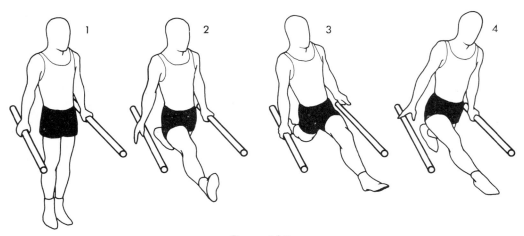

Figure 10.3
Handwalking Exercise while Striding

Hand Hops (Figure 10.4)

From his shoulders the performer swings his body back and forth in a small swinging motion; on a forward swing he quickly flexes at his knees and hips and jumps both hands forward as his body, hips and legs are approaching the peak of the forward swing and his hands are supporting only a portion of his body weight. The spotter should spot the performer's upper arm and shoulder and be alert that he does not collapse when landing from his hop. After one hop has been mastered, the performer should attempt two or more hops, hopping on each successive forward swing. With practice the performer can increase his amount of body swing and

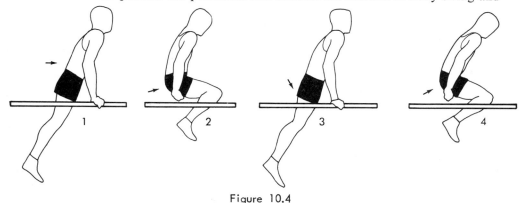

Figure 10.4
Hand Hops

the distance traveled on each hop. The performer should next practice a single hop backward during his backward swing and later, consecutive backward hops.

Piked Inverted Hang (One-Half Inverted Hang) (Figure 10.5)

In the middle of and under the bars the performer assumes a cross-hang position with an outside hand grip. Keeping his body tucked he next inverts it until he is in an upside down position. He then flexes his head forward, tucking his chin next to his chest and extends his legs while his hips are flexed in a piked position. He maintains this position, keeping his legs straight and his feet and toes pointed.

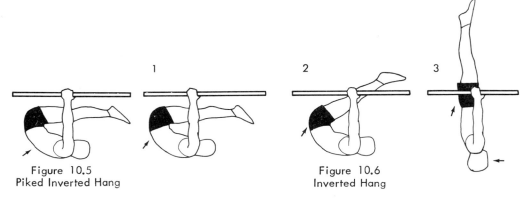

Figure 10.5
Piked Inverted Hang

Figure 10.6
Inverted Hang

Inverted Hang (Figure 10.6)

From the piked inverted hang the performer extends his legs toward the ceiling and holds his body in a straight position with his body slightly arched and his head extended and in line with his body. His eyes should be forward on the mat below him while holding the inverted hang position. While little danger is involved in this balancing stunt, a spotter should spot the performer's shoulders during the learning stage. If the performer falls off balance backward (toward his back) he should retain his grasp and arch his body and legs, landing in a semistand; if falling forward (toward his stomach), he should retain his grasp and tuck his body and legs, again coming to his feet.

Bird's Nest (Figure 10.7)

From a hanging position in the middle of the bar, the performer pikes his legs and places the instep of each foot on the bar nearest each of his

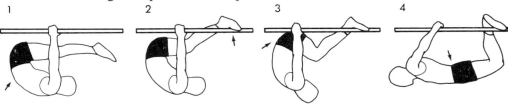

Figure 10.7
Bird's Nest

hands. He then slides his feet away from his body and extends his back and head, so inverting his body that his stomach faces the mats. The spotter spots the hand grip of the performer.

Intermediate Swing with Hop (Figure 10.8)

From a support position between the bars, the performer swings his body back and forth, letting the movement originate from his hips. Keeping his arms extended, he extends his body on the back swing, flexes it at the hips on the front swing and as he nears the end of the front swing he releases his grip and hops forward, regrasping the bars while keeping his arms extended as much as possible. The spotter should remain alert that the performer does not miss his regrasp or does not collapse immediately after catching the bars.

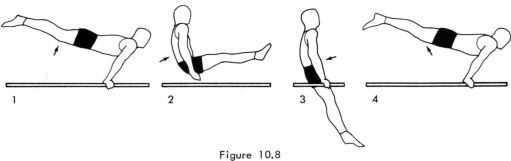

Figure 10.8
Intermediate Swing with Hop

Jump to Cross Rest (Figure 10.9)

The performer takes a short run toward one end of the parallel bars and, using a two-footed take-off, jumps forward as for a dive-and-roll on the tumbling mat, landing on his upper arms in the middle portions of the bars with his body leaning forward. He immediately grasps the bars with his hands and swings forward and then backward, keeping his degree of

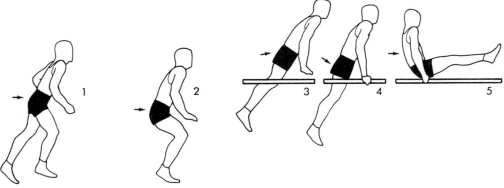

Figure 10.9
Jump to Cross Rest

arm bend constant. The spotter spots the performer from underneath the bars and if he collapses on the forward swing, the spotter lifts on the performer's chest.

Single Leg Cut-Off (Figure 10.10)

With his arms completely extended, the performer, facing the middle of the parallel bars, assumes a cross-support position at one end of the parallel bars and develops an intermediate swing. As the forward swing is completed, he pushes his legs, hips and body backward and at the same time raises one leg and swings it sideward, performing a cut-off above the bar while simultaneously releasing his grasp on that bar. He then regrasps the bar and retaining his grasp on both bars drops to a landing on the mat behind the bars. When doing this stunt the performer should keep his head back in order that his face is in no danger of hitting a bar. The backward lean taken by the performer before the cut-off is made is an essential action in the execution of this stunt. For this stunt, the spotter stands a short distance behind the performer and spots both of his shoulders during the dismount.

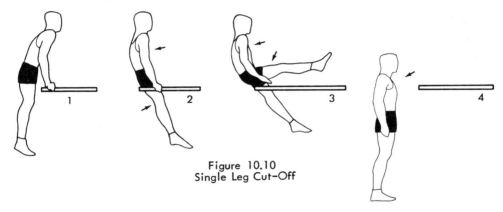

Figure 10.10
Single Leg Cut-Off

Double Leg Cut-Off (Figure 10.11)

The performer duplicates the movements as for the single leg cut-off except that as he is swinging backward he raises both extended legs above

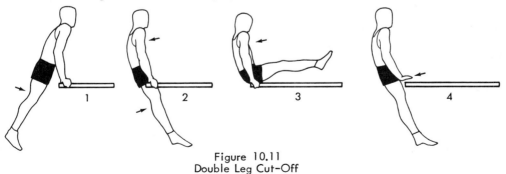

Figure 10.11
Double Leg Cut-Off

the bars and cuts them sideward and backward, releases both hands, and regrasps the end of the bars before landing on the mat behind the parallel bars. He must have a slight backward lean during the time that he performs the double leg cut-off and he must decisively execute the double leg cut without any hesitation. Again the spotter should stand behind the performer and spot him at his shoulders.

Straddle Vault (Split-Off) (Figure 10.12)

With his arms completely extended the performer, with his back to the middle of the bars, takes a cross-support position at one end of the parallel bars. He develops an intermediate swing from the shoulders and at the back of the back swing he leans forward and raises his hips to just below shoulder height and, keeping his head up, he splits his legs sideward and vigorously swings his hips and legs forward. At the instant that his thighs touch his arms (or slightly before this time), he releases his grasp on the ends of the bars and does a straddle vault dismount to his feet. He slightly flexes his knees and hips upon landing and extends his arms sideward. The spotter stands toward one side of and in front of the performer, facing him, and spots the chest, shoulders, and upper arms of the performer during the dismount.

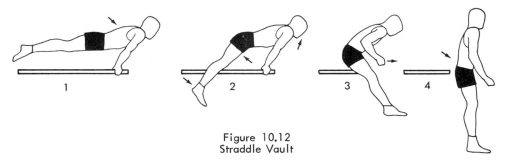

Figure 10.12
Straddle Vault

Kidney Roll (Figure 10.13)

The performer takes a straddle seat position on the middle of the parallel bars, bends forward, and reaches forward with his right hand and places it, palm up, on the left bar between his left hand and thigh. He twists onto the small of his back, positioning his head under the left bar and his legs

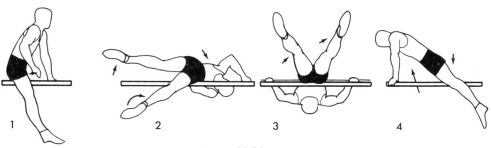

Figure 10.13
Kidney Roll

toward the ceiling. He continues to twist in this direction until he has returned to a straddle sitting position on top of the bars, but facing in the opposite direction from which he originally faced. The spotter should spot the legs of the performer while this stunt is being performed.

ELEMENTARY PARALLEL BARS STUNTS

Monkey Walk (Figure 10.14)

The performer takes a cross hanging position underneath the middle of the bars. He turns his toes out and from the inside hooks them on the bars, placing him in a position of hanging from his hands and toes. He releases his right hand and places his left foot in its previous location by twisting his body, his chest and stomach toward the floor. He next flexes his body at his hips and knees and reaches up behind and grasps the bar with his right hand, placing himself in a position in which he is toe hanging on one bar and hanging upside down from his hands on the other bar. He last releases his left hand and places his right foot in the location just vacated by his left hand, thus completing a one-half turn of his body. He regrasps the other bar and he is now hanging and facing the opposite direction from which he originally started.

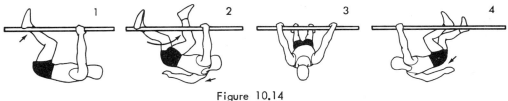

Figure 10.14
Monkey Walk

Single Knee Circle (Figure 10.15)

The performer shifts his weight to the left (or near) bar and hooks his left knee around it. Holding tightly to the bar with his left hand and with

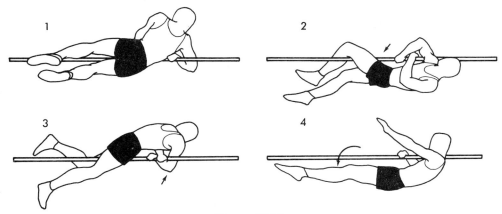

Figure 10.15
Single Knee Circle

his left arm flexed, he reaches over the left bar with his right arm and hand. Keeping his body close to the bar he then swings his right leg forcibly around the left bar and catches his right leg under the right bar. The circling motion is done on the knee of his left leg and the under-arm portion of his right arm. From the position in which his right leg is fixed under the right bar, he turns his left shoulder and completes a one-quarter turn and then drops into an upper-arm-hang position. The spotter stands next to and to one side of the performer and spots his shoulders and chest.

Forward Swinging Dip (Figure 10.16)

The performer develops an intermediate swing and at the end of the back swing flexes his arms, dropping his shoulders as close as possible to his hands. He holds the flexed arm position during his forward swing and as he completes his forward swing he completely extends his arms. During the backward swing of his body his arms are extended and he repeats the forward swinging dip several times. This is an excellent exercise for developing the triceps muscles located on the back of the upper arms and the pectoralis major and minor muscles of the chest.

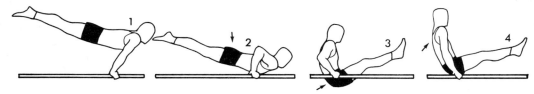

Figure 10.16
Forward Swinging Dip

Rear Vault to Right (Figure 10.17)

From a cross-support position in the middle of the parallel bars and with his arms extended, the performer develops an intermediate swing while keeping his legs together and completely extended. At the end of a forward swing he pikes and passes the rear portion of his body over the right bar. As he passes over the right bar, he changes his grasp on it, releasing his right hand and grasping it with his left hand. He lands facing in the same direction, and does a partial knee bend with his left hand on the right bar and his right arm extended sideward.

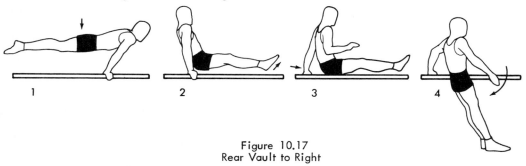

Figure 10.17
Rear Vault to Right

Rear Vault to Right with One-Quarter Twist (Figure 10.18)

The performer executes a rear vault to the right and immediately after he passes over the right bar he turns his left shoulder toward the bar and lands with both hands grasping the bar.

Figure 10.18
Rear Vault to Right with One-Quarter Twist

Rear Vault to Right with One-Half Twist (Figure 10.19)

The performer does a rear vault with a one-half twist until his right side is facing the right bar. He lands with a partial knee bend with his right hand grasping the bar and his left hand extended to the side.

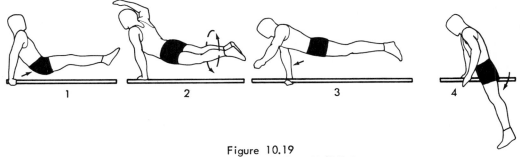

Figure 10.19
Rear Vault to Right with One-Half Twist

High Front Vault (High Face Vault) (Figure 10.20)

Keeping his arms straight the performer develops an intermediate or high swing and as he comes to the back of the swing, he pushes his body sideward, passing, stomach downward, over the right bar. As he passes to the outside of the bar he releases his right hand grasp and regrasps with the left hand on the right bar. He lands with his side facing the bar while retaining his grasp on that bar. As he lands the right arm is extended sideward and he does a partial knee bend.

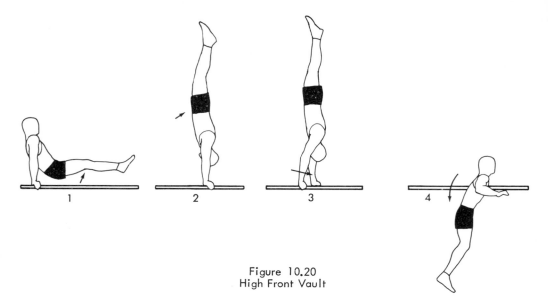

Figure 10.20
High Front Vault

Shoulder Stand (Upper-Arm Stand) (Figure 10.21)

From a cross-riding seat position on the middle of the bars the performer leans forward and, keeping his elbows extended directly sideward, rocks up onto his upper-arms while maintaining his grasp on the bars. While rocking upward the legs may be extended and piked or they may be tucked. The hips are slowly raised and then the legs are aligned with the body while the performer looks down at the mat directly below him throughout the performance of the stunt. If the performer keeps his upper arms extended sideways he is in no danger in performing this stunt. Should he overbalance and fall forward, he should immediately tuck his body as tightly as possible, extend his arms sideward and roll forward to an upper-arm hang.

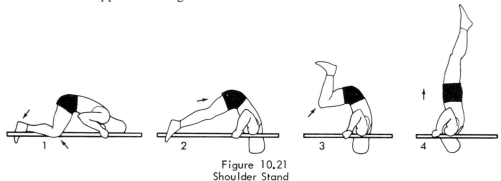

Figure 10.21
Shoulder Stand

S Vaults (Figure 10.22)

The performer (who is right-handed) takes a front-stand facing the nearest bar and grasps it with his left hand in an underhand grip, and his right hand in an overhand grip. He does a front vault to the right into a cross-rest position between the bars, and immediately as he swings forward he does a rear vault to the right, dismounting on the far side of the parallel bars. (The front vault and rear vault are described in detail in Chapter 9, Side Horse Stunts.)

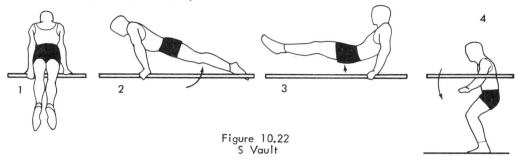

Figure 10.22
S Vault

Forward Roll from Sit (Figure 10.23)

From a cross-riding-seat position the performer spreads his elbows as wide apart as possible and places his hands on the bars about eight inches in front of his hips. He raises his hips and slowly rolls forward, attempting for an instant to balance his body in a pike position while changing his hand grasp from in front of his shoulders to behind them. Keeping his elbows pointing outward and his upper arms resting over the bars, he grasps his hands behind his back and then continues to roll forward until he returns to a riding-seat position. Throughout the forward roll the performer keeps his legs extended and spread wide apart.

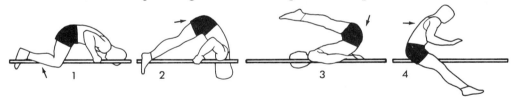

Figure 10.23
Forward Roll from Sit

Backward Roll from Sit (Figure 10.24)

With his legs spread apart and extended, the performer assumes a cross-riding-seat position and grasps the parallel bars just behind his thighs. He

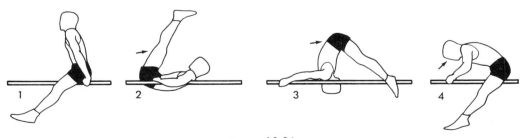

Figure 10.24
Backward Roll from Sit

extends his elbows directly sideward and rolls back, piking his legs up and over his body. He then raises his hips and moves them backward, pushing hard with first his hands and then the back of his arms as he keeps his legs spread apart and extended. He comes to a cross-riding-seat position.

Back Thigh Roll (Figure 10.25)

The back thigh roll is actually done on the legs. From a cross-riding seat position, the performer grasps his hands behind his back, pikes at his hips and rolls backward and between the bars while raising his legs behind him as he starts the backward roll. As his upper body rolls backwards and passes underneath the bars, he grasps the bars from below with his hands. He keeps his legs extended and spread and as his thighs start to rest on top of the bars, he hooks his heels under the bars and with his arms and legs, raises his body until he is in a cross-riding-seat position.

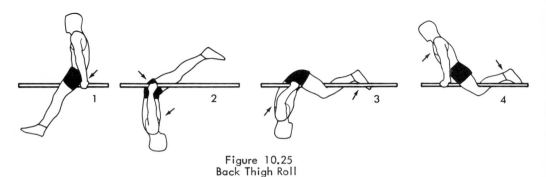

Figure 10.25
Back Thigh Roll

Single Leg Scissors (Figure 10.26)

While in a front-leaning rest position with his thighs resting on the near bar and his hands underneath his chest and grasping the far bar, the performer places his left leg between the bars. He swings his left leg high to his left and turns on his right thigh. He then transfers all his weight to his right arm, scissors his right leg under his left leg, and makes a one-half twist to his left, arriving at a sitting position on top of the bars.

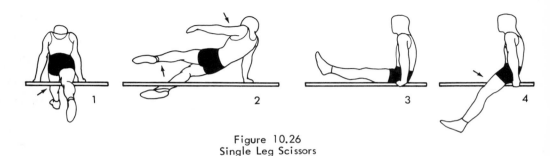

Figure 10.26
Single Leg Scissors

INTERMEDIATE PARALLEL BARS STUNTS

Skin the Cat (Back Hip Pullover) (Figure 10.27)

With the back of his thighs resting against the bar, the performer assumes an inverted-hang position along the middle of one of the parallel bars. He arches his body to the maximum degree possible, keeps his head well back and slowly does an inverted pullup, sliding the back of his body along the bar until he is sitting on top of the parallel bars.

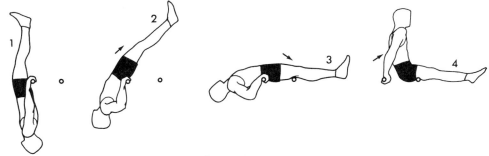

Figure 10.27
Skin the Cat

Forward Swinging Dip; Back Somersault Dismount (Figure 10.28)

A spotter should always be ready to assist the performer during all phases of this stunt. The spotter must be especially alert to give aid as the performer completes the dip and commences the back somersault. Grasping the ends of the parallel bars and facing the bars, the performer does a forward swinging dip but during the last half of the dip keeps his hands close to his shoulders and raises only his legs and hips. When his legs begin to rise above the bars he allows his upper body to drop backward as his legs are piked over his chest and face and at the same time his hand position is changed from above to below the bars. He completes the back somersault and drops to a feet landing directly behind the parallel bars.

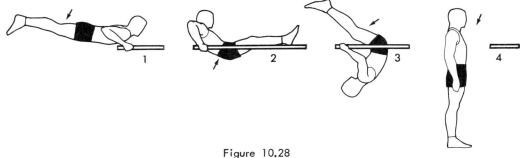

Figure 10.28
Forward Swinging Dip; Back Somersault Dismount

Forward Thigh Roll Mount (Figure 10.29)

The performer stands at one end of the parallel bars and so places his hands over the end of the bars that his weight is supported by his wrists (not his hands). He lifts his legs, coming to a one-half inverted hang, spreads his legs apart, and with his toes positioned over his face he supports his weight on his thighs. He then rolls his entire body forward by pulling vigorously with his arms while attempting to look between his legs.

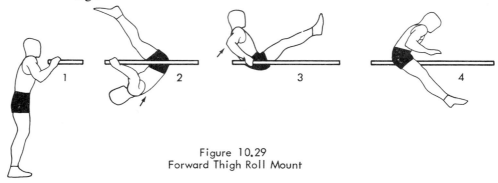

Figure 10.29
Forward Thigh Roll Mount

Front Hip Circle Mount (Belly Grinder) (Figure 10.30)

From a front-standing position in which the performer stands alongside of and faces the middle of the parallel bars, he reaches under the near bar and grasps the far bar with an over grip (regular grasp). He places one foot on the floor in front of and underneath the far bar and kicks the other foot over the far bar. As his body swings underneath the far bar he pulls up while vigorously piking his body and comes to a front-lying position on top of the bars. He then pushes up to a front-leaning-rest position.

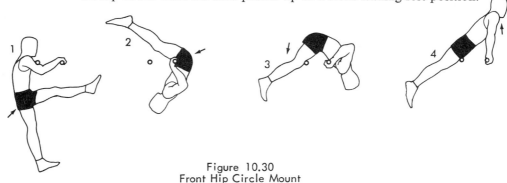

Figure 10.30
Front Hip Circle Mount

Extension Back Roll (Figure 10.31)

The mastery of this stunt provides an excellent basis for learning a back roll to a shoulder stand. The performer assumes a face-down cross-lying position on top of the parallel bars in which his partially flexed elbows are outside of the bars. He brings his legs together and from an upper-arm-hanging position swings his body downward between the bars. He continues his swinging motion by swinging his legs forward and piking them as they swing upward overhead while pushing down vigorously with his hands. The performer should finish in a cross-riding-seat position on top of the bars. When first learning this stunt the performer may experience some difficulty in rolling to and past an inverted position above the bars. This difficulty can be alleviated if the spotter will push with as much force as necessary against the back of the performer as he is approaching the upsidedown position.

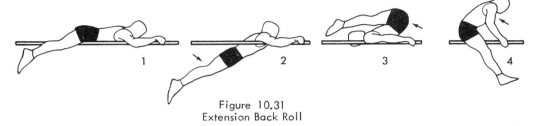

Figure 10.31
Extension Back Roll

Upper-Arm Kip (Figure 10.32)

From an upper-arm-hang position the performer swings back and forth and on a forward swing pikes his legs until his shins are directly above his face and his hips are above the bars. As his body comes to a standstill he quickly extends it by throwing his piked legs forward and slightly upward, lifting his hips and rotating his body around them as is done in a floor kip. He then slightly arches his body and comes to a cross-rest support position.

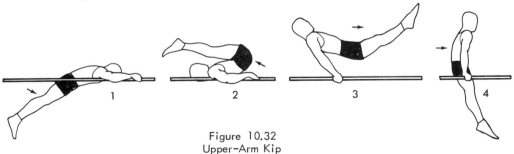

Figure 10.32
Upper-Arm Kip

Back Uprise (Stem Rise) (Figure 10.33)

The performer takes an upper-arm kip position with his body piked as depicted in the first figure. While his body is momentarily at rest, he straightens himself from shoulder to feet and extends his body slightly forward upward. He swings his extended body forward, downward, and backward while supporting himself in an upper-arm-hang position. At the end of his back swing he arches his body as much as possible and simultaneously pushes down forcefully with his hands and comes to an extended arm support. He then swings forward while in this position.

During the learning stage the back uprise may be performed by swinging back and forth a few times while in an upper-arm-hang position and then doing a back uprise on a high backward swing.

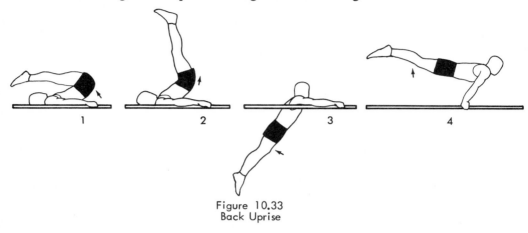

Figure 10.33
Back Uprise

Front Uprise (Hip Rise) (Figure 10.34)

From either an upper-arm support position or from an upper-arm kip position, the performer develops an intermediate swing while in an upper-arm hang position. He swings backward as far as possible and at the end of the front swing he quickly raises his hips as high as possible, pushes vigorously downward with his hands and arms, and forces his head and shoulders forward and upward coming to a cross-rest position. When performing this stunt it is important that the performer utilize the lift of his hips on his forward swing.

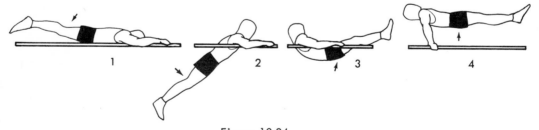

Figure 10.34
Front Uprise

Drop Kip (Figure 10.35)

The performer assumes a cross-rest position at the end of the bars and then lifts up and pikes his legs. Holding the piked position the performer leans back and swings downward and backward while keeping his thighs near his hands by rotating his body at the hips. The performer should not permit his hips to swing back too far. At the completion of the back swing, he extends his body by thrusting his legs first upward and forward and then downward while simultaneously pushing down forcefully with his hands thus rotating his body forward. The spotter should carefully watch the performer when he drops back preparatory to executing the kipping motion, and the spotter may need to give some assistance by lifting against the performer's back during the kipping action.

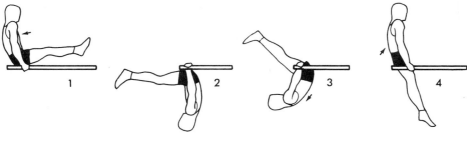

Figure 10.35
Drop Kip

Double Cut and Catch (Figure 10.36)

The double cut and catch is merely a straddle vault with a catch to a cross-rest position at the end of the bars. The performer jumps and pushes forward and upward with his hands while avoiding leaning too far forward in order to prevent catching his heels on the bars. As soon as his legs have cleared the bars he regrasps the ends of the bar with his hands. This stunt may first be practiced by performing a double cut to a seat-rest position on the thighs. Once the performer has mastered this to the point of attaining considerable height on the double cut above the bars, he then brings his legs together before catching the end of the bars. For the first few attempts of the complete stunt the performer should be closely spotted by the spotter who places his hands around the performer's waist and stands back and to one side to avoid the possibility of being kicked.

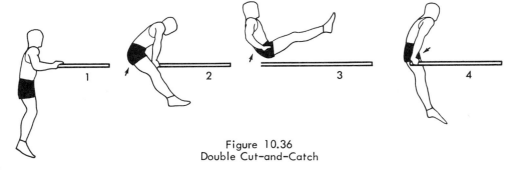

Figure 10.36
Double Cut-and-Catch

Handstand (Figure 10.37)

Before attempting a handstand on standard height parallel bars, the performer should first practice many intermediate swinging movements in the middle of the parallel bars. He should gradually develop a higher and higher swing until he can attain a vertical position. In swinging to a handstand the performer should grasp the bars tightly and keep his head up. When swinging to a handstand the performer, if he is underbalanced, should swing down between the bars keeping his legs and feet together and his shoulders forward of his hands. If he overbalances he should quickly transfer his weight to one arm, and while looking at that hand he does a one-half twist while still upside down. He then pikes his legs and lands in a standing position still retaining his grasp (usually with his right hand if right-handed) on the one bar. Because of the possibility of overbalancing the handstand should first be learned while grasping the ends of the parallel bars and facing outward. A skilled spotter can be helpful in assisting the performer to find the correct handstand position. The use of low- or medium-height parallel bars is recommended when learning to hold a handstand on the parallel bars.

Figure 10.37
Handstand

Handstand and Split-Off (Figure 10.38)

The performer does a handstand at one end of the parallel bars with his back toward the end of the parallel bars. While in the handstand he leans forward until slightly overbalanced and, keeping his head up, he pushes forward with his hands and brings his body downward by piking sharply at his hips and quickly spreading his legs apart. This stunt may be learned with increased ease if the mule kick is first mastered on the mats.

Front Toss to Upper Arms (Forward Airo to Upper Arms) (Figure 10.39)

The performer develops an intermediate swing in the middle of the parallel bars and at the back of the backswing he sharply pikes his body while lifting his hips, ducking his head, and pushing hard with his hands. As he lands on his upper arms (elbows held out to the side), he grasps the bars with his hands in order to prevent or minimize sliding on the bars. As soon as the performer pushes off the bars he must be sure to extend his arms to the side to avoid the possibility of slipping through the bars on the landing. With sufficient practice and height, the performer may be able to complete the somersault motion to a catch with the hands. When

Figure 10.38
Handstand and Split-Off

first learning the stunt hanging a mat over each bar directly in front of the performer's hands will allow him to practice with increased safety. If the performer positions himself at the end of the parallel bars while facing outward, he may do this stunt as a dismount—in which case he should be carefully spotted during his first few landings.

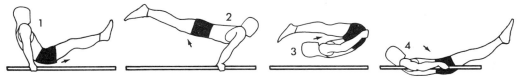

Figure 10.39
Front Toss to Upper Arms

Triple Rear Dismount (Figure 10.40)

The fact that the legs cross over the bar three times—the legs cross the bar in back of the right hand, in front of the right hand, and then over the left bar in the rear position—gives this name to the dismount. The per-

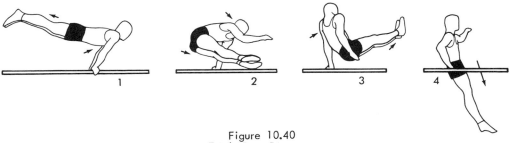

Figure 10.40
Triple Rear Dismount

former develops an intermediate swing and as his body passes the vertical on the back swing, he starts shifting his weight to his left, leans on his left arm, raises his hips high, and pikes at his hips while circling his legs counter-clockwise over the rear right bar, forward right bar, and then brings his legs under his body in a rear-vault as the last movement of the dismount. As his body passes over the left bar, he releases his left hand from the bar and regrasps it with his right hand, extending his left arm sideward. The important movement in performing this stunt is to first transfer most of the body weight to the left arm and as the leg circling movement is started to move the body to the left and forward.

Glide Kip (Figure 10.41)

The performer stands in a front-cross position, facing the parallel bars and grasps the inside portion of the end of the bars, keeping his thumbs alongside the inside of the bars and not around them. With his back arched, he jumps backward and upward and pikes at his hips. He glides forward while keeping his feet a few inches above the floor. At the end of the forward swing when his body is completely extended, he immediately pikes his legs and comes to a kip position. He holds this kip position until the completion of the back swing when he quickly kips his body by thrusting his legs upward and forward and then downward while pushing down hard with his hands. He comes to a cross-rest position between the bars.

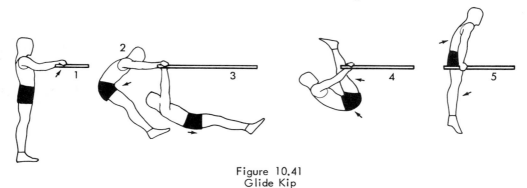

Figure 10.41
Glide Kip

Reverse Kip (Figure 10.42)

The performer assumes a back-cross stand position between the parallel bars and about eighteen inches in from the end of the bars as illustrated in the first figure. He then reaches his hands under the bar and grasps the bars from the outside. He jumps up and goes into a kip (or piked) position and swings forward while maintaining this position. At the end of the front swing, he quickly extends his body by forcing his head and shoulders back and up and as his body is extended he pushes down forcefully with his hands. These actions bring him to a cross-rest position and if his timing and movements are correctly executed he should have his arms completely extended. The spotter must be alert and ready to assist the performer during the time he does the reverse kip and particularly as he is coming to the cross-rest support position. After the regular reverse kip has been mastered the performer may attempt to shoot his legs vertically upward and thus come to a handstand position.

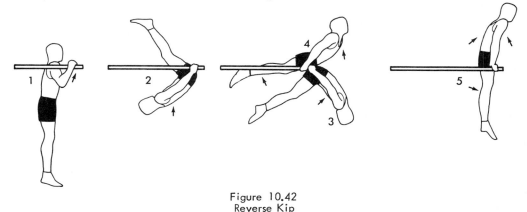

Figure 10.42
Reverse Kip

Peach Basket to Upper Arms (Figure 10.43)

This stunt can be performed from either the cross-rest or front-stand position. If executed from the cross-rest position, the performer raises his legs to a horizontal position as his body starts to drop back as illustrated in the first figure. If executed from the kip position, the performer swings down from a front stand position. With either start, at the highest point of the forward swing the performer pulls hard with his arms and vigorously extends his body in the same manner as when doing a reverse-kip. When the body is extended all parts of it reach for the ceiling—the heels, legs, trunk, shoulders and head. The momentum of the swing and the upside-down kipping action should raise the performer's body above the bars from which position he drops on his upper arms. With increased speed and kipping action this stunt can be accomplished at sufficient height to enable the performer to drop to his hands. Although this stunt can be hand spotted by any experienced spotter it is best spotted in the overhead mechanic.

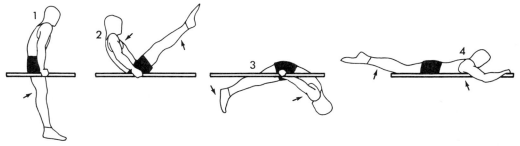

Figure 10.43
Peach Basket to Upper Arms

CHART FOR RATING PARALLEL BARS SKILLS

Beginning Parallel Bars Stunts	Rating of Stunt Performance*				
	1	2	3	4	5
Handwalking Exercise with Legs Motionless					
Handwalking Exercise with High Knee Lift					
Handwalking Exercise while Striding					
Hand Hops					
Piked Inverted Hang					
Inverted Hang					
Bird's Nest					
Intermediate Swing with Hop					
Jump to Cross Rest					
Single Leg Cut-Off					
Double Leg Cut-Off					
Straddle Vault					
Kidney Roll					
Sub-Total					

Elementary Parallel Bars Stunts	1	2	3	4	5
Monkey Walk					
Single Knee Circle					
Forward Swinging Dip					
Rear Vault to Right					
Rear Vault to Right with One-Quarter Twist					
Rear Vault to Right with One-Half Twist					
High Front Vault					
Shoulder Stand					
S Vault					
Forward Roll from Sit					
Backward Roll from Sit					
Back Thigh Roll					
Single Leg Scissors					
Sub-Total					

Intermediate Parallel Bars Stunts	1	2	3	4	5
Skin the Cat					
Forward Swinging Dip; Back Somersault Dismount					
Forward Thigh Roll Mount					
Front Hip Circle Mount					
Extension Back Roll					
Upper Arm Kip					
Back Uprise					
Front Uprise					
Drop Kip					
Double Cut and Catch					
Handstand					
Handstand and Split-Off					
Front Toss to Upper Arms					
Triple Rear Dismount					
Glide Kip					
Reverse Kip					
Peach Basket to Upper Arms					
Sub-Total					
Grand Total					

*The Simplified Points System containing the description of the five categories of ratings appear on pages 76-77.

(Figure 10.44)

ROUTINES ON THE PARALLEL BARS

Routine Consisting of Beginning Stunts on the Parallel Bars

Jump to cross-rest position, go to pike position; bird's nest, inverted hang, return to pike position. Jump to cross-seat position, kidney roll, forward roll to end of parallel bars, straddle vault.

Routine Consisting of Elementary Stunts on the Parallel Bars

Jump to cross-seat position, forward roll from seat, to the right bar, single leg scissors, cross-seat position, shoulder stand, roll to cross-seat position, rear vault to right with one-quarter twist.

Routine Consisting of Intermediate Stunts on the Parallel Bars

Reverse kip, scissors extension back roll, hip rise, handstand, swing to cross-support position, front toss, back uprise, triple rear dismount.

11 THE HORIZONTAL BAR

INTRODUCTION

The horizontal bar was invented by Frederick Jahn of Germany in 1812. Before this time the limbs of trees were used as horizontal bars. Performances and routines on the horizontal bar are considered by many to be the most spectacular and demanding of all competitive gymnastics events.

Three types of horizontal bars are commonly used for practicing horizontal bar stunts: the high bar, the low bar, and the adjustable bar. The low horizontal bar, from hip to chest level in height, is extremely useful for learning with the greatest safety many horizontal bar stunts. The adjustable horizontal bar is normally set at a low height and used as a low bar. The adjustable horizontal bar can be quickly set up and taken down, occupies little floor space, and because it is adjustable in height from two to eight feet permits the practice of horizontal bar stunts at the safest height level. The fixed high bar is used for performing advanced gymnastics stunts because it is strongly supported and has a flexible bar that permits performing on it with minimum effort. Only the high bar is used in gymnastics competition on the horizontal bar. The tempered steel bar is one-and-one-eighth inches in diameter, is 80 to 96 inches wide, and is usually located eight feet above the floor.

Regular workouts on the horizontal bar especially develop the muscles of the forearms, upper arms, shoulders, chest, and back. A fulfillment of the sense of daring and an acute sense of timing are other benefits that may be derived by working on the horizontal bar.

When performing most horizontal bar stunts the performer uses a regular or normal grasp in which the thumbs are parallel to each other and in which the palms of the hands face to the rear when the arms are hanging at the side. For some stunts a reverse grasp in which the little fingers are next to each other (or in which the palms of the hands face forward when the arms hang down at the side) is used, and for a few stunts a combination or mixed grasp in which the palms face each other is used. Unless otherwise stated the performer should use a regular grasp for all the stunts listed in this chapter. Normally, for any stunt in which the performer circles the bar his thumbs lead in the direction of the rotary motion and the fingers trail, because this hand position best enables him to retain his grip on the bar.

The performer should rub or dust a layer of carbonate of magnesium chalk on his hands before performing any stunts on the horizontal bar because it is essential that his palms do not become sweaty at any time. Although the presence of chalk on the bar is helpful in maintaining a strong grasp, a heavy coating may cause so much friction on the performer's hands as he rotates his grip on the bar that the skin on the palms may rip or tear. For this reason, a heavy coating of chalk should not be allowed to accumulate on the bar but should be sanded off with emery paper in horizontal back and forth motions. If the performer's hands are not tough and the skin tends to tear easily, he should use hand straps made of leather or cotton, to protect the palms. If his skin does tear then he should trim off the torn portion and apply petroleum jelly on this area and stay off the horizontal bar until the bruise heals.

LOW HORIZONTAL BAR STUNTS

The horizontal bar should be adjusted to chest height of the performer for all the stunts included in the first half of this chapter.

BEGINNING STUNTS

Modified Pull-Ups from Hand-Lying Position (Figure 11.1)

With the bar adjusted to a height of about three feet and using a reverse grasp, the performer grips the bar with his arms fully extended, his chest underneath the bar, and his body straight and at an angle to the bar. He flexes his arms until his chin or chest touches the bar and he then lowers his body. He repeats these movements as many times as possible.

Figure 11.1
Modified Pull-Up from Hang-Lying Position

Forward Turn-Over from Front-leaning Rest Position (Figure 11.2)

Using a reverse hand position, the performer grasps the bar and jumps upward and forward while pushing with his hands. His body comes to rest on the bar supported only by his arms and hands. Retaining a tight grasp on the bar he leans forward, pikes his body and allows it to fall forward.

As his body rotates forward over the bar he keeps his arms semiflexed and does not relax them thus assuring that his face does not hit the bar. He muscles his piked body and slowly lowers his feet to the mat in order to avoid having his heels slam down on the mat.

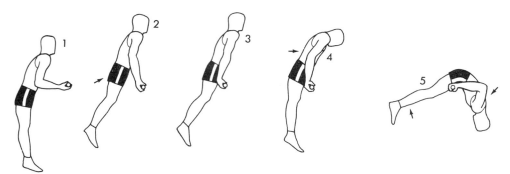

Figure 11.2
Forward Turn-Over from Front-Leaning Rest Position

Jump to Sitting Position (Figure 11.3)

The jump to a sitting position is an excellent balance exercise in which the performer jumps up to the bar as described for the preceding stunt but during which jump he keeps most of his weight on his right arm and does a one-half twist of his body before coming to a sitting position on top of the bar. As he executes the one-half twist he quickly changes his hand position to a reverse grasp. As he completes the stunt the performer tightly grasps the bar with both hands in order to retain his sitting position, and he may have to flex or extend his legs in order to retain his balance. When learning this stunt the performer may wish to use a mixed grasp in which his left hand is palm up and his right hand is palm down. The spotter should be ready to assist the performer in case he starts to fall backwards. Should the performer fall off balance forward, he merely pushes forward off the bar and lands on his feet.

Figure 11.3
Jump to Sitting Position

Knee Hang (Figure 11.4)

From a hanging position under the bar the performer tucks his body, and lifts his legs and hips, placing the back portion of his knees over the bar as illustrated in the third figure. He forcefully and continuously flexes his lower legs, releases his hands, and extends his body downward, remaining in a knee-hang position. When ready to dismount, he places his hands on the mat, straightens his legs, and then tucks them under the bar and drops them to the mat behind his hands.

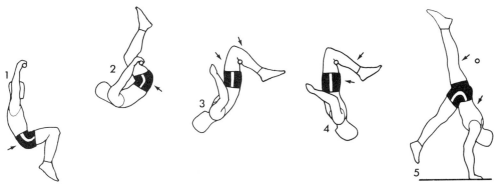

Figure 11.4
Knee Hang

Travel Forward from Front-leaning Rest Position (Figure 11.5)

Using the grasp of his choice the performer jumps to a front-leaning rest position. He then leans on his left arm and raises his right leg over and onto the other side of the bar. He next leans on his right arm and raises his left leg over the bar thus coming to a back-leaning rest position.

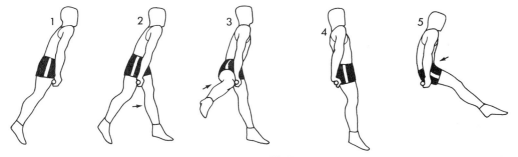

Figure 11.5
Travel Forward from Front–Leaning Rest Position

Forward Side-Riding Seat to Backward Side-riding Seat (Figure 11.6)

The performer grasps the bar, jumps, does a one-quarter twist and lands sitting on the bar. He places both hands on the bar behind his back and, while retaining his balance, kicks both extended legs to the side and over the bar. He is now facing in the opposite direction in a back-leaning rest position. The spotter stands behind the performer and assists him if he loses his balance.

Figure 11.6
Forward Side–Riding Seat to Backward Side–Riding Seat

One-Half Inverted Hang and Turn-Over to Back Hang (Figure 11.7)

Employing a regular grasp on the bar, the performer raises his legs and extends them between his hands. This places his body in a piked or inverted L position in which his head is flexed forward, his legs are extended, and his toes pointed. He then turns his body backwards forcefully stretching his shoulders and extending his legs as far behind him as possible. He finally releases his grasp and drops to his feet. The bar should be raised to head height for this stunt.

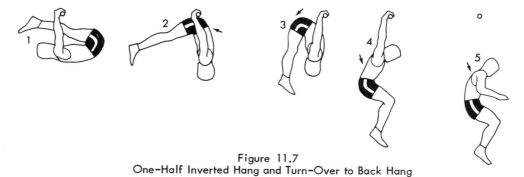

Figure 11.7
One-Half Inverted Hang and Turn-Over to Back Hang

Turn-Over to Back Hang and Return (Figure 11.8)

The performer executes a back hang but instead of dropping off the bar he returns to an inverted piked position.

Bird's Nest (Figure 11.9)

The performer grasps the bar and comes to an inverted pike position. He next flexes his knees, places his toes over the bar and forces his hips between his arms as shown in the third figure. He then arches his back and comes to a bird's-nest position as illustrated in the fourth figure.

Figure 11.8
Turn-Over to Back Hang and Return

Figure 11.9
Bird's Nest

Glide and Shoot (Figure 11.10)

The glide and shoot can be initiated in several different ways; the instructions given here are for the least difficult way. The performer assumes the position illustrated in the first figure in which his body is inclined backward, his feet are on the floor directly under the bar, and the weight of his body is supported by his arms, which are extended. The performer vigorously extends his right leg forward and upward, pushes off his left foot, and allows his body to swing downward and forward and simultaneously raises his left leg and positions it alongside his right leg. He then

Figure 11.10
Glide and Shoot

swings both legs forward, arches his body, and when his body is extended pushes away from the bar with his hands. With practice this stunt may be performed for the purpose of shooting as far away from the bar as possible.

Flank Vault (Side Vault) (Figure 11.11)

Facing the bar and grasping it at arm's length, the performer jumps upward and forward, leans his weight on his extended left arm, releases his right hand and raises both legs up and over the bar while attempting to keep his legs and body in a straight line. His left side faces the bar during the vault and he lands with his back to the bar as shown in the last figure. As he lands, he extends both arms sideward and bends his legs slightly in order to absorb the force of his landing.

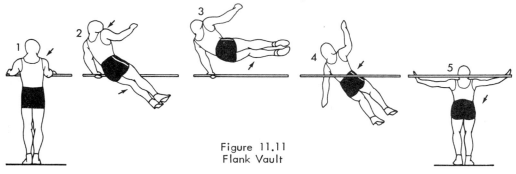

Figure 11.11
Flank Vault

Front Vault (Face Vault) (Figure 11.12)

The performer initiates a vault as described for the flank vault and as he passes over the bar his face and the front of his body face the bar. If he vaults to his right, his left hand remains on the bar during the landing, and his right hand is extended to the right.

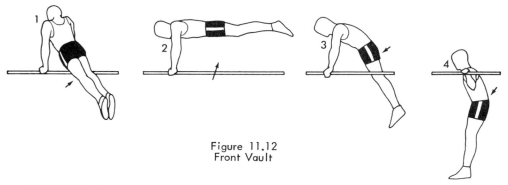

Figure 11.12
Front Vault

ELEMENTARY STUNTS

Glide and Shoot from Upright Start (Figures 11.13 and 11.14)

The performer does the same actions as for the Jump and Shoot (the tenth skill) except that he starts from an upright position. When the glide and shoot is learned to the point where a long under-shoot can be done, the performer initiates this stunt by jumping off both feet. By executing a higher jump on the take-off, pulling the arms with increased force, and extending the body with increased speed, the performer can do the glide and shoot for a considerable distance.

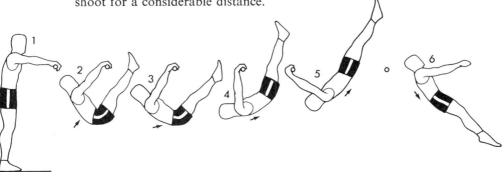

Figure 11.13
Glide and Shoot from Upright Start

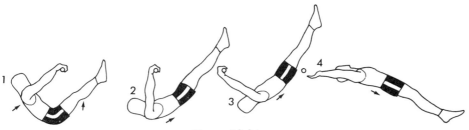

Figure 11.14
Glide and Shoot for Distance

Shoot from Front-leaning Rest Position (Under Swing from Front-leaning Rest Position) (Figure 11.15)

From a front-leaning rest position on the bar rotate the body backward while falling below the bar as shown in the first figure. During this initial phase keep the arms straight, the hips tense and close to the bar, and the

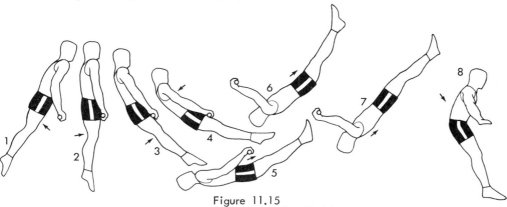

Figure 11.15
Shoot from Front-Leaning Rest Position

legs piked. As the shoulders pass under the bar, let the hips drop away from the bar and extend the legs upward and then forward. As the body reaches full extension, push away from the bar and arch the body, coming to a standing position.

Backward Hip Circle (Figure 11.16)

The performer assumes a front-leaning rest position on the bar with his arms slightly bent in order that his hips rest on the bar. The performer takes a slight cast by piking his legs forward and then extending his body and pushing with his arms, thus lifting his hips and legs backward and upward a short distance. He then pulls his hips to the bar and as the bar is contacted he throws his head and body backward after he first whips his legs under the bar while pulling the bar tightly against the angle formed by his trunk and thighs. As his flexed body passes under the bar his weight transfers to his thighs and he then forces his legs downward over the bar while raising his shoulders and head and thus returns to a front-leaning rest position in which his arms are straight. The successful performance of this stunt requires the performer to concentrate on keeping his legs in the correct position because the piked leg position aids in keeping the body in the proper position on the bar. A more advanced stunt, the free hip circle, is performed by driving the body toward the bar with increased speed and by keeping it and the arms fully extended and the hips close to the bar but not touching it during the complete rotation around the bar. The backward hip circle may be easily learned by performing the lead-up stunt depicted in the figures in which the performer takes a standing position and then kicks one leg upward and pulls his hips into the bar.

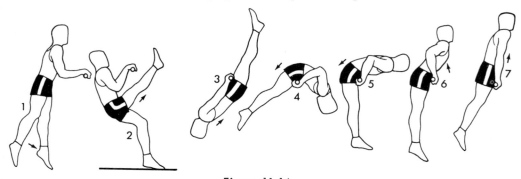

Figure 11.16
Backward Hip Circle

Glide and Single Knee Mount (Figure 11.17)

The performer, using either grasp, glides his body forward in an under-shoot. At the end of the glide, he flexes his right leg and raises it between his arms and over the bar. He hooks the back of his right knee on the bar as shown in the third figure and at the end of the back swing he swings his extended left leg downward and rotates his flexed body and head forward and over the bar, stopping on top of the bar in a semisitting position. The spotter should be ready to assist the performer in case he rotates past the top of the bar and falls forward. In this case the performer should tuck his body close to the bar, flex his arms, and attempt to check his rotation.

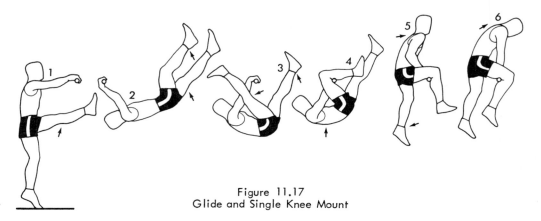

Figure 11.17
Glide and Single Knee Mount

Single Knee Circle Backward (Figure 11.18)

The performer assumes a single knee support as shown in the first illustration. From this position the performer raises his hips, pushes his flexed legs back against the bar, and keeps his other leg extended and high behind him. He extends his head backward and drops his body backward while maintaining this position. As his body rotates under the bar, he kicks his free leg forward and over the bar, flexes his body and hips, and pulls into the starting position. The spotter may need to lift against the performer's back during the last half of the swing in order to help him come to an upright position, and the spotter may need to support the performer at the end of his swing in order that he can maintain his upright position. Should the performer swing past an upright position he should perform another knee circle; if he should fail to rotate to an upright position and start to swing forward, he should tuck his body, flex his arms, and stop his swing underneath the bar. With practice several consecutive back knee circles may be performed.

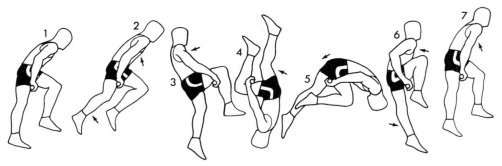

Figure 11.18
Single Knee Circle Backward

Single Knee Circle Forward (Figure 11.19)

From a two-hand and one-knee support position, the performer raises his hips and body and fully extends his arms, hooks one knee against the bar and falls forward. On the upswing, he bends his arms, and forces his head and shoulders forward and over the bar, stopping in the starting position. If the performer cannot stop on top of the bar he may perform another circle if he circles forward or if he circles backward he should tuck his body, flex his arms, and stop his motion underneath the bar. With practice several forward single-knee circles may be performed in succession.

Figure 11.19
Single Knee Circle Forward

Crotch Circle (Figure 11.20)

Taking a reverse grasp, the performer sits on the bar in a straddle position with one leg forward and the other leg back of the bar as shown in the first figure. He then leans his head and body forward (the direction in which he is facing) and swings downward head first. On the upswing he flexes his arms, tucks his body forward, and forces his head and shoulders above the bar, coming to the starting position. He may perform several crotch circles in succession.

Airplane Spin (Mill Circle) (Figure 11.21)

The performer straddles the bar, crosses his ankles, and places both hands (palms facing each other) in front of him as shown in the first figure. He flexes his body sideward to his left and drops sideward as fast as possible. As he starts to swing up on the other side of the bar he flexes his arms and leans slightly forward, finishing in the starting position. With practice several circles can be performed in succession without stopping between circles.

Front Hip Pull-Over (Belly Grind) (Figure 11.22)

The performer assumes an inverted hang in a frontway position as depicted in the first figure. Keeping his head back and his body sharply piked, he slowly pulls his body over the bar, coming to a front-support position. The stunt may also be performed from a hang in which case as

Figure 11.20
Crotch Circle

Figure 11.21
Airplane Spin

Figure 11.22
Front Hip Pull-Over

the performer pikes his legs upward he does a semipullup with his arms and at the same time extends his head back.

Back Circle (Figure 11.23)

Using a reverse grip the performer jumps to a sitting position on the bar. He kicks his extended legs forward and upward as shown in the third figure and drops back to the bar with the small of his back resting against the bar. Holding his body in this position against the bar, he simultaneously swings his legs backward and over the bar. As his body swings over the bar he pushes with his arms and lifts in order to return to a sitting position on the bar. The performer must attempt to hold tight and keep the small of his back against the bar throughout the stunt.

Figure 11.23
Back Circle Forward

Vaults from a Standing Position

Vaulting stunts may be performed over the low horizontal bar in a similar manner to the vaults performed over the side horse except that raised pommels are not available for the hand grasp and the height of the horizontal bar may be varied more than can the height of the side horse. The vaults described in this section include only some of the elementary vaults and the listing is by no means complete. For almost all vaults the spotter should stand on the far side of the bar either to one side of or in front of the performer in order to give instant assistance should the vaulter trip as he passes over the bar.

Squat vault (Figure 11.24). The performer vaults forward and upward, raises his hips as high as possible and swings his tucked legs between his arms and over the bar. He lands with his arms extended sideward and with his legs slightly bent.

Rear vault. Using a regular grasp the performer stands at arm's length from the bar, facing it. He jumps upward and forward, pulling forward with his extended arms. He passes over the bar in an L position, doing a one-quarter twist to his right in order that his back and hips face the bar as he passes over it. He lands on his feet on the other side of the bar, grasping it with his right hand while extending his left arm sideward and flexing his legs slightly.

Straddle vault (Figure 11.25). The performer vaults upward and forward, raising his hips as high as possible and spreading (straddling) his legs wide, keeping them extended at all times. He lands with his back to the bar, dipping his legs slightly and extending his arms sideward.

Wolf vault. The performer vaults over the bar while holding one leg in the straddle position and the other leg in a position in which the foot rests on the inside of his other knee.

Corkscrew vault. Using a mixed grip with the left hand in a reverse grasp position, the performer takes off (using a beat board if he wishes) as

Figure 11.24
Squat Vault from Standing Position

Figure 11.25
Straddle Vault from Standing Position

though he were going to do a front vault. As soon as the front of his body passes over the bar he executes a one-half twist counter clockwise and lands with his right side parallel with the bar, his right hand grasping the bar and his legs slightly bent.

Vaults from a Front-rest Position

Vaults on the horizontal bar that are performed from a standing position can usually be done from a front-leaning rest position—and the height of the bar from the floor does not adversely affect the performer in passing over the bar. The most important phase of all vaults performed from a front-leaning rest position is the cast employed to enable the vaulter to clear safely the horizontal bar. Once the cast has been mastered, proficiency in vaulting from the front-leaning rest position should be rapidly acquired. From a front-leaning rest position with his arms extended, the performer flexes at his waist and swings his extended legs forward underneath the bar. He then quickly swings his legs backward and when his entire body is in a straight line he pushes forcibly with his arms. The first three figures demonstrate the actions used in performing a cast. The beginner should often practice performing casts on the horizontal bar, attempting to cast his body as high as possible. When returning to the bar after a practice cast, he should resist the descent of his hips to the bar by muscling with his shoulder and back muscles. With practice, sufficient leg swing and arm push can be generated in order that the performer's body ascends into a handstand position. The spotter spots the arm and shoulder of the performer in case he overthrows and starts to fall forward. The squat, rear, front, corkscrew, and straddle vault should be practiced from a cast in which the performer deliberately leans far forward during the cast in order to shift his center of gravity ahead of the horizontal bar and thus pass safely over the bar during the vault.

INTERMEDIATE STUNTS

Undershoot with One-Half Twist (Figure 11.26)

Using a mixed grasp the performer initially performs a regular under-shoot and when his body is completely extended at the end of the under-swing, he twists his hips, shoulders, and arms, and executes a one-half twist, landing facing in the opposite direction. The performer should do the undershoot with decreased distance and increased height.

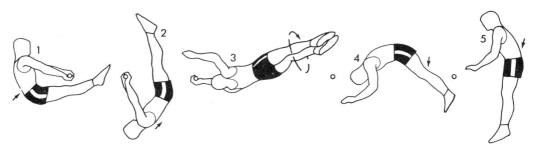

Figure 11.26
Undershoot with One-Half Twist

Double Knee Circle Forward (Figure 11.27)

The performer sits on the bar and grips it with a reverse grasp. He lifts his body and hips as high as possible, pulls his hips back, places the back of his knees against the bar, and drops forward, diving head first. As he begins to swing upward he flexes his arms and tucks his body, which shortens his radius of rotation and thus increases his speed of revolution. As he completes the circle he brings his body to an erect position and

Figure 11.27
Double Knee Circle Forward

stops in a sitting position on top of the bar. If he circles past this position he may quickly push with his hands and vault forward to his feet or he may do another circle. If he is short and starts to circle backward, he should tuck his body and flex his arms in order to stop in a hanging position underneath the bar. Using a regular grasp a double knee circle backward may be executed. With practice successive knee circles may be performed.

Heel Circle Forward (Figure 11.28)

Using a reverse grasp, the performer takes a seat position on the bar. He pikes his body and raises his hips high behind him until the back of his heels rest against the bar. He leans forward and starts a forward heel circle. As his body starts its upswing, he shoots his legs over the bar and comes to an erect position, stopping in a sitting position on top of the bar. The spotter should be alert to assist the performer in the event that he requires aid or spotting. With practice several forward heel circles (or backward if a regular grasp is used) may be performed in succession.

Figure 11.28
Heel Circle Forward

Back Hip Pull-over (Skin the Cat) (Figure 11.29)

From a one-half inverted hang position, the performer extends his head, arches his body as much as possible and slowly pulls his hips up and over the bar as shown in the first figure. In performing this stunt the weight of the legs and the flexibility of the body are essential elements in maintaining the body's center of gravity on the opposite side of the bar from the hips.

Figure 11.29
Back Hip Pull-Over

One-Half Seat Circle (Skin the Cat From Seat Drop) (Figure 11.30)

From a sitting position on the bar the performer extends his arms, raises his hips as high as possible, pikes his legs, and swings back and under the bar. As he attains the peak of his forward swing, he rapidly extends his body over the bar and as his weight shifts to the far side of the bar, he comes to a sitting position on top of the bar. He then pushes off the bar, jumping forward to his feet. The spotter should closely spot the performer's shoulders during his backswing.

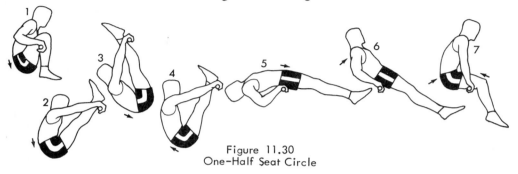

Figure 11.30
One-Half Seat Circle

Glide Kip (Figure 11.31)

From a standing position near the bar the performer jumps upward (with a one- or two-footed push off) and glides forward, coming to a full extension of his body and never letting his heels rise more than ten inches above the mat. As soon as his body is fully extended, he flexes at his waist, and brings his insteps to the bar. As his shins contact the bar and when his body has come to the apex of its backswing, he vigorously extends his legs forward and downward and strenuously pushes down with his hands. He continues to pull the upper portion of his body toward the bar as he pushes with his hands until he comes to a front-leaning rest position on the bar. The spotter should grasp the performer's shoulders and assist him to a front-leaning rest position during the first few attempts.

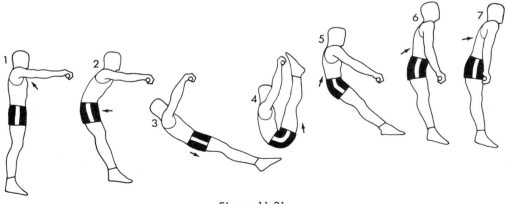

Figure 11.31
Glide Kip

Drop Kip (Figure 11.32)

From a front-leaning rest position, the performer, keeping his arms straight, drops backward, flexing sharply at his hips and raising his shins to the bar. Keeping his legs straight, he holds his insteps to the bar until he passes directly underneath the bar on his return swing. At this instant he kips by extending his body rapidly, thrusting his legs forward and downward and pushing down with his hands. He continues to push down with his hands until he comes to a front-leaning rest position on the bar. The spotter should spot the performer's shoulders, and the spotter may need to lift slightly on the performer's back during the learning stages of this stunt.

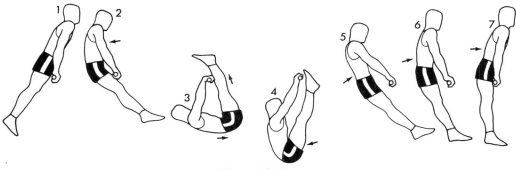

Figure 11.32
Drop Kip

Instep Circle Forward (Figure 11.33)

From a front-leaning rest position and using a reverse grasp, the performer casts upward, raising his hips a sufficient height that he can hook his instep on the bar while keeping his legs extended (the legs may be spread as far apart as desired). Keeping his arms straight, he holds tight with his hands and keeps his insteps tightly against the bar as his body drops forward. As he swings upward he bends his arms slightly, flexes his body and lowers his hips into the bar. When learning the forward instep circle at least two mats should be placed under the horizontal bar in case the performer's insteps slip off the bar during the downswing. With sufficient momentum several instep circles in succession may be done.

Figure 11.33
Instep Circle Forward

Sole Circle Forward (Figure 11.34)

From a front-leaning rest position and using a reverse grasp, the performer flexes at his waist and does a high cast, raising his hips sufficiently high to place the soles of his feet on the bar outside of his hands. He holds tightly, keeps his legs straight and drops forward. On his upswing, he pulls hard with his arms, bends his legs and arms while reaching forward with his head and shoulders and comes to a front-leaning rest position. The spotter should spot from behind the performer and should spot his shoulders, being particularly alert at the bottom of the swing. With practice several successive sole circles may be performed. Backward sole circles may be done by using a regular grasp.

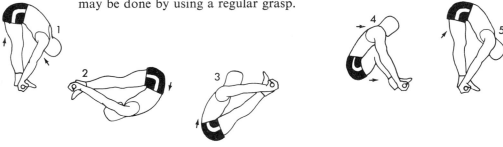

Figure 11.34
Sole Circle Forward

Cast to Momentary Handstand (Figure 11.35)

From a front-leaning rest position the performer flexes sharply at his waist, leans forward, and very vigorously extends his legs to the rear and upward while pushing vigorously with his arms and keeping his head in line with his body. If the performer underthrows his cast he may muscle back to a front-leaning rest position on the bar or he may push away from the bar as he falls downward and land on his feet while retaining his grasp on the bar. If he overthrows he should look at his hands, do a half-twist of his body while upside down, and release one hand and then regrasp it in a regular grasp after the half-twist is completed. He then loosely tucks his

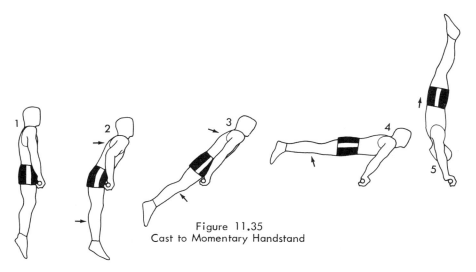

Figure 11.35
Cast to Momentary Handstand

Beginning Low Horizontal Bar Stunts	Rating of Stunt Performance*				
	1	2	3	4	5
Modified Pull-ups from Hang-Lying Position					
Forward Turn-Over from Front Leaning Rest Position					
Jumps to Sitting Position					
Knee Hang					
Travel Forward from Front-Leaning Rest Position					
Forward Side Riding Seat to Backward Riding Seat					
One-Half Inverted Hang and Turn-Over to Back Hang					
Turn-Over to Back Hang and Return					
Bird's Nest					
Glide and Shoot					
Flank Vault					
Front Vault					
Sub-Total					

Elementary Low Horizontal Bar Stunts	1	2	3	4	5
Glide and Shoot from Upright Start					
Shoot from Front-Leaning Rest Postiion					
Backward Hip Circle					
Glide and Single Knee Mount					
Single Knee Circle Forward					
Single Knee Circle Backward					
Crotch Circle					
Airplane Spin					
Front Hip Pull-Over					
Back Circle					
Squat Vault					
Rear Vault					
Straddle Vault					
Wolf Vault					
Corkscrew Vault					
Fence Vault					
Sub-Total					

Intermediate Low Horizontal Bar Stunts	1	2	3	4	5
Undershoot with One-Half Twist					
Double Knee Circle Forward					
Heel Circle Forward					
Back Hip Pull-Over					
Skin the Cat from Seat Drop					
Glide Kip					
Drop Kip					
Instep Circle Forward					
Sole Circle Forward					
Cast to Momentary Handstand					
Sub-Total					
Grand Total					

*The Simplified Points System containing the description of the five categories of ratings appears on pages 76-77.

(Figure 11.36)

body and comes to feet landing, pushing away from the bar as he descends but retaining his grasp on the bar.

ROUTINES ON THE LOW HORIZONTAL BAR

Routines are not ordinarily performed on the low horizontal bar as it is used to learn, with increased safety, stunts and skills to be employed on the high horizontal bar. Although the performer may wish to construct

209

one or more routines to be practiced on the low horizontal bar, it is suggested that he concentrate his efforts on learning and perfecting routines on the high horizontal bar.

HIGH HORIZONTAL BAR

If an adjustable bar is used as the high horizontal bar, the performer should so adjust its height that it is just a few inches higher than his reach in order that at the bottom of all swinging movement (in which his feet and toes are pointed) there is no possibility that his toes will touch the mat.

BEGINNING STUNTS

Short Swings (Figure 11.37)

Standing two to three feet behind the bar as illustrated in the first figure, jump, grasp the bar (second figure), and swing forward, swinging from the shoulders and waist and slightly piking the body (third figure). Arch the body and swing backward (fourth figure) and continue to repeat the swinging motion. The spotter stands to one side of the performer and slightly in front of the bar and is particularly prepared to spot the performer at the end of each forward swing.

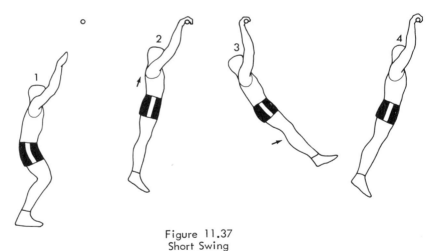

Figure 11.37
Short Swing

Knee Hang Between Hands (Figure 11.38)

The performer jumps up and grasps the bar. He pulls up to a one-half chinning position and, with his knees bent, raises his legs. Keeping his hips low and his head forward he brings his legs through his arms and under the bar. He then bends his legs, placing the back of his knees over the bar, and hangs in this position. The spotter spots the head and shoulders of the performer.

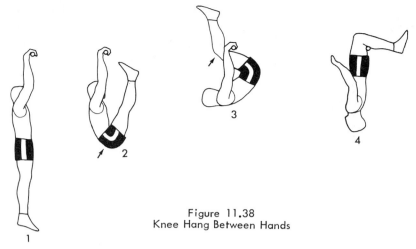

Figure 11.38
Knee Hang Between Hands

Knee Hang Outside Hands (Figure 11.39)

The performer comes to a knee-hang position by following the instructions given for the preceding stunt except that he spreads his legs and places them outside of his arms and hands.

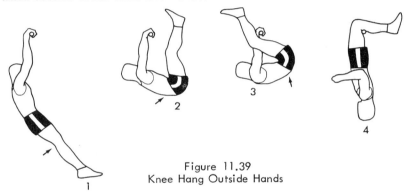

Figure 11.39
Knee Hang Outside Hands

Two-Hand Pull-ups (Figure 11.40)

Using either a regular or a reverse grasp, the performer does as many pull-ups as possible, doing each one through a full range of motion. He

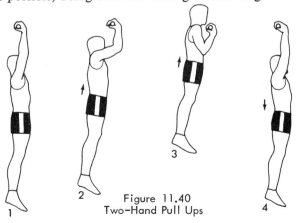

Figure 11.40
Two-Hand Pull Ups

should practice pull-ups with both grasps because the performance of various stunts requires maximum pull-up strength with either grasp.

Pull Through to Hang Rearways (Figure 11.41)

The performer jumps to a hang position, pulls up to a one-half chin position, and then flexes his legs and inverts his body, coming to a one-half inverted hang or pike position. He lowers his legs behind him and comes to a rear-hang position which he holds momentarily before reversing his movements and coming to a regular hang position. The spotter should spot the head and shoulders of the performer.

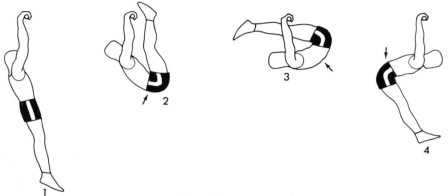

Figure 11.41
Pull Through to Hang Rearways

Leg Raise (Raise Feet to Bar) (Figure 11.42)

Grasping the bar the performer keeps his legs straight and pikes them forward and upward, touching his insteps to the bar. Leg raises are an excellent exercise for developing abdominal and hip flexor strength and may be used as a test in partially evaluating the benefits derived from previous gymnastics practice.

Figure 11.42
Leg Raise

High Swings (Figure 11.43)

The performer takes a regular grasp and develops a large swinging movement, doing several repetition swings and then dismounting at the end of a forward swing. The spotter should be alert to give spotting assistance toward the end of each front swing.

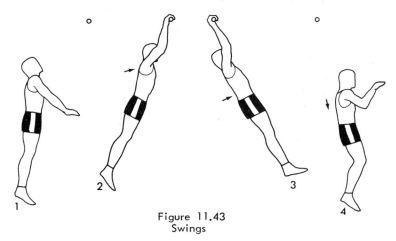

Figure 11.43
Swings

High Swing with Half-Twist on Front Swing (Figure 11.44)

To perform this stunt the performer may use a regular grasp or for a twist to his right a mixed grasp in which he has a regular grasp with his right hand and a reverse grasp with his left hand. As his body swings under the bar (second figure) the performer begins to pike his legs at his hips. He then tightly grasps the bar with his right hand and scissors his left leg over his right leg, twisting his body by means of leg and hip action while pushing with his left hand (third figure) and then releasing his left hand grasp. As soon as the half-twist is completed he regrasps with his left hand (fourth figure) and releases his right hand grasp, turns his right

Figure 11.44
High Swing with Half-Twist on Front Swing

hand over and regrasps (fifth figure). With practice the performer can do several half-twists in succession, twisting on either side of the bar at the end of each front swing. The spotter closely spots the performer during the twisting phase of this stunt.

Single Knee Swing-Up (Circus Mount) (Figure 11.45)

Standing approximately twenty inches behind the bar, the performer jumps, grasps the bar, swings forward, and raises his left leg higher than his right leg as depicted in the second illustration. As his body swings backward he keeps his hips low until his right leg passes under the bar, at which time he raises it to a position to the right of his right arm as shown in the third illustration. He hooks his right knee over the bar, forces his extended left leg downward and backward, tucks his body and lifts his head and shoulders up and over the bar, coming to a walk-stride-seat position. The spotter spots the performer in the event that he overswings and falls forward.

Figure 11.45
Single Knee Swing-Up

Single Knee Circle Forward (Figure 11.46)

Taking a reverse grasp, the performer sits on the bar in a walk-stride position (first figure). He lifts his body, pushing up to a straight-arm position, raises his hips, hooks his top knee against the bar and falls forward (second figure). As his body starts its upward swing (third figure), he tucks his body and pulls his head and shoulders over the bar while simultaneously driving his free leg downward and backward (fourth figure). He then comes to a sitting position on top of the bar. If the performer is unable to generate sufficient swing to come to a sitting position on the bar, he should immediately tuck his body and flex his arms and wrists, stopping his reverse swing underneath the bar; if he swings past the sitting position then he may repeat his actions and do a second forward knee circle or he may tuck his body and flex his arms and stop his forward

Figure 11.46
Single Knee Circle Forward

swing underneath the bar. The spotter should spot the middle of the performer's back as he is swinging upward to the sitting position on top of the bar. With practice the performer can do several consecutive forward knee circles. If a regular grasp is employed, single knee circles backward may be done.

Front Hip Pullover (Belly Grinder) (Figure 11.47)

The performer jumps, grasps the bar and hangs (first figure). He swings his legs forward and simultaneously does a semipullup (second figure). He then pikes at his hips (some beginners may have to also flex their knees) (third figure) and brings his legs over the bar while continuing to pull up with his arms (fourth figure). As his legs and hips slide over the bar, he rotates around the bar, raises his head and shoulders, and comes to a front-leaning rest position (sixth figure). The spotter may at first need to assist the performer by lifting slightly on the upper portion of his back.

Figure 11.47
Front Hip Pull-Over

Airplane Spin (Mill Circle) (Figure 11.48)

The performer takes a cross-riding position on the bar and grasps it in a mixed grasp with both hands positioned in front of him as depicted in the first illustration. He straightens his arms and sits tall (illustration two), then falls to the side (illustration three). As he begins his upward swing, he tucks his body and pulls in to the bar (illustration four), returning to the starting position. The spotter spots the performer's arm and shoulder during the upswing.

Figure 11.48
Airplane Spin

ELEMENTARY STUNTS

Lower Self Below Bar with Legs Raised (Figure 11.49)

The performer, keeping his legs raised, lowers his body below the bar as depicted in the figure. This exercise demands considerable power for its successful execution and is hence developmental in nature.

Drop Back to Knee Hang from Sitting Position (Figure 11.50)

From a sitting position on the bar the performer, while grasping the bar, slowly drops back and comes to a knee-hang position. When performing this stunt, in order to prevent his body from dropping backward too rapidly and hence perhaps falling off the bar, the performer must lower his hips while keeping his head and shoulders up as shown in the third illustration. The spotter should spot the performer's head and shoulders as he releases his hand grasp.

Hip Circle Backward (Figure 11.51)

From a front-leaning rest position on the bar the performer pikes his body slightly and leans into the bar, which is positioned at his hip joints as shown in illustration two. He swings his legs and hips backward (illustration three) and then whips them forward and as his hips contact the bar he swings his legs up and around the bar, throwing his head and shoulders backward while pulling the bar against his hips (illustration four). The momentum from these motions should be sufficient to rotate his body a complete circle and return him to the starting position. During the entire

Figure 11.49
Lower Self Below Bar with Legs Raised

Figure 11.50
Drop Back to Knee Hang from Sitting Position

Figure 11.51
Hip Circle Backward

backward hip circle the performer is in a slightly piked position and he continues to vigorously push his hips against the bar. The spotter should spot the performer's shoulders as he completes the last half of the hip circle. With practice and by keeping his body almost completely extended, the performer may perform two or more hip circles without stopping.

Hock Circle Dismount (Penny Drop) (Figure 11.52)

There are many methods of doing a hock circle dismount. One easy method is for the performer, from a knee-hang position with his body extended, to develop a swing by starting with his arms flexed then extending them toward the ceiling (illustration two). He next swings his arms forward and downward (illustration three), and lastly returns them to the flexed position. This arm movement cycle is repeated until a knee swing of sufficient height is obtained. At the end of a forward swing, the performer releases his legs by extending them and simultaneously arches his head and upper body upward. He slowly somersaults backward and lands on his feet with his body semitucked. The spotter should closely spot the performer's arms and shoulders, particularly immediately before, during, and after he releases his legs. Once the performer has mastered this dismount he may practice starting from a sitting position on the bar from which he does a knee swing backward and finishes with a hock circle dismount.

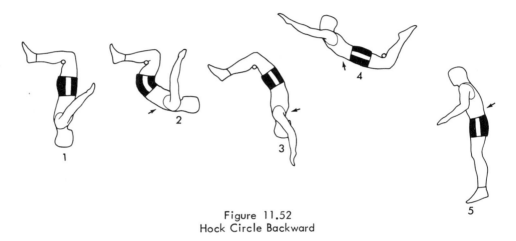

Figure 11.52
Hock Circle Backward

Seat Circle Backward (Figure 11.53)

The performer assumes a sitting position on the bar (illustration one). He then extends his arms and raises his hips off the bar (illustration two). Retaining his hand, body, and leg relationship (piked body), he rotates his body by dropping his head and trunk backward (illustration three). He swings under the bar and on his upward swing he pulls with his hands, drops his legs, and forcefully arches backward (illustration four), coming to

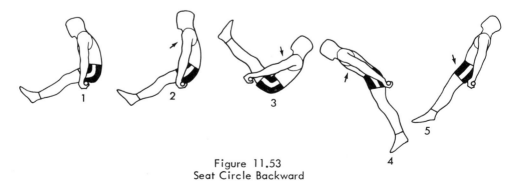

Figure 11.53
Seat Circle Backward

a back-leaning rest position on the bar (illustration five). The spotter should carefully spot the performer throughout the stunt, especially at the bottom of the swing and the last half of the stunt. The spotter should be alert to give assistance in the event that the performer changes the relationship of his hands and legs. With practice several backward seat circles in succession may be performed.

Hip Circle Forward (Figure 11.54)

Starting from a front-leaning rest position the performer pushes his extended body upward to a position where the bar crosses his upper thighs (illustration one). Keeping his body extended, he leans forward and circles the bar forward until his body is parallel to the floor. At this point he sharply pikes his upper body downward, pulls the bar tightly against the area where his hips are bent and circles the bar (illustrations two and three). As his momentum ceases, he bends his arms, leans forward and comes to a front-leaning rest position (illustrations four, five, and six). The spotter may need to lift on the performer's hips during his first few attempts. With practice, the performer may be able to perform two or more forward hip circles in succession.

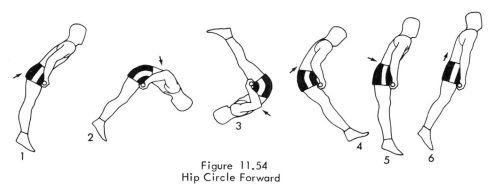

Figure 11.54
Hip Circle Forward

Double Heel Circle Forward (Figure 11.55)

From a rear seat position the performer takes a reverse grasp, pushes his body up to a full-arm extension and raises his hips until his heel tendons are pressing against the bar (illustration two). Keeping his legs extended

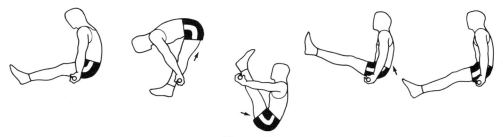

Figure 11.55
Double Heel Circle Forward

he swings forward and downward and as his body passes under the bar he pulls strongly with his arms and drives his legs over the bar (illustration four), coming to a rear seat position (illustration five). The spotter should spot the performer for a possible overshoot—if this occurs the performer can tightly tuck his body and stop his swing or he can do another forward double heel circle. With practice several successive forward double heel circles may be performed. If a regular grasp is used the performer may do backward double heel circles.

Cast (Figure 11.56)

The cast is used to quickly and easily develop a large swinging motion on the high horizontal bar. Standing approximately three feet behind the bar, the performer jumps grasps the bar, and swings forward (illustration one). At the end of the back swing he does a pullup while arching his body (illustration two). He immediately flexes his hips and arms (illustrations three and four). He then pikes his legs forward and forcibly extends his legs upward (illustration five), which action is followed by a forceful extension of his arms (illustration six). These actions should generate a large swing. The spotter must spot closely at the bottom of the downward swing.

A second method of casting is for the performer to grasp the bar, do a quick pullup and then thrust his head and upper body backward while piking his legs and thrusting them forward and upward at a 45 degree

Figure 11.56
Cast

angle, keeping his chest near the bar during the initial thrusting action. As his legs and body shoot forward he extends his arms behind him.

Another method of casting is for the performer to hang motionless and, keeping his arms straight throughout, pike his extended legs sharply and then immediately swing them forward, downward and backward. While still swinging backward the performer repeats the piking and swinging action of his legs while his hips are some distance behind the bar, thus creating a large swing. This method requires better timing but less strength than does the second method.

Kip (Figure 11.57)

The mastery of this stunt marks the point where the novice has truly started to become proficient on the high bar. The performer jumps forward, grasps the bar and swings forward (illustration two). On his forward swing he attempts to touch his toes to the mat directly under the bar and then forcefully arches his body. Pressing down on the bar he vigorously pikes his legs forward and upward and raises his shins or insteps to the bar (illustrations three and four). He holds this position momentarily until his hips have swung back under the bar at which time he thrusts his legs forward and downward, rotates his body and immediately reaches over the bar with his head and shoulders coming to a front-leaning rest position. The beginner must avoid the common mistakes of rushing his timing by attempting to raise his feet to the bar too soon or kipping before his hips pass directly under the bar. It is almost impossible to be too late in the timing of this stunt. The spotter should spot the performer and lift his shoulders and hips, if needed, as the kipping action takes place.

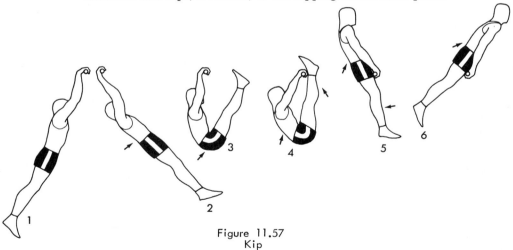

Figure 11.57
Kip

Reverse Kip (Figure 11.58)

From a standing position about twenty inches behind the bar, the performer jumps, grasps the bar, and swings forward (illustration one). As he swings forward, he pikes his body, raising his extended legs (illustration two), passing them between his arms and under the bar (illustration three). He starts his backward swing with his body piked, and he quickly extends his body over the bar by unpiking at his hips (illustration four). He then flexes at his waist and pushes his hips back with his hands and comes to a rear seat position. The spotter should spot the performer carefully in case he overshoots past the rear seat position—in which case the performer does a rear seat circle.

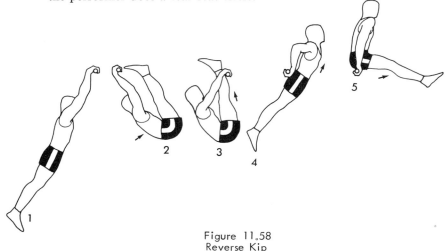

Figure 11.58
Reverse Kip

Back Uprise (Stem Rise) (Figure 11.59)

The performer executes a high cast and as his body starts to swing backward he flexes slightly at his waist (illustration one). As he completes his back swing, he arches his body and pushes down with his arms, pulling his body into the bar (illustration two). He comes to a front-leaning rest position on the bar (illustration four), flexing his body slightly as he contacts the bar at his hips. The spotter should be alert that the performer does not lose his grasp toward or at the end of the back swing.

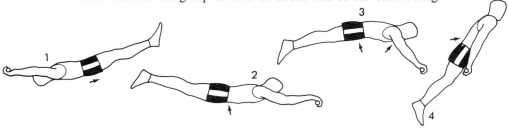

Figure 11.59
Back Uprise

Shoot-through to Double Heel Circle Forward (Figure 11.60)

For this combination of stunts the performer, using a reverse grasp, first performs a shoot-through or reverse kip as previously described and then immediately performs a double heel circle forward, which has also been previously described.

Figure 11.60
Shoot-Through to Double Heel Circle Forward

INTERMEDIATE STUNTS

Kip and Hip Circle Backward (Figure 11.61)

The performer should first review the techniques for performing this combination of stunts that were previously described and are illustrated in this chapter. When performing this combination he should not pause after completing the kip but should immediately transfer his momentum from the completion of the kip to the rotary action of the backward hip circle.

Figure 11.61
Kip

Half Twist and Kip (Figure 11.62)

From a front-leaning rest position in which his hands are close together, with a mixed grip the performer does a small cast (illustration one). After passing under the bar and at the end of his back swing, he changes the grip of his left hand and twists (illustration two). He then pikes his body (illustrations three and four) and does a kip (illustrations five and six).

The spotter may, if needed, assist the performer by lifting on his upper back or shoulder as he begins his kip.

Figure 11.62
Half–Twist and Kip

Half-Twisting Back Uprise (One-Half Twisting Stem Rise) (Figure 11.63)

From a front-leaning rest position, the performer executes a rather high back cast (illustrations one and two) and, while at the top of his cast, crosses his left hand immediately on the other side of his right hand. Holding this crossed-hand position, he swings down and under the bar and upward. When he reaches the end of his front swing, he releases the right hand and twists to his left, pulling hard with his left hand (illustration four). He regrasps with his right hand, shifts his left hand to a regular grasp and pulls his hips to the bar, coming to a front-leaning rest position. The spotter should be especially alert to spot the performer as he starts swinging upward from the bottom of his swing and during the changing of his hand positions.

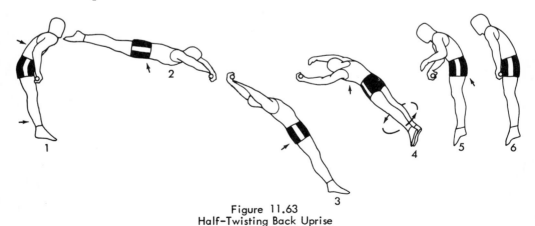

Figure 11.63
Half–Twisting Back Uprise

Instep Circle Forward (Figure 11.64)

From a front-leaning rest position the performer, who has a reverse grasp, does a back cast then immediately sharply pikes his body (illustration two), spreading his legs and bringing them toward the bar so that he can place his insteps under the bar (illustration three). Keeping his arms fully extended, he circles his body forward and downward and under the bar (illustration four). As he completes his upward swing he straightens his body by extending his legs, flexes his arms, and comes to a front-leaning rest position (illustrations five and six). The spotter takes the normal precautions in spotting the performer.

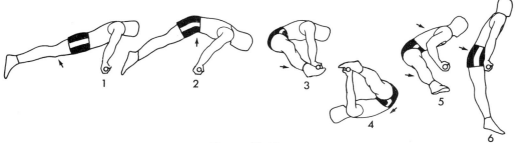

Figure 11.64
Instep Circle Forward

Sole Circle Backward (Figure 11.65)

Using a regular grasp, the performer does a cast then sharply pikes his body (illustration three), placing his feet (while keeping his legs straight) on the bar between his hands (illustration four). Retaining a tight grasp at all times and keeping his legs stiff, he swings backward and downward (illustration four). On his upward swing, he flexes his legs and comes to a squat on the bar (illustrations six and seven). The spotter should spot the performer closely during the upward swing of the sole circle.

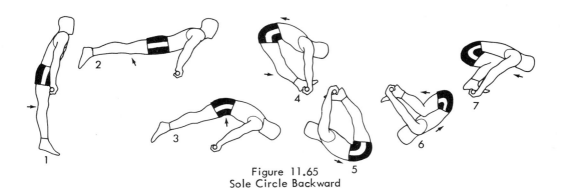

Figure 11.65
Sole Circle Backward

Sole Circle Backward and Dismount (Figure 11.66)

The performer, using a regular grasp, does a backward sole circle as previously described and as illustrated, but instead of flexing his body on the upward swing and coming to a squat position, he keeps his legs extended and as his swing stops just short of a balanced standing position on top of the bar, he jumps forward off the bar (illustrations four and five). The spotter carefully spots the performer throughout his upward swing and dismount.

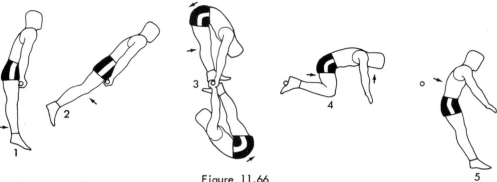

Figure 11.66
Sole Circle Backward and Dismount

Heel Circle Forward and Dismount (Figure 11.67)

From a sitting position on the bar with his legs extended, the performer, using a reverse grasp, fully extends his arms and raises his hips, placing his heel tendons against the bar (illustration one). He swings forward and under the bar (illustrations two and three). As his body completes its upward swing, he releases his grasp and dismounts forward, coming to a stand position in front of the bar (illustration five). The spotter should carefully spot the arms and shoulders of the performer during his upswing and dismount.

Figure 11.67
Heel Circle Forward and Dismount

Back Cast to Handstand (Figure 11.68)

From a front-leaning rest position the performer pikes his legs (illustration one) and then vigorously extends them while pushing his body upward with his arms (illustrations two and three). As his body reaches its maximum extension, he pushes into an inverted or handstand position (illustration four) in which he is slightly under-balanced. Throughout the cast and extension to a handstand the performer should keep his head up and slightly back, and he should watch the bar. The performer then muscles his body back to a front-leaning rest position on the bar. The spotter should stand in front of the bar and spot the performer in the event that he overthrows and starts to fall forward off the bar. If this should occur the performer, while upside down, should release one hand, do a half-twist, regrasp, pike his body and either muscle to a front-leaning rest position or drop to a stand behind the bar (illustrations five and six).

Back Cast to Handstand and Front Vault (Figure 11.68)

Using whatever grasp he desires the performer takes an extremely high back cast as previously described but deliberately overthrows past a handstand position. As he begins to swing forward and downward he does a one-quarter twist to either side (illustrations five and six), and comes to a side-stand.

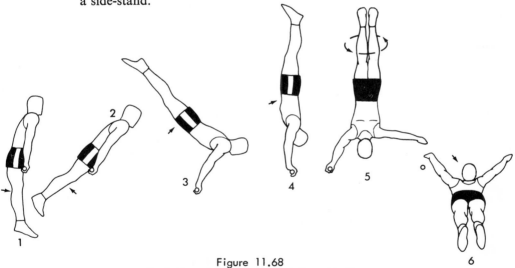

Figure 11.68
Back Cast to Handstand and Front Vault

Half Giant Swing Forward (Three-Quarter Swing) (Figure 11.69)

Using a regular grasp the performer flexes his body (illustration one) and does a high back cast with a slight underbalance (illustration two). He completely extends his body, swings downward (stomach first) and under the bar, keeping his body fully extended and stretched (illustration three). As his upward swing gets underway he pikes his body (as illustration four depicts) while keeping his arms extended and brings his hips to the bar (illustration four), coming to a front-leaning rest position on the bar (illustration five), and being careful not to flex his arms too much. The spotter should stand in front of the bar and spot the performer for a possible fall from the bar as he swings upward.

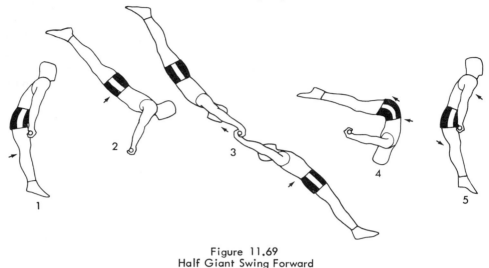

Figure 11.69
Half Giant Swing Forward

Giant Swing Forward (Front Giant Swing) (Figure 11.70)

Using a regular grasp the performer casts to a near handstand position (illustration one). He then extends his body, tightens his grip and drops forward in the direction of his chest (illustrations two and three). As he swings upward, as soon as his body is in a horizontal position, he flexes slightly at his hips, pulls hard with his arms, pulls his head back, and rotates his grip to above the bar (illustrations four and five). He comes to or slowly past a handstand, focuses his eyes on the bar (illustration six), and he may either lower his body to a front-leaning rest position on the bar or he may do another giant swing. The spotter should be alert to aid the performer in case he slips off the bar during his upswing.

Giant Swing Backward (Reverse Giant Swing) (Figure 11.71)

Using a reverse grasp, the performer slightly overthrows a back cast and slowly swings backward past a handstand position (illustrations one, two, and three). Keeping his head positioned between his arms, he stretches his body as much as possible and continues into his downward and backward swing (illustration four). The performer continues to swing backward and on his upswing, when his body comes to a horizontal position, he pikes slightly at his hips (illustrations six and seven) and then extends his legs to a vertical position and thrusts his head forward (illustration eight). (If necessary the performer may flex his arms slightly in order to lower his body and hence swing past the handstand position—the sticking point.) After completing one giant swing the performer may retard his

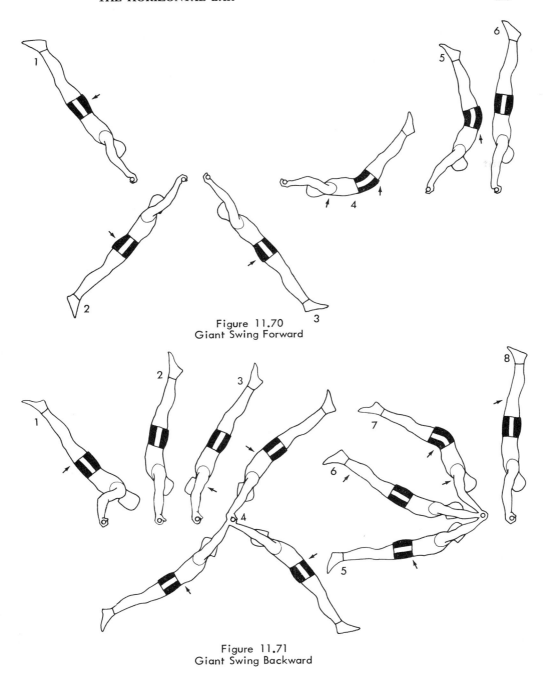

Figure 11.70
Giant Swing Forward

Figure 11.71
Giant Swing Backward

swing by lowering to a front-leaning rest position while piking his body or he may continue by doing one or more additional giant swings, extending his arms and body as much as possible at the start of each swing. The spotter must be ready to spot the performer in case he does not complete a full circle and starts to drop frontward behind the bar.

HIGH HORIZONTAL BAR ROUTINES

Routine of Beginning Stunts on High Horizontal Bar

Front hip pull-over, straddle bar, airplane spin, drop to hang, single knee swing-up, single knee circle forward, pull through to hang rearways, dismount by dropping to feet.

CHART FOR RATING HIGH HORIZONTAL BAR SKILLS

Beginning High Horizontal Bar Stunts	Rating of Stunt Performance*				
	1	2	3	4	5
Short Swings					
Knee Hang Between Hands					
Knee Hang Outside Hands					
Two Hand Pull-Ups					
Pull Through to Hang Rearways					
Leg Raises					
High Swings					
High Swing with Half-Twist on Front Swing					
Single Knee Swing-up					
Single Knee Circle Forward					
Front Hip Pull-Over					
Airplane Spin					
Sub-Total					

Elementary High Horizontal Bar Stunts	1	2	3	4	5
Lower Self Below Bar with Legs Raised					
Drop Back to Knee Hang from Sitting Position					
Hip Circle Backward					
Hock Circle Dismount					
Seat Sircle Backward					
Hip Circle Forward					
Double Heel Circle Forward					
Cast					
Kip					
Reverse Kip					
Back Uprise					
Shoot-Through to Double Heel Circle Forward					
Sub-Total					

Intermediate High Horizontal Bar Stunts	1	2	3	4	5
Kip and Hip Circle Backward					
Half Twist and Kip					
Half Twisting Back Uprise					
Instep Circle Forward					
Sole Circle Backward					
Sole Circle Backward and Dismount					
Heel Circle Forward and Dismount					
Back Cast to Handstand					
Back Cast to Handstand and Front Vault					
Half Giant Swing Forward					
Giant Swing Forward					
Giant Swing Backward					
Sub-Total					
Grand Total					

*The Simplified Points System containing the description of the five categories of ratings appears on pages 76-77.

(Figure 11.72)

Routine of Elementary Stunts on High Horizontal Bar

Cast, kip, hip circle backward, hip circle forward, drop to hang, cast, shoot-through to double heel circle forward, drop back to knee hang from sitting position, hock circle dismount.

Routine of Intermediate Stunts on High Horizontal Bar

Cast, stem rise, half twisting back uprise, hip circle backward, giant swing forward, instep circle forward, giant swing backward, sole circle backward and dismount.

12 STUNTS ON THE RINGS

The rings are sometimes referred to as the Roman rings, indicating that they existed in some form in the time of ancient Rome. In 1842 Spies first described them as they are presently used.

Stunts on the rings may be performed without any swing of the rings (still rings) or when the rings swing back and forth (swinging or flying rings). The rings, which are normally seven or eight inches in diameter and are made of wood or iron covered with rubber, may be suspended from the ceiling from either steel cables or ropes, which are not as strong but which have a tendency to provide a small bounce. These rings are generally attached to the steel cable or rope by strong straps of webbing that allow the height of the rings to be adjusted over a range of four feet. The steel cables or ropes are attached to the ceiling by a swivel housing equipped with a unique ball thrust-bearing eye-fitting from which the rope or cable is suspended with a strong metal hook.

Except for the legs, regular exercise on the rings develops most of the muscles of the entire body—the muscles of the forearms, upper arms, shoulders, chest, and upper back are especially developed.

Unless otherwise indicated the stunts listed in this chapter should be learned on the still rings before they are attempted on the flying rings. After a stunt has been mastered, it should be performed on rings adjusted to regular height (just above the performer's reach).

BEGINNING RING STUNTS

Pull-up; Release Right Hand; Grasp Left Wrist (Figure 12.1)

In performing this stunt on the still rings the performer should remember to keep his left arm flexed and his left hand near his chin when he releases his right hand.

Backward Circle to Back-Hang (Figure 12.2)

The performer flexes his arms, tucks his body by flexing his hips and legs, and rotates his body backward as far as possible. The beginning ring performer will usually discover that it is nearly impossible to do a

Figure 12.1
Pull Up; Release Right Hand; Grasp Left Wrist

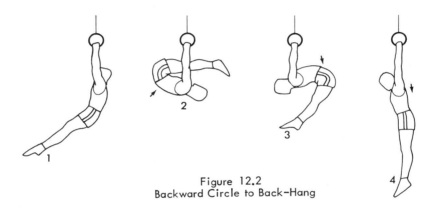

Figure 12.2
Backward Circle to Back-Hang

backward circle to a back-hang if he keeps his arms straight at all times. As his strength increases the performer should attempt this stunt while keeping his arms completely extended.

Fundamental Swing (Figure 12.3)

The actions necessary to develop correctly a swing with the correct timing on the flying rings are described below. The height of the rings should be about six inches less than the height of the performer's reach. As the performer's body moves forward on the forward swing, it is in an arched position as shown in the first illustration. The performer then flexes at his hips and pikes his legs forward. As the rings start to swing backward he lets his legs swing back and he reaches with one foot for the mat area underneath the rings support as shown in the second and third illustrations. He takes one large backward step and pushes himself backward into a sitting position (fourth illustration), and as he reaches the end of the backward swing of the rings he swings his legs back placing his body in a hyperextended position as shown in the fifth illustration. As the rings begin to swing forward he flexes his body, reaches forward with his feet, and takes two steps, pushes his chest forward and arches his body at the front of the forward swing. These actions are repeated for each cycle of the swing of the rings. It is important that the performer take a beat on each forward and backward swing by taking directly underneath the rings support a running forward or backward step.

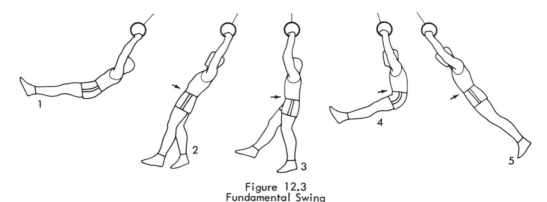

Figure 12.3
Fundamental Swing

Swing with Twist (Figure 12.4)

The performer develops a swing as previously described. He extends his body on the backward swing of the rings and does a one-half twist by dropping his right shoulder, raising his left shoulder and rotating his head to the right.

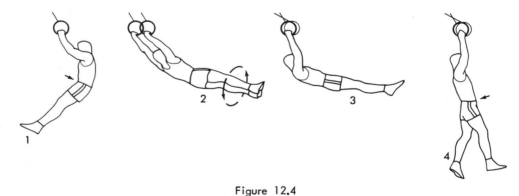

Figure 12.4
Swing with Twist

Pull-up at End of Swing (Figure 12.5)

With the height of the rings slightly below the reach of the performer, he develops a short to intermediate swing by taking a beat on each forward and backward swing. As the end of a front swing is attained, the performer flexes his arms and brings his body to a pull-up position. He then holds the pull-up position for two or more complete swings if possible.

This stunt is a developmental exercise that should be practiced often by those of below normal strength.

Figure 12.5
Pull-Up at End of Swing

Pull-up at End of Frontswing; Lower at End of Backswing (Figure 12.6)

The performer performs the stunt previously described but as he reaches the end of the backswing he extends his arms, lowering his body to a hanging position. This sequence of pulling-up on the frontswing and lowering on the backswing should be repeated until the performer is fatigued.

Figure 12.6
Pull-Up at End of Front Swing; Lower at End of Backswing

Inverted Hang and Return (Figure 12.7)

This stunt should not be attempted on the swinging rings until it has been completely mastered on the still rings. The performer first assumes an inverted pike position (one-half inverted hang) with his chin on his chest as depicted in the first illustration. From the pike position his legs are slowly extended upward until the performer is upside down and his body is slightly arched. The performer may assume the upside down position with increased ease if he extends his feet inside of and along the ropes or steel cables and keeps his head flexed until he is upside down. Once the inverted hang position is obtained, he should press the rings against the outside of his thighs. Should he start to fall he should pike his body and quickly return to a pike position, which is the method used to make a normal recovery from an inverted hang position. When this stunt is first attempted on the flying rings, the performer should avoid allowing his body to go too far forward.

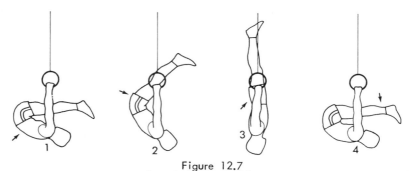

Figure 12.7
Inverted Hang and Return

Bird's Nest (Crow's Nest) (Figure 12.8)

The performer assumes a pike position and then hooks both feet in the rings, placing his toes just in front of his hands. He next forces his hips between and through his arms, extends his back by arching his body and extends his head backward.

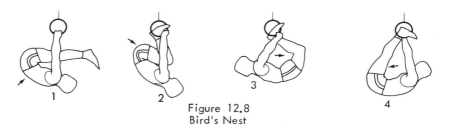

Figure 12.8
Bird's Nest

Inverted Hang to Bird's Nest and Return (Figure 12.9)

On the still rings the performer goes to a pike and inverts his body until he is in an inverted hang. He then returns to a pike and hooks his feet in the rings and forces his hips forward until he is in a bird's nest position. He returns to a pike and then extends his body slowly into an inverted hang. Throughout this exercise series the arms are extended.

Forward Swing to Pike; Return to Hang (Figure 12.10)

The performer develops a swing on the swinging rings and on the forward swing he hyperextends his body and immediately takes a beat or foot tap at the bottom of the swing. He then swings his legs forward and

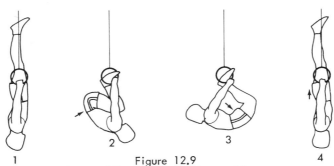

Figure 12.9
Inverted Hang to Bird's Nest and Return

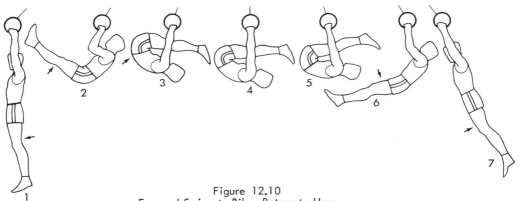

Figure 12.10
Forward Swing to Pike; Return to Hang

swings his body into a pike position. As he and the rings begin to swing back, he unpikes his body at the hips, comes to a hanging position and takes a beat at the bottom of the swing. Throughout this stunt the performer ordinarily holds his arms in full extension although he may flex them slightly during the learning stages in order to facilitate piking and swinging back to a hanging position. When this stunt is performed correctly the forward swing of the body will assist greatly in moving the body into the pike or one-half inverted-hang position. The important action position of this stunt is shown in the first illustration.

Bird's Nest from Swing and Dismount (Figure 12.11)

The performer develops a small to intermediate swing on the flying rings and on the forward swing he assumes a pike position. He then flexes his legs and places the insteps of his feet in the rings. He next extends his head, and pushes his knees forward as far as they will go as depicted in the third illustration. After holding this position a short time he recovers to a pike position by flexing at his hips, and at the end of the forward swing he extends his legs forward and comes to a hang, dropping off the rings at the end of the backward swing.

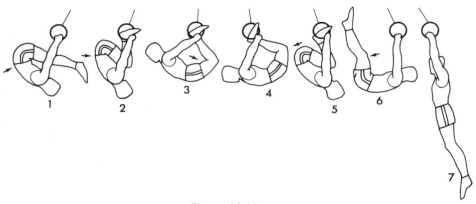

Figure 12.11
Bird's Nest from Swing and Dismount

Single Leg Cut and Catch (Figure 12.12)

From a pike position on the still rings the performer quickly rolls his body forward and hooks his left leg over his left forearm. As his leg is hooked over his left arm, he rolls up on his left arm by flexing both elbows and trying to chin himself, at which time his head should be almost between the rings. While still rolling forward and holding fast with his right arm and hand, he releases the left ring with his left hand, whips his left leg forward and downward, and regrasps the left ring with his left hand. In performing this stunt the performer must remember to roll his body upward and forward on his left arm and to continue this movement with a strong effort with his right arm when the cut-and-catch is executed. The left ring is released—never thrown—in order that it remain in the same location for a quick regrasp. When learning this stunt the performer will find it helpful to practice rocking forward to almost a sitting position on the left arm without actually performing the cut. By making two or three rock-ups in rhythm, the cut-and-catch on the next rock-up requires only normal effort.

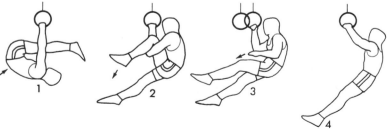

Figure 12.12
Single Leg cut-and-Catch

Double Leg Cut-Off on Forward Swing (Figure 12.13)

The performer stands about twelve inches behind the still rings which are at a height of about six to twelve inches less than the performer's reach. He grasps the rings tightly and falls forward off balance. As he falls forward he pulls up with his arms, extends his head backward, and whips his extended legs quickly upward, piking at his hips. He rotates his body as far backward as possible and then quickly rocks forward, rolling as far forward as possible while riding his thighs upward on his arms. While still retaining a slight forward somersault motion, he releases both rings and curls his head and body forward, looking for the mat underneath him. The spotter spots the performer carefully by placing one hand on the performer's upper arm and the other hand on the small of his back.

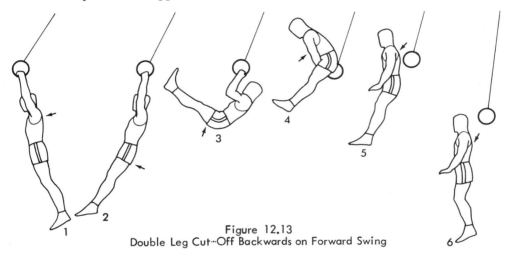

Figure 12.13
Double Leg Cut-Off Backwards on Forward Swing

ELEMENTARY RING STUNTS

Single Leg Cut-and-Catch on Backward Swing (Figure 12.14)

The performer develops a small swing on the flying rings and assumes a pike position at the end of the forward swing. At the instant that he comes

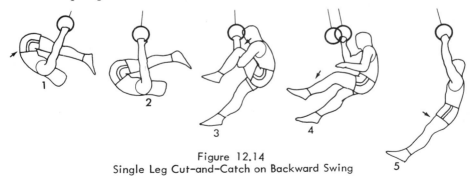

Figure 12.14
Single Leg Cut-and-Catch on Backward Swing

to the end of the backswing of the rings he rocks his body forward and hooks his left leg over his left arm. He rocks his body as high as possible on his left arm and attempts to place his chin between the rings. He then releases the left ring with his left hand and passes his left leg forward. He quickly regrasps the left ring with his left hand and swings his body forward and downward to a straight-arm hanging position. The spotter should spot the performer with both hands by lifting him momentarily by the small of his back as he makes his recatch.

Cut-Off (Split-Off) Forward on Backward Swing (Figure 12.15)

This stunt is essentially a double cut without a recatch. As the performer completes a low forward swing on the flying rings he swings his legs forward and upward and comes to a pike position (illustration one). Just before he reaches the end of his back swing he rocks forward, riding upon his arms and hooking his knees while spreading his legs (illustration two). He rolls his body forward and upward until his chin is close to the rings. As he approaches the top of his rock-up and as his body is still rotating forward, he releases the rings and somersaults forward, placing his feet on the mats underneath his hips (illustrations three and four). The spotter positions himself underneath the performer and places one hand on his back and one on his upper arm and lifts as much as necessary to enable the performer to land on his feet.

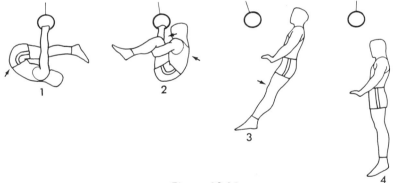

Figure 12.15
Cut-Off Forward on Backward Swing

Cut-Off (Split-Off) Forward on Still Rings (Figure 12.16)

From a pike position the performer should do a very vigorous rock-up onto his arms and he should keep his body tightly tucked after his release until he can extend his legs directly underneath his hips. The difficulty of the forward cut-off is increased when performed on the still rings because without a swing the performer's body is nearer the mat, he is more upside down, and there is no swinging motion to aid him on his rock-up. The spotter should grasp an upper arm or armpit of the performer and give him whatever assistance is needed.

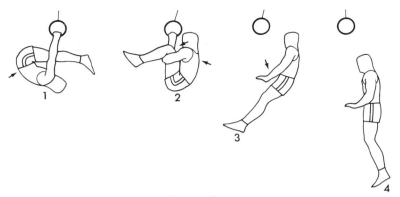

Figure 12.16
Cut—Off Forward on Still Rings

Back (Reverse) Straddle-Off on Still Rings (Figure 12.17)

With the height of the rings just above head level, the performer grasps the rings from the outside and falls off-balance forward (illustration two). As he starts to fall off-balance, he pulls up to a one-half bend (illustration three), throws his head back, and rapidly pikes his split legs upward (illustration four). He retains his grasp during the backward rotation of his body until after his thighs contact his arms and he sees the mat underneath the rings. At this instant he releases his grasp and lands in a tucked position on his feet. This is not a difficult stunt to master if the correct timing is employed. The spotter places one hand on the performer's upper arm and with his other hand the spotter lifts against the performer's chest as needed.

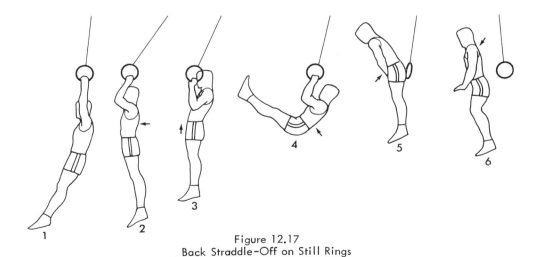

Figure 12.17
Back Straddle-Off on Still Rings

Back Straddle-Off on Backward Swing (Figure 12.18)

The performer takes a small swing on the flying rings and at the end of the forward swing swings his legs forward and does a pull-up as depicted in the third illustration. As the rings swing backward he swings his body backward and lowers it and if he wishes, he places his feet on the mat below the rings support just before the rings swing past the perpendicular. He then immediately and vigorously performs a back somersault movement by swinging his body forward–upward, quickly piking his legs at his hips while spreading them well apart, and throwing his head and shoulders backward (illustration four). His legs should ride up high on his wrists and he releases his grasp on the rings while his body is still rotating backward. The spotter spots by reaching over the performer's left arm and placing his right hand on the performer's chest and his left hand on the small of the performer's back. The spotter then lifts with his left hand and rotates the performer with his right hand being careful to avoid overthrowing the performer past a feet landing on the back somersault movement. In learning this stunt the correct timing on the swing should first be mastered. This stunt can also be performed at the end of the forward swing, in which case a regular beat is taken. It requires somewhat less of a somersaulting action and is probably easier than when performed at the end of the backswing.

Figure 12.18
Back Straddle–Off on Backward Swing

Dislocate on Still Rings (Figure 12.19)

From a pike position the performer rapidly extends his legs at a 45 degree angle upward and backward while supinating his hands (turning his thumbs away from his body) and forcefully spreading his arms as far apart as possible. He continues to hold his hands apart while the dislocate movement is completed. By keeping his arms flexed throughout the stunt, the performer can muscle his arms (resist their tendency to straighten) and thus avoid the shock that might occur if his falling body were suddenly stopped by his extended arms as his body falls through the dislocate. The wider apart the hands are spread, the easier will the dislocate be as this prevents the body from falling freely for any distance. The spotter spots the beginning performer by placing his hands on his hips and lifting as he shoots his legs upward and backward. He then lifts on the performer's chest as he swings forward after the dislocate. In order to get a forceful shoot of his body before doing the actual dislocate, the performer should rhythmically unpike his body partially two or three times, settling into a pike after each movement. A fear of hurting the shoulders is a major obstacle in learning this stunt but this may be overcome by proper spotting and the correct understanding of all the movements involved.

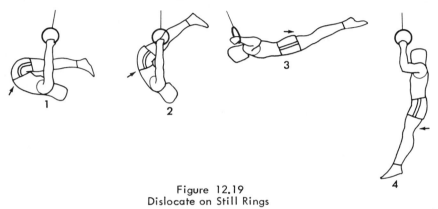

Figure 12.19
Dislocate on Still Rings

Dislocate on Backward Swing (Figure 12.20)

The dislocate performed at the end of the backswing on the flying rings is identical to one performed on the still rings except that if the timing is correct it is somewhat easier because the performer's body is in motion from the swing and the effects of gravity are lessened at each end of the swing. At the end of the forward swing the performer assumes a pike

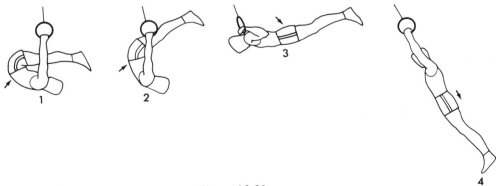

Figure 12.20
Dislocate on Backward Swing

position. As he nears the end of the backward swing he forcefully extends his legs backward in order that they continue the swinging motion of his body. At the same time he pulls up with his arms, spreads them as wide apart as possible, and supinates his hands (rotates his thumbs away from his body). He should at first hold his arms slightly flexed (later they should be straight) as his body begins to swing downward in order to absorb the force of his fall through the dislocate. The spotter carefully spots the performer as he swings forward after dislocating; the danger point being when the performer is in the position depicted in the sixth illustration.

Toe Snap on Forward Swing (Figure 12.21)

To do this dismount the performer should first master the toe-hang on the still rings. To practice the toe-hang he assumes a hand-and-toe hang, turning his toes upward toward his knees and placing the top of his instep on the rings as close to his ankles as possible. He then releases his hand grasp and while closely spotted by a spotter slowly lowers his upper body until he is in a toe-supported upside down position. He then walks his hands forward, drops his toes from the rings and tucks his body, landing in an all-fours position. The performer next practices these actions on the flying rings in which only a small amount of swing is taken. He then takes a larger swing and, at the end of the forward swing, instead of merely dropping off the rings he instead arches his body, head, and arms forward and upward. As his body approaches a horizontal position and while it is still swinging upward, he releases his feet and tucks his legs, dropping to a tucked feet landing. The spotter should grasp one shoulder or upper arm of the performer and spot his head and shoulders when he is dismounting.

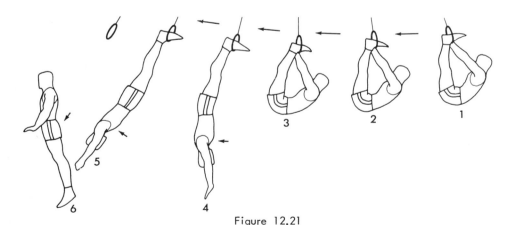

Figure 12.21
Toe Snap on Forward Swing

Toe Snap on Backward Swing (Figure 12.22)

Before attempting a toe-snap at the end of the backward swing the performer should master it from the still rings and from the end of the forward swing on the flying rings. In order to perform this stunt successfully the performer uses a different technique to develop the forward somersault movement which has to be done with increased speed because a larger somersault rotation is required to get to a feet-first position. From a small swing the performer, on the backward swing, goes to a toe hang. He then flexes his trunk, chest, and head toward his feet, and while his upper body is still moving upward he releases his toes and quickly extends his legs forward and downward. Keeping his chin on his chest at all times, he immediately semitucks his legs and drops to the mat, landing on his feet. The spotter should place his hands under the shoulders of the performer during this dismount and give whatever assistance is needed.

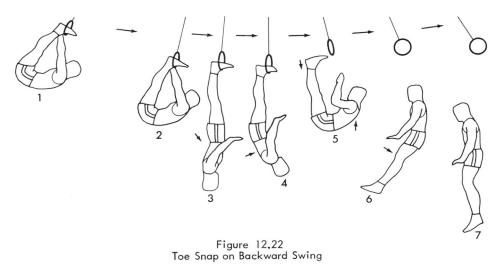

Figure 12.22
Toe Snap on Backward Swing

Double Leg Cut-and-Catch on Backward Swing (Figure 12.23)

This stunt is the same as the forward cut-off previously described except that the performer regrasps the rings after cutting both legs forward. With the height of the rings adjusted at chest height, the performer takes a low swing and from a pike position executes a cut-off at the end of the backward swing, as described earlier for Figure 12.16. He should make certain that he rocks as high on his arms as possible. In releasing the rings

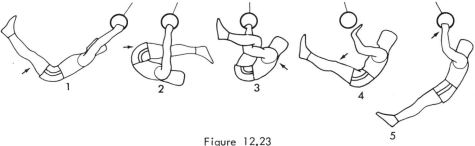

Figure 12.23
Double Leg Cut-and-Catch on Backward Swing

when doing the cut-off the performer must not throw the rings but instead should leave them in place in order to regrasp them immediately after his legs have passed beyond them. The performer should do a cut-off to a regular feet landing if he should miss regrasping one or both rings. During the first few attempts the spotter should grasp the performer's upper arm and assist him as needed.

Forward Roll on Still Rings with Arms Flexed (Figure 12.24)

This stunt requires more-than-average strength; consequently the novice gymnast may not be able to master it unless he has engaged in a program of weight training or has increased his strength through other strength-building programs. With the rings set at shoulder-height position the performer takes a cross-rest position as shown in the first illustration. Without turning or rotating his hands he tucks his body, lowers his shoulders and raises his hips (illustration two). As his body begins to roll over as shown in the third illustration he supinates (turns his thumbs away from his body) his hands but does not allow his shoulders to drop while his body rotates forward. As he completes his forward roll he pulls up as high as possible and at the same time pronates (turns his thumbs toward his body) his hands (illustration five). These actions should complete his forward somersault movement and he should finish with his chest above the rings and his weight resting on his arms. He returns to his original cross-rest position by doing a push-up movement, extending his arms completely. During the first few attempts of the stunt it may be necessary for the spotter to assist by lifting the performer as he completes the last half of the forward roll.

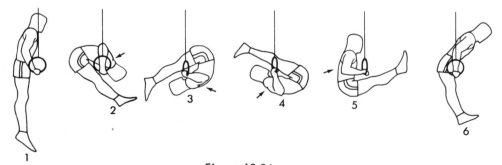

Figure 12.24
Forward Roll on Still Rings with Arms Flexed

INTERMEDIATE RING STUNTS

Shoulder Stand on Still Rings (Figure 12.25)

When learning a shoulder stand the height of the rings should be adjusted to about three feet above floor. The performer grasps the rings from the inside as illustrated in the first figure. He then jumps his hips upward and raises them slowly as he lowers his shoulders to the rings as illustrated in the second figure. Keeping his eyes on the mat below him at all times, he slowly arches his back and brings his feet together while keeping the rings in contact with his shoulders at all times. When first learning the shoulder stand the performer may steady his body by locking his legs around the ropes or steel cables. The performer should never flex his head forward because placing his chin on his chest will cause him to lose his sense of balance and will tend to cause him to overbalance and fall. If the performer does start to somersault forward, he should tuck his body and muscle his arms while the spotter prevents him from somersaulting too rapidly.

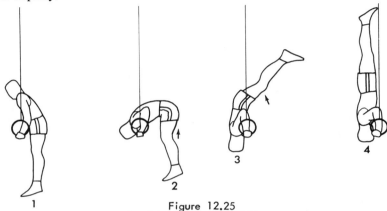

Figure 12.25
Shoulder Stand on Still Rings

Muscle-Up (Figure 12.26)

With the rings at the height of his reach, the performer grasps the rings with a false or high grasp as illustrated in the first figure. For this grasp the performer sharply flexes his hands and holds the rings as close as possible

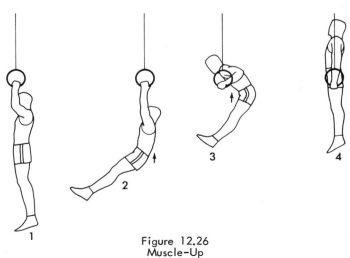

Figure 12.26
Muscle-Up

to his wrists. He quickly does a rapid pull-up until the rings are at shoulder height and at the same time he pikes his extended legs forward, raising them to an angle of about 30 degrees from the vertical. He then quickly lowers his legs and pronates his hands while turning his hands inward (rotates the right ring clockwise and the left ring counter-clockwise), spreading his elbows, and shifting his wrists above his hands. This action places his shoulders just above the rings. Continuing his upward motion, he does a quick push-up with his arms, arches his back and holds his head up and slightly back positioning the rings just behind his hips. The spotter may need to assist the performer by lifting slightly as he shifts from the pulling to the pushing motion as illustrated in the third figure.

Kip on Still Rings (Figure 12.27)

With the rings at chest height, the performer grasps them from the outside. He takes a half-step backward, lifts one leg and then the other into a pike (illustrations one and two). He rapidly unpikes his legs by extending them slightly upward and forward while pushing down and inward with his hands, and forcing his head and shoulders forward and upward (illustrations four and five). The performer comes to a cross-rest position. During the first few attempts of the kip the performer may have to come to a cross-rest position with his arms flexed and his hands near his shoulders —from this position he should then extend his arms. The kip may also be practiced on still rings. At all times the performer must be careful not to allow the rings to spread too far apart. The spotter may need to lift against the middle of the performer's back during the kipping action.

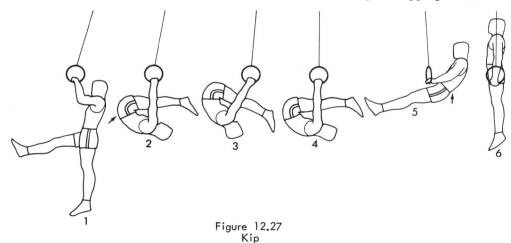

Figure 12.27
Kip

Kip on Swinging Rings (Figure 12.28)

With the rings set at a low height for ease in spotting, the performer, at the end of the back swing, executes a kip as previously described. The spotter does not lift the performer but instead watches that the performer does not overthrow the kip and thus fall through the cross-rest position and possibly lose his grasp on the rings as he falls forward. In such an event the performer tucks his body and muscles his arms.

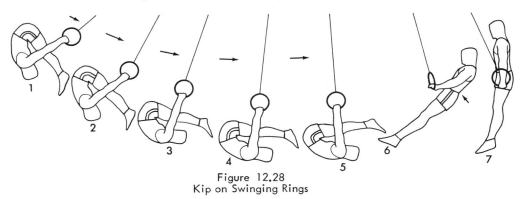

Figure 12.28
Kip on Swinging Rings

Dislocate on Backward Swing from Inverted Hang Position (Figure 12.29)

This is actually a backward fall-out from an inverted hang. The performer obtains a swing and goes into a pike position (illustration one) as the rings pass the perpendicular portion of the backward swing, he extends his body and goes into a momentary inverted-hang position (illustration two). With his body and arms fully extended and with his hands spread as wide apart as possible, he continues to fall past this position and as he reaches the end of his back swing he supinates his hands (rotates his thumbs away from his body) and does a dislocate (illustrations three and four). The spotter should watch that the performer does not lose his grasp during or immediately after the dislocate is completed.

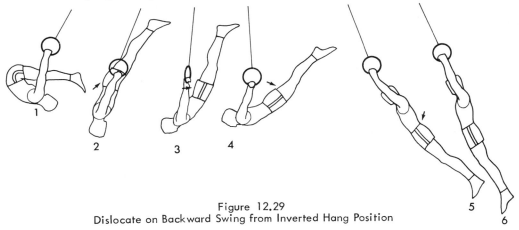

Figure 12.29
Dislocate on Backward Swing from Inverted Hang Position

Dislocate on Forward Swing (Figure 12.30)

In performing a dislocate at the end of the forward swing of the flying rings, the performer should duplicate the movements used when doing a dislocate on the backward swing, doing the body extension movement just before the peak of the front swing is attained in order that the dislocate is done at the peak of the front swing. The spotter should closely spot the performer immediately after he completes the dislocate because this is the point at which he is most apt to lose his grasp on the rings. During the first few performances of this stunt the arms should be slightly bent and tense at all times. The figures illustrating this stunt depict from right to left the sequence of movements.

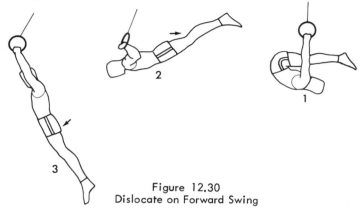

Figure 12.30
Dislocate on Forward Swing

Front Inlocate and Cut-Off (Figure 12.31)

The illustrations of this stunt combination read from right to left. With the rings adjusted to head height level the performer takes a small swing. As the rings swing forward and just before they have attained a vertical position, the performer places his feet on the mat, jumps up and pikes his body into a forward rotation, coming to a pike position in a movement that is the reverse of a dislocate (illustrations two, three and four). As the jump is made the performer spreads his hands apart and rotates them inward (the right thumb turns clockwise, and the left hand turns counterclockwise) and tucks his head. As soon as the pike position is attained and while his body is still rotating forward the performer rocks forward, spreads his legs apart, and does a cut-off dismount (illustrations four and

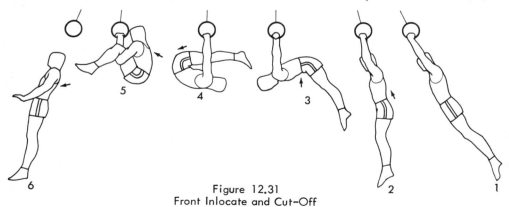

Figure 12.31
Front Inlocate and Cut-Off

five). The sequence of movement for this combination of stunts is quite rapid and the performer must not hesitate before doing the cut-off. The spotter should carefully spot the performer as he does the cut-off dismount. When learning this combination the performer must first master the in-locate by itself. It may also be performed in a similar manner on the flying rings by swinging backward in a pike position and just before the end of the back swing is attained, the performer extends his body and swings his hips and legs downward and then backward as for a back uprise. However, instead of lifting the entire body, the hips are raised, the arms spread, the head tucked, and the body piked sharply in order to inlocate.

Back Uprise (Stem Rise) on Still Rings (Figure 12.32)

The performer should keep a tight grip on the rings when doing this stunt. The performer assumes a pike position and then extends his legs and body to a momentary inverted hang position in which his legs and feet are somewhat forward of the rings. Keeping his body arched, he drops his hips and legs forward and downward, and then backward (illustrations two and three). He then whips his legs backward and upward and pushes downward forcefully with his hands, which action brings him to a cross-rest position. The spotter may need to lift the performer's body at the end of his back swing, and the spotter must be alert to spot the performer in case he falls forward through the rings after completing the back uprise. The inexperienced ring performer may have difficulty in obtaining an efficient cast from a pike position that will provide a large backward and upward swing of his body and legs. If this is true the performer may for a while simply develop a large swinging motion while hanging from the rings and as he nears the end of a back swing, he hyperextends his legs and pushes hard against the rings. With the same actions, this stunt may be done with less effort on the backswing of the flying rings if the correct timing is employed.

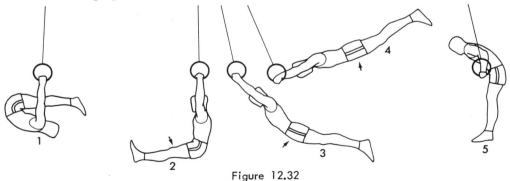

Figure 12.32
Back Uprise on Still Rings

Back Kip (Reverse Uprise) (Bird-Up) (Figure 12.33)

Using a false grasp, the performer takes a small swing and as he approaches the end of the forward swing he swings his body into a pike position (illustration two) and immediately, without any hesitation at all, lifts his hips above the rings by quickly pulling up with his arms. He simultaneously shoots his legs upward and backward and extends his head and shoulders forward so that his body is in an arched position (illustrations three and four). At the same time he pushes vigorously downward and inward with his hands, exerting as much force as possible. His body pivots about his hands and he comes to a cross-rest position (illustrations four, five, and six). The illustrations that depict the movements involved in the performance of this stunt should be intently studied. The spotter spots the performer under his shoulders as he does the reverse uprise.

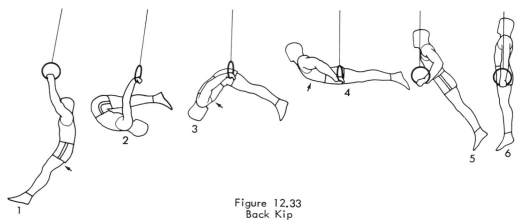

Figure 12.33
Back Kip

High Straddle-Off (Cut-Off) on Forward Swing (Figure 12.34)

With the height of the rings adjusted to the height of his reach (during the learning stages only) the performer takes a fairly high swing, and as he swings forward he takes a walk beat or two-footed beat at the bottom of the swing as depicted in the second illustration. He then arches his body forward (as depicted in the third illustration) and then pikes his legs forward and upward while spreading them (illustration four). He quickly

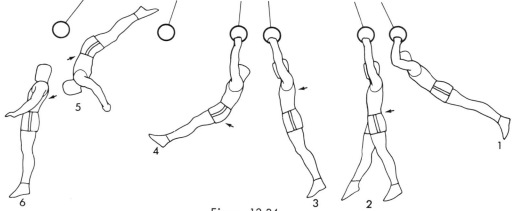

Figure 12.34
High Straddle-Off on Forward Swing

extends his head backward and looks for the mat underneath him, and pulls vigorously with his arms. He releases his grasp as his body passes a horizontal position, just before his thighs reach his arms, and while his body retains a considerable back somersault rotation. The spotter should carefully watch the performer's landing, and should grasp his upper arm as a precautionary measure because this dismount can easily be over-thrown past a feet landing.

Flyaway on Forward Swing (Figure 12.35)

This stunt is very similar to the straddle-off described in the last para-graph except that the legs are not spread apart, the lift of the body is increased, and the body is arched during the flyaway. In doing a flyaway utilize the mechanics and actions employed for the straddle-off until reaching the point of piking the legs forward near the end of the forward swing. Instead the performer arches his body and throws his head and shoulders back. When he sees the mat, he so pikes his legs that he lands on his feet. Although an experienced spotter will have little difficulty in hand spotting the performer during a flyaway, the performer should make use of an overhead safety belt during his first few attempts of the flyaway from the flying rings. By swinging his body vigorously forward the per-former can do a flyaway on the still rings where it is often preceded by a dislocate.

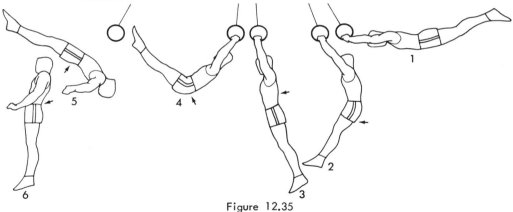

Figure 12.35
Flyaway on Forward Swing

ROUTINES ON THE RINGS

Routine of Beginning Stunts on the Still Rings

Inverted hand and return, bird's nest, pike, single leg cut-and-catch, double leg straddle-off backward.

Routine of Elementary Stunts on the Flying Rings

Swing, dislocate on backward swing, pike, single leg cut-and-catch on backward swing, pike, double leg-cut-and-catch on backward swing, extend body on forward swing, beat, straddle-off on backward swing.

Routine of Intermediate Stunts on the Still Rings

Hang, pike, back uprise, shoulder stand, pike, back kip, lower forward to pike, inlocate, dislocate to flyaway.

CHART FOR RATING RINGS SKILLS

Beginning Rings Stunts	Rating of Stunt Performance* 1	2	3	4	5
Pull-Up; Release Right Hand; Grasp Left Wrist					
Backward Circle to Back-Hang					
Fundamental Swing					
Swing with Twist					
Pull-Up at End of Swing					
Pull-Up at End of Front Swing; Lower at End of Backswing					
Inverted Hang and Return					
Bird's Nest					
Inverted Hang to Bird's Nest and Return					
Forward Swing to Basket; Return to Hang					
Bird's Nest from Swing and Dismount					
Single Leg Cut-and-Catch					
Double Leg Straddle-Off on Forward Swing					
Sub-Total					

Elementary Rings Stunts	1	2	3	4	5
Single Leg Cut-and-Catch on Backward Swing					
Cut-Off Forward on Backward Swing					
Cut-Off Forward on Still Rings					
Straddle-Off on Backward Swing					
Dislocate on Still Rings					
Dislocate on Backward Swing					
Toe Snap on Forward Swing					
Toe Snap on Backward Swing					
Double Leg Cut-and-Catch on Backward Swing					
Forward Roll on Still Rings with Arms Flexed					
Sub-Total					

Intermediate Rings Stunts	1	2	3	4	5
Shoulder Stand on Still Rings					
Muscle-Up					
Kip on Still Rings					
Kip on Swinging Rings					
Dislocate on Backward Swing from Inverted Hang Position					
Dislocate on Forward Swing					
Front Inlocate and Cut-Off					
Back Uprise on Still Rings					
Back Kip on Still Rings					
High Straddle-Off on Forward Swing					
Flyaway on Forward Swing					
Sub-Total					
Grand Total					

*The Simplified Points System containing the description of the five categories of ratings appears on pages 76-77.

(Figure 12.36)

13 ADVANCED GYMNASTICS

The stunts contained in this book are prerequisites to the more advanced skills of competitive gymnastics or are in themselves useful elements in the advanced stages of gymnastics. Therefore, the practice and mastery of these stunts, together with the exercises and routines, should provide the performer with the knowledge and the firm, broad foundation needed to progress rapidly to advanced gymnastics.

The gymnast who aspires to become a champion should definitely work toward style, finesse, and a complete mastery of his routines; he should not include in his routines difficult stunts and movements of which he is unsure. He should work all events and then decide which are his best. Although he may decide to specialize in these, the inclusion of an all-around event in American gymnastics competition and the requirement of being an all-around performer in international competition strongly dictates that he be an all-around gymnastics performer. He therefore should spend extra time and effort in upgrading the gymnastics events in which he is weak. For men the individual events normally included in all-around competition are (1) Floor Exercise, (2) Long Horse, (3) Side Horse, (4) Horizontal Bar, (5) Parallel Bars, and (6) Still Rings. These events are often referred to as artistic gymnastic events. Trampolining or rebound tumbling, tumbling, and the flying rings are individual events only and these events are not always included in gymnastics competition, especially the flying rings.

The long horse is essentially a raised side horse, without pommels, that is turned in the direction that the long horse vaulter runs in making his approach for the vault. Many of the vaults listed in Chapter 9 may be performed on the long horse but their performance is much more difficult when done on the long horse. Because a vault of considerable height and distance is required to perform these vaults successfully, a beat board is provided to be used for the take-off.

The gymnast who would like to find information concerning advanced gymnastics may consult several sources.

Books

Baley, James A. *Gymnastics in the Schools* (Boston: Allyn and Bacon, Inc., 1965).

Frey, Harold J. and Charles J. Kenney. *Elementary Gymnastics Apparatus Skills Illustrated* (New York: Ronald Press Co., 1964).

Holzaepfel, Norman R. *Gymnastics, How to Do It* (Schiller Park, Illinois: Porter Athletics Equipment Co., 1964).

Kenney, Charles J. *Fundamental Tumbling Skills Illustrated* (New York: Ronald Press Co., 1966).

Ladue, Frank, and Jim Norman. *This is Trampolining* (Cedar Rapids, Iowa: Nissen Trampoline Co., 1954).

Loken, Newton C., and Robert J. Willoughby. *Complete Book of Gymnastics* (Englewood Cliffs, N.J.: Prentice-Hall, Inc., 1959).

Griswold, Larry. *Trampoline Tumbling* (St. Louis: Fred Medart Manufacturing Co., 1948).

Price, Hartley D., Joseph M. Hewlett, and Newt Loken. *Gymnastics and Tumbling* (revised) (New York: Ronald Press Co., 1950).

Ryser, Otto E. *A Teacher's Manual for Tumbling and Apparatus Stunts* (Dubuque, Iowa: William C. Brown Co., 1961).

Szypula, George. *Tumbling and Balancing for All* (Dubuque, Iowa: William C. Brown Co., 1957).

Periodicals

Amateur Athletic Union Official Gymnastics Guide and Handbook, 231 West 58th St., New York, N.Y. 10019.

The Modern Gymnast, P. O. Box 611, Santa Monica, Calif.

The Official National Collegiate Athletic Association Gymnastics Guide, The National Collegiate Athletic Bureau, New York, N.Y.

The U.S. Gymnast, P. O. Box 53, Iowa City, Iowa 52240.